D0758978

American River College Library
47 College
Sacramento, California   95841

WITHDRAWN

Magical Muse

Magical Muse

Millennial Essays on Tennessee Williams

Edited by

Ralph F. Voss

The University of Alabama Press
Tuscaloosa and London

Copyright © 2002
The University of Alabama Press
Tuscaloosa, Alabama 35487-0380
All rights reserved
Manufactured in the United States of America

Typeface: Stone Serif and Stone Sans

∞
The paper on which this book is printed meets the minimum requirements of
American National Standard for Information Science–Permanence of Paper for
Printed Library Materials, ANSI Z39.48–1984.

Library of Congress Cataloging-in-Publication Data

Magical muse : millennial essays on Tennessee Williams / edited by Ralph F. Voss.
    p.   cm.
    Includes bibliographical references and index.
    ISBN 0-8173-1127-0 (alk. paper)
    1. Williams, Tennessee, 1911–1983—Criticism and interpretation. I. Voss,
Ralph F.
    PS3545.I5365 Z756 2002
    812'.54—dc21

                          2001005097

British Library Cataloguing-in-Publication Data available

Permission for the use of the cover photo has been generously given by the Harry
Ransom Humanities Research Center, The University of Texas at Austin.

The following publisher has generously given permission to use extended quotations from the play *Cat on a Hot Tin Roof* (© 1954, 55 renewed 1982, 1983 The University of the South; unpublished material © 2000 The University of the South;
published by New Directions, reprinted by permission of The University of the
South, Sewanee, Tennessee). All rights whatsoever in this play are strictly reserved
and application for performance etc., must be made before rehearsal to Casarotto
Ramsay & Associates Ltd., National House, 60–66 Wardour Street, London W1V
4ND. No performance may be given unless a licence has been obtained.

Dedication

For my grandchildren:
Alexandra Elizabeth Voss
Kyler Mathias Voss
Zachary Malone Voss

A Party at Tennessee's

It was a blues trumpet hot night in the Quarter
When the old white-plumed bird
Threw a party for friends
As close to himself
As Dumaine is to Toulouse.
Around the patio he hung
Colored lights and Chinese lanterns
Pulsating against dancers' and dreamers' bodies
Fresh from the Paradise Dance Hall.

Several gnädiges fräuleins fanned themselves
Like Sybil with the eyes of a phoenix
From the Garden District.
Catharine entertained royalty and wealth:
The Princess Kosmonopolis and Mrs. Goforth
Escorted by double dildoes Chris and Chance.

At a table for two
Sat forget-me-not-girls
Waiting for a dance,
Sipping Moon Lake water laced with absinthe,
Eccentricities of nightingales.
Laura languished for Jim; and Alma for a John.
Both accepted Archie Kramer's invitation—

Sudden intimacy in a double-breasted suit.
Rose languished for a Tennessee waltz.

Faster-paced married couples swung
To liquored jazz
Played by Val Xavier and his Delta Brilliants.
Mangiacavallo caressed the buttocks
Of plump Serafina, who slapped
His invited pinches.
Brick Delta-kissed Maggie,
Winking at all her lies,
As Gooper and Mae
Inhaled color-coordinated cigs.
Stanley adjusted Stella's
Thin shoulder strap falling
Just beneath her luxuriously-swelling breasts.
Big Daddy elephant-stepped out
With Big Mama under
A star-colored canopy,
And the birds howled with laughter.

Near the fountain in the square,
Chicken had his first white date.
Myrtle stole from the corner
Where Lot plotted with Jabe and Archie M.
In the hearts of their darkness

To underwrite a new gin,
Cuckolds Three.
The smell of embalmed wealth.
Frosted Baby Doll's perfumed trail
Meandering to a mustachioed-grinning Vacarro
and Lady sang the blues for Val
Her baby inside exulting in the rhythm.

Near the bird himself
Gathered all the boys of desire:
Sebastian, Allan, Skipper,
Lance, and Moise's reasonable friend;

Frankie, Pancho, Donald
And the little young man who
A long time ago lived
In the Vieux Carré,
Primping and cruising.

Blanche worked the bird's tables
Selling honeymoon corsages:
Florid lilies, wreathed with rosemary,
Escapist gentility.
Her most grateful customers
Kilroy and Quixote,
Hannah and Zelda.
Magnolia-scented words
Regaled the night at Tennessee's
When Heavenly sang of earthly love
Just before dawn scattered
All the bird's shades.

                        —Philip C. Kolin

Contents

Acknowledgments

A project of this size and scope could not be taken on without assistance of commensurate size and scope. Fortunately, I had help equal to that challenge, and I am grateful for it. Foremost among those I want to thank is my colleague Donald Noble, who first broached the idea of codirecting an Alabama Symposium in honor of Tennessee Williams and who then brought his experience, patience, and good judgment to our combined efforts to make that symposium a successful reality. As I pulled together this collection, I had the able efforts of four outstanding graduate student research assistants in succession: first Lex Ames, then Don Gilliland and Dan Kaplan, and finally, Stephanie Chatelain. All of my colleagues in the English Department at Alabama have proved encouraging and supportive along the way, particularly the chair, Sara D. Davis. I am especially grateful to the University of Alabama administration, first for continued funding and support from the provost, Dr. Nancy S. Barrett, for this and other Alabama symposia; and also for granting me a sabbatical leave to finish editing this work.

On a more personal note, I want to thank my wife, Glenda Brumbeloe Weathers, whose support and patience have been and continue to be of incalculable value; my three sons—John, Walker, and Collin and their families; and my longtime friend and collaborator Michael Keene of the University of Tennessee at Knoxville.

Magical Muse

Introduction

Ralph F. Voss

"I don't want realism! I want magic!"
—Blanche DuBois, *A Streetcar Named Desire*

"Snatching the eternal out of the desperately fleeting is the great magical trick of human existence."
—Tennessee Williams, "The Timeless World of the Play," Introduction to *The Rose Tattoo*

As the bloodiest century in the history of the planet wound down, few things seemed magical and even fewer seemed certain; death and taxes held their usual reliable places, but almost everything else was up in the postmodern air. Scholars of American drama, however, could largely agree on two points: (1) Emerson's call for an American Renaissance in literature may have come to pass in poetry and fiction shortly after he called for it in the nineteenth century, but it didn't begin to happen in drama until the twentieth, when Eugene O'Neill found his way to Provincetown. (2) The Renaissance having finally occurred, reaching its peak in the years between the end of World War II and the end of the Vietnam War, two playwrights seem now to tower above many other gifted twentieth-century American dramatists: O'Neill and Thomas Lanier "Tennessee" Williams. Both created magic in full view of theater and, especially in Williams's case, film audiences.

O'Neill and Williams are gone now, having died thirty years apart, in 1953 and 1983, respectively, and they will write no more;

but unlike O'Neill, who saw to it that many of his unpublished manuscripts were destroyed, Williams left behind many manuscripts that were being examined, as the century closed, by readers who hoped to find hitherto undiscovered treasure. Indeed, one of Williams's very first plays, *Not About Nightingales,* saw production on Broadway in 1998 and publication that same year. Yet another early play, *Spring Storm,* was published by New Directions in 1999; and another, *Stairs to the Roof,* saw production at the Krannert Center for the Performing Arts at the University of Illinois–Urbana in 2000, and was then published. Though no one was claiming that these newly discovered plays were likely to join the magical company of *The Glass Menagerie, A Streetcar Named Desire, Cat on a Hot Tin Roof* or *Night of the Iguana,* among Williams's greatest creations, interest in the discoveries was high. Such attention to previously unheard-of work is itself testimony to canonical greatness—whatever canonical means at the millennium—because only the truly great writers provoke such feverish attempts to find more that they have written. In Williams's case, perhaps such seeking may yet provide us with additional truly great work; perhaps his legacy won't suffer as has, for example, Hemingway's, with breathless rushes to publish what should probably have remained unpublished.

Questions about literary leftovers aside, and granting that no one is likely to settle the question of which playwright, O'Neill or Williams, is the greater figure, there remains a consensus that these two are the greatest American playwrights of the twentieth century. And this consensus, along with Williams's achievement, comparable to that of his fellow Mississippian William Faulkner, in making his southern settings and characters vibrant with universal appeal, gave life to the idea that Williams and his work should be the focus of the Twenty-seventh Alabama Symposium on English and American Literature during the last year of the century. This end-of-an-epoch symposium gathered both established and neophyte scholars to reflect on old perspectives, generate new ones, and perhaps anticipate future views of the contributions wrought by the "Magical Muse" of Tennessee Williams, born at the outset of only the second decade of the twentieth century in Columbus, Mississippi, only sixty miles west of our symposium site in Tuscaloosa.

It is an especially propitious time for the development of new perspectives on Williams because of signal events in the 1990s, including the passing of Maria St. Just, Williams's contentious literary executor, which freed access to previously unexamined source material; and the publication of *Tom*, the first volume of Lyle Leverich's meticulously detailed authorized biography of Williams, which afforded a fuller picture than ever before of the playwright's life in the years leading up to the initial triumph of *The Glass Menagerie* in 1945. Moreover, the publication in 2000 of *The Selected Letters of Tennessee Williams, Volume 1: 1920–1945*, edited by Albert Devlin and Nancy Tischler, two of our contributors and symposium participants, promised an even fuller understanding of Williams's life during those crucial years. Then, too, the rise of gender studies in the academy found rich soil in Williams's imaginary delta, where the shackled sexuality not only of Williams's characters but also of Williams himself always provided potent motivation and incident, bringing yet more ways of understanding brilliant creations like Blanche DuBois and Big Daddy Pollitt. The 1990s also saw a greater fascination with the popular culture of the 1950s, Williams's—and Broadway's—most successful single decade. These interests, and more, are echoed here in original essays, most of which were read and discussed at our symposium.

For this collection I have grouped the contributions roughly according to bibliographical and biographical, critical and theoretical, and, finally, broadly cultural considerations. Nevertheless, the individual pieces, as well as the remarks of symposium participants in the "Afterwords" at the end of the book, can all be read fruitfully apart from the whole. The beginning selections are primarily bibliographical and biographical.

First, noted Williams bibliographer George W. Crandell reviews fin de siècle Williams scholarship, acknowledging the enduring interest in Williams's work, much of it mentioned above, and also detecting an apocalyptic strain in this work that has not yet been widely explored. Crandell's concluding bibliography is extensive and certain to be very useful for Williams students in the early twenty-first century.

Another established Williams scholar, Albert Devlin, demonstrates, as he has impressively done elsewhere with his longtime collaborator Nancy Tischler, how meticulous discovery and examination of correspondence can illuminate our understandings. Here Devlin combines Williams's own letters with the Williams-related correspondence of others to reveal insights into the year 1939, which was pivotal in Williams's creative life and career. Devlin draws prescient parallels between Williams in that year and two of his then-celebrated (but now nearly forgotten) contemporaries, the poet Vachel Lindsay and the travel writer Richard Halliburton. Devlin suggests that the celebrity engines that drove Lindsay and Halliburton, men of similar verbal gifts and similar sexuality, also drove Williams—in ways both creative and cautionary.

Nancy Tischler provides a fascinating view of how the imperatives of Hollywood's midcentury mass-audience censorship affected the filming process and eventual release of *A Streetcar Named Desire*. She reminds us that then, as now, Hollywood's "conscience" has always been commercially driven, regardless of questions regarding actual morality or artistic vision. Williams, like his friend William Inge, enjoyed much greater recognition for his work because of Hollywood's treatment of his plays, but, also like Inge, he believed that this treatment did violence to the integrity of his creations.

Williams scholar Michael Paller offers an insightful exploration of a subject long of keen interest to Williams watchers: the relationship between Williams and his sister, Rose. Paller goes well beneath the easily drawn surface conclusions about this relationship. He suggests that Rose Williams was not only her brother's chief "magical muse" but also his captor, carefully marshaling evidence for this view from several of Williams's works.

Next, meticulous researcher Jeff Loomis concludes the bibliographical and biographical group of essays by examining several different manuscript versions of *Cat on a Hot Tin Roof* in several different manuscript collections to show how these varying manuscripts reveal Williams's varying intentions as he readied his Pulitzer Prize–winning story for stage and screen. Loomis sees the influence of Elia Kazan on these versions but also discerns some creative turmoil at work in Williams's responses to these characters, whom Loomis likens to Luigi Pirandello's *Six Characters in Search of an Author* in seeming to dictate to Williams how they wanted to be presented.

Robert Siegel opens the critical and theoretical group of essays with an absorbing examination of the tensions between spirit and flesh in Williams's plays. Siegel's essay, originally presented at our symposium but reprinted here courtesy of *American Drama*, argues that the Apollonian and Dionysian impulses so central to the conflicts of Williams's characters are what make his work so durably memorable in the public consciousness.

In the next essay, veteran Williams scholar Philip Kolin examines a species of male characters in Williams's work that Kolin calls "unsuitable suitors." Sometimes penetratingly, sometimes playfully, but always insightfully, Kolin demonstrates that Williams, known as a brilliant student of women, was every bit as much a student of what constitutes—or does not constitute—masculinity. Thus Kolin gives a provocative spin to gender criticism.

In her contribution, Allean Hale, who has researched and written extensively about Williams and his work, bucks the critical tide about one of Williams's late-produced plays, *In the Bar of a Tokyo Hotel*, arguing that it is not the embarrassment most critics claim it to be. Hale notes that almost all critics of the production seized upon it as an opportunity to attack Williams and to lament his decline—as though Williams had used a new form to lodge an old complaint, thus enacting in his personal life a demonstration of the play's theme. But Hale finds the interpretive key to this play in Japanese Noh dramatic form, with which Williams was familiar. She builds a plausible explanation that this is not a demonstration of his own decline but rather Williams's crucifixion story, an evocation of the idea that the artist figure in our culture seems inevitably destined to become a martyr to his muse.

Then, using a late Williams play, *Clothes for a Summer Hotel*, as his point of departure, Jackson Bryer, a noted scholar of F. Scott Fitzgerald and of American theater, offers a bridge from the critical and theoretical group to the broadly cultural group of essays. Bryer accomplishes this feat by developing striking comparisons between Williams's work and that of Fitzgerald, not only via *Clothes for a Summer Hotel*, a play that focuses on Scott and Zelda Fitzgerald, but also via what most observers would consider these two writers' greatest works: *A Streetcar Named Desire* and *The Great Gatsby*. The thematic similarities that Bryer develops speak to the visions of the American Dream that compelled the greatness of both writers and remind us that any people's culture is brightly illuminated by its creative writers regardless of genre.

According to Williams scholar Barbara Harris, Williams's "place as America's greatest playwright appears secure"; she discovers a catalog of references to Williams's work buried in the popular culture of America at the turn of the century. Harris shows us that Williams references are ubiquitous in some of the most unlikely places and take some highly amusing forms; television sitcoms and advertisements yield Williams allusions that, to some viewers, may be as obscure as those made in their college literature classes but offer convincing testimony to the lasting cultural impact of Williams's best-known works, especially *Streetcar.*

W. Kenneth Holditch, the editor of the *Tennessee Williams Literary Journal* and a resident of New Orleans, delighted symposium attendees with a slide-and-commentary presentation on New Orleans sites significant in Williams's life and works. In his contribution here he marshals his Crescent City expertise to recapture in print the kind of intimate "tour" that could be given only by an insider who blends love of the playwright's work with love of the city that inspired so much of it. Williams is as much a part of New Orleans culture as jazz and cuisine, a fact celebrated by the annual gathering of Williams scholars, each spring, in the city that lured first Williams, then Blanche DuBois, toward destiny.

Longtime *Los Angeles Times* drama critic Dan Sullivan, who originally served as the symposium's keynote speaker, concludes the cultural grouping and the collection of individual essays with an interesting perspective from outside the academy. Likening the two sides of Williams's creative personality to an angel and a crocodile, Sullivan discusses why and how American theater in particular and popular culture in general benefited from the angel side, however difficult the crocodile part may have been. Perhaps more than any of the other writers represented in these pages, Sullivan reminds us that, after all, many regard Williams as this country's greatest playwright so far because of the appeal of his work, not only to scholars, but also to theater and film audiences everywhere.

In keeping with Alabama Symposium traditions, the program concluded with a panel discussion of the ramifications of ideas that had been mentioned in earlier sessions. This discussion, which was ably moderated by Colby Kullman of the University of Mississippi, yet another Williams scholar, comprises the "Afterwords" section, which concludes the book and helps to begin the further examination and appreciation of Williams's work in the twenty-first century.

To date, the Alabama Symposia on English and American Literature have previously celebrated only one playwright—Shakespeare himself—and thus it seems only fitting that a symposium honoring a great English playwright should finally be matched by a symposium honoring a great American playwright. As these millennial essays suggest, the magical muse of Tennessee Williams made him remarkably successful at what he called "the great magical trick of human existence"—which, again in his own words, is "snatching the eternal out of the desperately fleeting."

1

Tennessee Williams Scholarship at the Turn of the Century

George W. Crandell

Part 1 of Tony Kushner's 1993 Pulitzer Prize–winning drama, *Angels in America: Millennium Approaches,* lends itself to this consideration of Tennessee Williams scholarship at the turn of the century, because as we enter the millennium, we can see that years ago the apocalyptic vision of Tennessee Williams inspired and first prepared the way for the epic extravaganza that Kushner subtitles "A Gay Fantasia on National Themes." Kushner, of course, has publicly acknowledged his debt to Williams, saying: "I've always loved Williams. The first time I read *Streetcar,* I was annihilated" (qtd. in Fisher 26), and James Fisher, tracing "images of homosexuality on the American stage," credits Williams with being "the dramatist most responsible for forcefully introducing sexual issues, both gay and straight, to the American stage" (13). Influential as well as innovative, Tennessee Williams continues to engage the attention of theater audiences as well as theater critics. Consequently, he is the subject of a significant and continuously growing body of scholarly work.

Since the late 1950s, when scholarship devoted to Williams first began to appear, critics have attempted to characterize the distinctive vision of Tennessee Williams, often employing such contradictory labels as romantic, realistic, surrealistic, expressionistic, and lyrical as well as poetic. It may now be appropriate, considering the new millennium, to introduce yet another label, by noting the *apocalyptic* tendency that characterizes so much of the playwright's mature work. Already critics have likened the cataclysmic events in plays such as *Battle of Angels* (later revised and retitled *Orpheus Descending*), *Clothes for a Summer Hotel,* and *The Red Devil Battery Sign* to an apocalypse.[1] Even in *A Streetcar Named Desire,* audiences witness what Anne Fleche describes as "Blanche's apocalyptic destruction at the hands of her 'executioner,' Stanley" (*Mimetic* 93). But apart from these events, the plays of Tennessee Williams (like the millennium) compel us to consider our relationship to time and history and even teleological concerns about the end of time. As Chance Wayne remarks at the conclusion of *Sweet Bird of Youth,* time is "the enemy . . . in us all" (124), the entity that threatens our destruction both individually and collectively as a civilization.

The impending doom sometimes signaled by Williams's apocalyptic vision is presented not necessarily by a chronological succession of events but rather by the *arrest* of time. As Williams explains in his preface to *The Rose Tattoo,* called "The Timeless World of a Play":

Carson McCullers concludes one of her lyric poems with the line: "Time, the endless idiot, runs screaming 'round the world." It is this continual rush of time, so violent that it appears to be screaming, that deprives our actual lives of so much dignity and meaning, and it is, perhaps more than anything else, the *arrest of time* which has taken place in a completed work of art that gives to certain plays their feeling of depth and significance. (*Rose* 259)

In the drama of Tennessee Williams, the arrest of time permits the juxtaposition of irreconcilable visions: of a past more glorious than the present but irretrievably lost, of a future more ominous than the present but seemingly inevitable, and of a future more hopeful than the present but one impossible to realize. Christopher Bigsby, in his critical history of American drama from 1945 to 1990, points to this kind of juxtaposition when he characterizes Williams's contrasting visions of the past and the future; plays such as *The Glass Menagerie* and *A Streetcar Named Desire* look backward in time and "suggest the end of a particular model of America and of individual character" (Bigsby, "Tennessee" 32). At the same time, these plays point to a future, according to Bigsby, that offers "little more than a bland materialism or a drugged conformity" ("Tennessee" 32). Offering a different characterization of the future toward which Williams directs his prophetic gaze, David Savran writes that Williams's plays "look forward to that utopian (or messianic) moment that will, in Walter Benjamin's words, 'blast open the continuum of history' and produce a new social and political order" (92).

For Williams, the arrest of time permits a period of repose in which theater audiences can contemplate what happens onstage and from that experience, if the playwright has been successful, see the relevance between the timeless world of the play and the actual "world in which time is *included*" (*Rose* 264). If this recognition takes place, as Williams hopes, something truly magical will happen: people will discover that which is eternal in the merely temporal. As Williams explains:

> About their lives people ought to remember that when they are finished, everything in them will be contained in a marvelous state of repose which is the same as that which they unconsciously admired in drama. The rush is temporary. The great and only possible dignity of man lies in his power deliberately to choose certain moral values by which to live as steadfastly as if he, too, like a character in a play, were immured against the corrupting rush of time. Snatching the eternal out of the desperately fleeting is the great magic trick of human existence. (*Rose* 262)

As much as the drama of Tennessee Williams provides audiences with multiple visions of the past and the future, so, too, does Tennessee Williams scholarship provide multiple, often conflicting, perspectives on Williams the playwright and his work. The diversity of this body of criticism resists easy summary and categorization, but foremost among recent efforts are works devoted to Williams's life and letters, studies tracing the textual and bibliographical history of his published and unpublished works, documentary accounts of the critical reception and production of his plays, and a multitude of critical essays (published singly or collected in anthologies) focusing on his drama. Although *A Streetcar Named Desire* and *The Glass Menagerie* have certainly garnered the most critical attention, Williams's other plays as well as his fiction and poetry have not been neglected. Recent studies of the poetry and short fiction typically highlight the features that help us understand Williams the dramatist or Williams the performer; Nancy Tischler, for example, suggests that Williams emulated the life of the poet Vachel Lindsay, casting himself in the role of the "vagabond poet" (75).[2] Elsewhere in this volume, Albert Devlin also elaborates comparisons between Williams and Lindsay.

The life of Tennessee Williams continues to be a source of great fascination and, for a significant number of writers, a key to understanding his work. For many years, scholars relied upon their own resources in the absence of a complete or reliable guide to Williams's biography. Benjamin Nelson's *Tennessee Williams: His Life and Work* (1961) provides only a partial account of Williams's life, and while Donald Spoto offers a more comprehensive view in *The Kindness of Strangers: The Life of Tennessee Williams* (1985), reviewers have not been kind to Spoto, whose informative but dispassionate account most importantly omits, as Terry Teachout remarks, "the voice of Williams himself" ("Irregular" 54). Ronald Hayman's more recent study *Tennessee Williams: Everyone Else Is an Audience* (1993), repeats an already familiar story without attempting a substantive reassessment of Williams and his work.

Scholars eagerly anticipated and enthusiastically welcomed the publication of *Tom: The Unknown Tennessee Williams,* the first volume in a projected two-volume biography of Williams by Lyle Leverich. Leverich, whom Williams authorized to write the biography in 1979, completed the first volume in 1989, but a protracted battle with Maria St. Just, cotrustee of the Rose Williams estate, delayed its publication until 1995 (Smith 75). In an illuminating essay published in the *New Yorker,* John Lahr details the battle between Leverich and Williams's "self-proclaimed . . . literary guardian" (Lahr 90). Lahr credits Maria St. Just with single-handedly setting back Williams scholarship by refusing "the right to quote from Williams' unpublished writings, or even to Xerox material from Williams' early papers" (88). As Lahr also reports, Cathy Henderson, research librarian at the Harry Ransom Humanities Research Center, participated in an unsuccessful effort to persuade St. Just to permit greater access to Williams's manuscripts. In a 1992 letter to St. Just, Henderson wrote: "Denying this group of users the option of doing at least a portion of their research from photocopies discourages critical attention and sets the stage for there being less of an audience for his works" (qtd. in Lahr 89).

The first volume of Leverich's biography is distinguished by its reliance upon primary materials, including Williams's private journals and voluminous correspondence. Consequently, it supersedes all previous attempts to document the development of the young Thomas Lanier Williams. Most critics, whose response to the book has been favorable, would agree with William Jay Smith, a personal friend of Williams, who writes that Leverich is sometimes "misled by his subject's imaginative fabrications" (76) but he has otherwise written a "faithful, thorough, sensitive, and carefully documented study" (75).

The Leverich biography has so far stimulated rather than stymied further biographical study of Williams. Allean Hale, for example, continues to unearth new information about Williams's early life.[3] Dakin Williams continues to fuel both investigation and controversy by providing details about the life of his older brother the playwright. In a 1995 interview with Robert Bray, Dakin discusses literary influences on Williams, their early lives together in St. Louis, and the playwright's religious beliefs as well as autobiographical details in Williams's work.[4]

As much as scholars looked forward to the publication of Leverich's biography, they also eagerly awaited the publication of more of his letters and journals. The publication of the *The Selected Letters of Tennessee Williams, Volume 1,* edited by Albert Devlin and Nancy Tischler, made publicly available much of what had previously been held privately or was only remotely accessible in libraries with substantial Tennessee Williams holdings. Carefully edited and easily readable, volume 1 provides readers with a remarkably candid portrait of Williams performing in a variety of roles as son, brother, student, aspiring writer, friend, poet, and playwright. The judicious selection of letters, coupled with informative notes that include excerpts from Williams's private journals, satisfies the need for a clear and coherent narrative in Williams's own words. At the same time, Devlin's and Tischler's informed commentary allows us to see Williams as he censors himself and modulates his tone for various audiences.

In an essay appearing in the *Tennessee Williams Annual Review* prior to the publication of volume 1 of *The Selected Letters,* Devlin emphasized the importance of the published letters for an understanding of Williams's life and work.[5] Since then, the number of letters collected has grown to 2,800, and from among these, Devlin and Tischler selected and annotated 330 that appear in volume 1. Covering the time period from 1920 to 1945, the letters in this first volume are addressed most frequently to members of the Williams family, to Williams's mother, and to Audrey Wood, Williams's agent from 1939 to 1971. Devlin suggests that the letters reveal a Tennessee Williams who enacts "a self-scripted drama of disclosure and disguise" (27). Devlin's characterization of Williams's performance in the letters reflects a current topic in Williams scholarship, namely Williams's unwillingness or inability (because of social prohibitions) to disclose the truth—at least onstage—about sensitive topics such as homosexuality or race relations. Devlin is also able to discern a "progress toward maturity" (29) that informs not only Williams's relationship with his agent but also his relationships with his collaborators, most significant among them Elia Kazan.

During the 1990s, critics have considered Williams not only as an independent artist but also as a collaborator influenced, favorably or unfavorably, by various theater professionals and contemporary writers. In her pioneering study *Tennessee Williams and Elia Kazan: A Collaboration in the Theatre,* Brenda Murphy chronicles the successes and failures of this uniquely dynamic relationship in an insightful analysis of the four major plays on which Williams and Kazan collaborated: *A Streetcar Named Desire, Camino Real, Cat on a Hot Tin Roof,* and *Sweet Bird of Youth.* Murphy's work, more than a supplement to existing biographical accounts of this relationship, also highlights the complex relationship between what Keir Elam has termed the "dramatic text," that is, textual material "composed *for* the theatre," and the "performance text," that is, textual material "produced *in* the theatre" (Elam 3). Marian Price, who likewise examines the relationship between Williams and Kazan, views their collaboration less positively than Murphy. Focusing more specifically on the production of *Cat on a Hot Tin Roof,* Price concludes that when Williams agreed to changes suggested by Kazan, he significantly compromised his artistic integrity in order to satisfy a personal desire for commercial success (334).

Williams's jealousy apparently turned many of his professional and personal relationships into rivalries. As Devlin demonstrates, Williams finally ended his long association with the agent Audrey Wood, jealously fearing that she was conspiring against him (Devlin 31). John S. Bak likewise characterizes Williams's relationship with fellow playwright William Inge as one that begins in friendship but ends in rivalry as the two of them became "jealous of each other's successes in the theatre" (23).

Even so, Williams remained friends for many years with Carson McCullers and may genuinely have benefited from an acquaintance with Japanese playwright Yukio Mishima, whom Williams first met in 1957 (Hale, "Noh" 37). Allean Hale suggests that Mishima's influence is first evident in *The Night of the Iguana* (1961) and subsequently in *The Gnädiges Fräulein* (1967), *In the Bar of a Tokyo Hotel* (1969), *The Two-Character Play* (1969), and *I Can't Imagine Tomorrow* (1970).[6] Likewise according to Hale, the most convincing evidence of Mishima's influence may be found in an unpublished work called "The Day on Which a Man Dies" ("Noh" 37–38).

Scholars can hope that more and more of Williams's unpublished manuscripts will be published, but from the time of Williams's death in 1983 until the death of Maria St. Just in 1994, only a few, minor plays appeared in print. In 1984, the *Missouri Review* published two one-act plays, both apprentice works: "Beauty Is the Word" and "Hot Milk at Three in the Morning." In 1991, *Antaeus* printed "The Chalky White Substance," another one-act play, probably written sometime in the 1970s (Kolin, "Existential" 8). Philip Kolin accurately describes it as an "existential nightmare," comparable to the "hapless" work of Beckett, Sartre, and Pinter (8). Not coincidentally, publication of Williams's manuscripts resumed following the death of Maria St. Just. In 1995, for example, New Directions released *Something Cloudy, Something Clear,* a play St. Just deliberately withheld from publication, "presumably because of its homosexual content" (Lahr 89). Two years later, the *Missouri Review* published *Will Mr. Merriwether Return from Memphis?* This was a comic play about a pair of women who entertain ghostly apparitions, including visits from Vincent Van Gogh and Arthur Rimbaud.[7] In the same year, 1997, Allean Hale edited and introduced *The Notebook of Trigorin,* Williams's adaptation of Anton Chekhov's *The Seagull,* and she has since edited *Not About Nightingales,* which opened in London to favorable reviews in March 1998; following its 1999 New York production, *Not About Nightingales* earned six Tony Award nominations and won the prize for best scene design. Dan Isaac's edition of *Spring Storm* was published in 1999 and was followed by a production of *Stairs to the Roof* in 2000 at the University of Illinois.

The production and/or publication of "new" works by Williams, such as *Not About Nightingales* and *Tiger Tail*, both in 1999, coupled with New York revivals of *Cat on a Hot Tin Roof* in 1990, *The Glass Menagerie* in 1991, *A Streetcar Named Desire* in 1992, *The Rose Tattoo* and *Suddenly Last Summer* in 1995, *Summer and Smoke* and *The Night of the Iguana* in 1996, and, more recently, *Small Craft Warnings* in 1999 and *Stairs to the Roof* in 2000, all attest to a revival of interest in Williams's plays and their production. Two works published in the 1990s document the critical reception of Williams's drama. George W. Crandell's *The Critical Response to Tennessee Williams* (1996) collects reviews of thirty New York productions and critical commentary on twelve major plays. Printing reviews of revivals as well as of original Broadway productions, this anthology allows readers to trace the changing critical response to Williams over a period of five decades. More recently, Robert A. Martin's *Critical Essays on Tennessee Williams* (1997) reprints reviews and criticism of nine plays, all but one produced before 1961. Six of its twenty-one critical essays are published in this volume for the first time.

Scholars in the 1990s have also drawn attention to historically important productions. Kolin documents the production history of *A Streetcar Named Desire* by collecting and reprinting reviews of the tryout performances in New Haven, Boston, and Philadelphia.[8] He also chronicles the various international productions of the play, describing the critical response to premiere performances in Great Britain, China, Cuba, Japan, Mexico, Poland, Spain, and Sweden.[9]

Scholars documenting the history of *The Glass Menagerie* in production have described, most importantly, experimental stagings of the play, for example, productions featuring all-black casts.[10] According to Kolin, the effect has been to "disclose political and social messages ignored by or impossible to incorporate in white productions" ("Black" 114).

For anyone interested in Tennessee Williams and his work, the textual studies, bibliographies, and reference works published in the last decade of the twentieth century have enabled students and other scholars to identify and locate primary and secondary resources with considerable ease. As many researchers know, the textual history of Williams's work is complicated by Williams's habitual practice of revision, a process that often continues beyond the first publication of a work. Thousands of pages of draft material, written over long periods of time (and frequently undated), make the task of tracing the development of works through the manuscript record a daunting but potentially rewarding undertaking. Readers are directed to the essay by Jeffrey Loomis in this volume for an example. The effort is further complicated by the fact that many of Williams's manuscripts are housed in depositories geographically distant from each other. Harvard University, the New York Public Library, Columbia University, the University of Delaware, the Harry Ransom Humanities Research Center on the campus of the University of Texas at Austin, the University of the South, and the University of California at Los Angeles all have significant collections of Williams material. So far, Brian Parker has accepted the challenge of collating the manuscripts and has produced preliminary stemma for *Suddenly Last Summer, The Rose Tattoo, Camino Real,* and *Cat on a Hot Tin Roof.*[11] Of course, the opportunity remains for scholars to assess the significance of the manuscript record and to relate this material to published versions and performances of the texts.

For published resources, Drewey Wayne Gunn's *Tennessee Williams: A Bibliography* continues to be a useful source listing works by and about Williams through the summer of 1990. In addition, Crandell's *Tennessee Williams: A Descriptive Bibliography* provides a comprehensive guide to the textual history of Williams's published work through 1991. It describes books (including all editions in English), collections, contributions to books, publications in periodicals and newspapers, interviews, articles quoting Williams, song lyrics, sound recordings, and translations.

Researchers have also been aided by the publication of *Tennessee Williams: A Guide to Research and Performance,* in 1998. Edited by Philip Kolin, this volume provides the most comprehensive guide to scholarship on Williams since the 1983 publication of John McCann's *The Critical Reputation of Tennessee Williams: A Reference Guide.*

As the twentieth century drew to a close, and the twenty-first century began, the critical response to Tennessee Williams exhibited some of the contradictory qualities of a paradox. Reviewers have noted, especially with each succeeding Broadway revival of a Williams play, that audiences generally no longer find Williams's drama shocking. The changing response to *Cat on a Hot Tin Roof* provides an illustrative example. Some reviewers in 1955 considered the play vulgar because of its language (especially the coarseness of Big Daddy's speech) and also because of its subject matter, in particular the suggestion of a homosexual relationship between Brick and Skipper (Watts 57). To some reviewers in 1974, however, Williams's treatment of homosexuality actually seemed dated (Crandell xxxiii), and by 1990, the presentation of sexual tension and the "hush-hush attitude toward cancer and scandal over childlessness" seemed to Linda Winer almost quaint (358). Paradoxically, at the same time that reviewers have noted that Williams's drama (in performance) seems more and more conservative, scholarly critics have discovered that Williams's plays are much more radical than previously supposed.

Adopting a centrist position, Christopher Bigsby affords Williams the status of a radical but with this qualification: "His radicalism was neither Marxist nor liberal. . . . indeed, it was profoundly conservative. . . . But even if his radicalism is better viewed as a celebration of the outcast or deprived, . . . his work reveals a consistent distrust of the wealthy and the powerful, a suspicion of materialism" ("Tennessee" 37). Taking a more liberal stance, David Savran believes that Williams's "radicalism is far more complex and vigorous than Bigsby makes it out to be" (80). In his provocative study *Communists, Cowboys, and Queers: The Politics of Masculinity in the Work of Tennessee Williams and Arthur Miller* (1992), Savran contends that Williams significantly "destabilizes mid-century notions of gendered subjectivity and dramatic form" (Savran 80). Even more important, he argues, Williams's plays "redefine . . . resistance" so that the potential for opposition is not so much the exclusive right belonging to a rebellious individual as it is a property inherent in "both social organization and dramatic structure" (81). While acknowledging that Williams was by no means a political activist, Savran nevertheless argues that the playwright was committed "to radical political change" because in Williams's view the individual is a component part of "a society that insistently 'rapes the individual'" (79).

Challenging critics to reevaluate Williams's drama, Savran observes how "most [critics] ignore the political implications and resonances of his plays as decidedly as they ignore his homosexuality, preferring to deal only with questions of characterization and theme, and hypostatizing character psychology to a stultifying degree" (79). Jacqueline O'Connor's thematic study *Dramatizing Dementia: Madness in the Plays of Tennessee Williams* (1997) is only the most recent example.

Since the publication of Savran's remarks in 1992, more and more writers are considering the social and political implications of Williams's message as well as the complex relationship between politics and sexuality. In one reassessment of Williams's work, Thomas P. Adler concludes that Williams is, indeed, revolutionary in his politics. "If politics can be understood very broadly as the relations of power that govern individuals, then . . . Williams would seem to qualify as a political playwright" ("Culture" 656). Joining Adler in commenting on Williams's politics, Robert Bray applies a Marxist reading to the "political and sociocultural context in which *A Streetcar Named Desire* appeared" ("*Streetcar*" 183). Similarly, Stephen Bruhm relates details of *Suddenly Last Summer* to the social and political climate in which it was written—the McCarthy era ("Blackmailed" 528). Contending that *Suddenly Last Summer* is "much more disconcerting and subversive than its critics have allowed," Bruhm echoes the sentiments of a growing number of writers who have begun to consider the evidence of subversive strategies in Williams's drama ("Blackmailed" 535).

John Clum, for example, observes that although "Williams was compelled to write about homosexuality," he was "equally impelled to rely on the language of indirection," that is, "if one's goal is the approbation, and financial reward, of a broad audience" (166). David Savran agrees that "Williams seems to practice a kind of double writing that, in turn, encourages a double reading" (118). For Savran, the Williams short story "Hard Candy" provides a reader's guide to Williams's drama, more specifically "to the way that homosexuality . . . is coded and decoded in [Williams's] writing for . . . the theater" (113–14). Mark Lily adds that gay readers who have experienced "victimisation [*sic*], social rejection and legal oppression" recognize what straight readers may not: "the often oblique strategies by which gay writers—unable through external censorship or, at least as often, self-censorship, to articulate their aspirations and desires openly—attempt the subverting of heterosexist culture" (153). Savran adds that Williams's oblique language also provides a basis for assessment, a view contested by Ruby Cohn (237). Savran, nevertheless, contends that "the fragmentation and incoherence" of the late plays may be attributed to "a pivotal change in [Williams's] public status: his coming out" (136). "The language of 'obscurity' and 'indirection' on which he had relied for thirty years was abruptly outmoded" (Savran 137).

Just as recent critics have begun to expose the subtleties of Williams's commentary on homosexuality, so, too, have writers begun to critique Williams's representations of black and ethnic characters. As I have suggested elsewhere, "the failure of Tennessee Williams to write explicitly about issues, such as 'race,' for example, should not be construed to mean that his works are silent about such matters" ("Misrepresentation" 338).

Philip Kolin, for instance, calls attention to the "strong social voice" that critics have overlooked in Williams's *Kingdom of Earth* ("Sleeping" 141), and he argues that in the film *Baby Doll,* Williams "champion[s] the rights of oppressed blacks" ("Civil" 10). Kimball King maintains, however, that although Williams considered "himself a liberal on social and racial issues, [he] steadfastly clung to the prevailing—and romantic—point of view of the white Southerner" (639). To David Savran, the interpretation of Williams's work is complicated by its own contradictions: "for all of Williams's no doubt sincerely held notions of social justice and equality, his work almost unfailingly objectifies and exoticizes the dark Other and, in that respect, clearly exemplifies a contradiction inherent within a certain liberal equalitarianism" (127). The covert strategy that characterizes Williams's treatment of homosexuality likewise applies to his representation of racial and ethnic alliances. In *A Streetcar Named Desire,* for instance, Williams describes the Polish-American Stanley Kowalski "with imagery traditionally associated with black characters" (Crandell, "Misrepresentation" 345). Thus "by means of a racialized discourse . . . Williams . . . covertly broaches the topic of miscegenation in a play ostensibly without an Africanist presence" (Crandell, "Misrepresentation" 345).

As early as *The Glass Menagerie,* Williams's plays have typically been staged more realistically than Williams asked in his production notes and stage directions. As a result, the plays have often been assessed by comparison with other realistic as well as naturalistic dramas. In the 1990s, as some directors have chosen to stage Williams's plays less realistically, reviewers and critics alike have had the opportunity to reassess Williams's work. Yet another facet of recent Tennessee Williams scholarship has sought to contrast Williams with the American realistic tradition.

In "Tennessee Williams's 'Personal Lyricism': Toward an Androgynous Form," Thomas P. Adler suggests that Williams's realism "resides in a tension . . . between characters conceived for their psychological verisimilitude and in a setting . . . almost invariably handled nonrealistically or even expressionistically" (173). Taking a different position, David Savran and Anne Fleche see Williams rejecting realistic drama and especially the temporal progression of events that so often characterizes it. As Savran remarks, "Williams's plays tend to undermine the purely linear and irreversible temporal progression on which . . . American realism in general depends" (92). Similarly, Fleche contends that Williams "makes meaning a matter not of consistency, but of montage, a spatialized time that sees via juxtaposition rather than persistence of vision" (66).

Commenting further on Williams's "deep antipathy to theatrical realism," Savran recognizes in Williams's work affinities with postmodernism: "In his fragmentation of narrative and the subject, his questioning of universalist claims, his subversion of the antitheses between high and low art, philosophy and kitsch, he seems to have anticipated many of the theatrical practices that now pass as postmodernist" (98). Fleche also distances Williams from the realistic tradition, contending that Williams lends himself to poststructuralist readings: "Williams's approach shares with poststructuralism its positive rethinking of the relation between reality and representation as the very sources of writing and dramatic innovation" (107). Savran would likely agree with Fleche that Williams's works are "harder to *read* . . . than the proliferating scholarship around them might lead one to expect" (18).

As much as recent scholars have exposed to view the subversive elements in Williams's drama, they have perhaps neglected to consider the seemingly invisible, shaping influence of the publishing industry on Tennessee Williams scholarship. A surprising number of works, all published between 1988 and 1998, bear the imprint of a particular series: *Readings on the "Glass Menagerie,"* published in 1998 and edited by Thomas Siebold, is one of Greenhaven Press's Literary Companions to American Literature. Matthew Roudané's 1997 *Cambridge Companion to Tennessee Williams* belongs to the Cambridge Companions to Literature. Robert A. Martin's *Critical Es-*

says on Tennessee Williams (1997) is part of the Critical Essays on American Literature. Crandell's *The Critical Response to Tennessee Williams* (1996) appears in Critical Responses in Arts and Letters. Similarly, Crandell's *Tennessee Williams: A Descriptive Bibliography* (1995) was published in the Pittsburgh Series in Bibliography. Kolin's *Confronting Tennessee Williams's "A Streetcar Named Desire": Essays in Critical Pluralism* is the fiftieth number in Greenwood's Contributions in Drama and Theatre Studies. Alice Griffin's *Understanding Tennessee Williams* (1995) is part of the Understanding Contemporary American Literature Series. Gunn's *Tennessee Williams: A Bibliography* (1991) is number 89 in the Scarecrow Author Bibliographies. Both *"A Streetcar Named Desire": The Moth and the Lantern* (1990), by Thomas P. Adler, and *"The Glass Menagerie": An American Memory* (1990), by Delma E. Presley, were published in Twayne's Masterwork Series; and finally, Dennis Vannatta's *Tennessee Williams: A Study of the Short Fiction* (1988) belongs to Twayne's Studies in Short Fiction. Scholars in the future may well want to consider whether the sometimes restrictive requirements and controlling influences of the publisher serve the best interest of Tennessee Williams scholarship.

While these recent full-length studies of Williams are characterized by varying degrees of conformity to publisher's standards, briefer articles continue to reflect the diversity of independent opinion. The *Tennessee Williams Literary Journal* and the *Tennessee Williams Annual Review,* as well as special issues of *Studies in American Drama, 1945–Present* (in 1993) and the *Mississippi Quarterly* (in 1995), are some of the many forums to which scholars have contributed in the last decade. Well over a hundred articles about Williams have appeared in print since 1990; the overwhelming focus has been on *A Streetcar Named Desire* and *The Glass Menagerie.* Critics have also selected for study the dramas *Cat on a Hot Tin Roof, Battle of Angels / Orpheus Descending, Suddenly Last Summer, The Night of the Iguana,* and *The Red Devil Battery Sign* but only occasionally the fiction, the poetry, or the other late plays of Tennessee Williams.[12]

Collecting some of the best recent work on *A Streetcar Named Desire,* Philip Kolin's volume *Confronting Tennessee Williams's "A Streetcar Named Desire": Essays in Critical Pluralism* (1995) includes fifteen original essays and considers Williams's most famous work from a variety of critical perspectives.

Separately published articles on *A Streetcar Named Desire* include, for example, comparative studies likening *Streetcar* to Oscar Wilde's *Salomé,* to Armistead Maupin's *Tales of the City,* and to Shakespeare's *The Taming of the Shrew* and *Measure for Measure.*[13] Character studies, almost all of them focusing on Blanche DuBois, take into account misogynic aspects of *Streetcar* and Blanche's complicity in her own victimization as well as Blanche's similarity to other literary and historical figures, for instance: Cleopatra, the Virgin Mary, and the Lady of Shallott.[14] The significance of paper, characters' names, dates, props, the "expressionistic uses of space" (Fleche 496), and the play's concluding scene have all been topics of recent discussion.[15] Even Alex North's musical score is the subject of an interview with Luigi Zaninelli, just as André Previn's operatic version of *Streetcar* was the topic of reviews in 1999.[16]

Many of the recent studies of *The Glass Menagerie* also make comparisons or engage in character analysis. Bigsby, following Gunn, comments on the similarity of *The Glass Menagerie* to Chekhov's *The Seagull,* while Laurilyn J. Harris notes how *Menagerie* resembles the work of Filipino playwright Nick Joaquin.[17] Analyses of the characters in *The Glass Menagerie* have identified types, such as the "belle" and "the crippled, maladjusted girl" (Taylor 110), or have indicated how each of the characters is imprisoned by her or her self-consciousness.[18] In other considerations, Reynolds observes that as much as technology has the potential to facilitate change and to make lives better in *The Glass Menagerie,* "the play consistently reiterates the failure of technology to achieve social or individual values" (523), while Crandell likens the structure of *The Glass Menagerie* to that of the classic cinema, which, in turn, is patterned after the patriarchal structure of society.[19]

Recent critical commentary on *Battle of Angels,* Williams's first professionally produced play, shows that Williams had already discovered the themes that would appear repeatedly in later works, but at this early stage in his career he did not yet have the skill to manage them successfully.[20] Adler, for example, claims that in *Battle of Angels* we see prefigured "all of the motifs that become central in the Williams canon":

> a romantic valorization of the poetic misfit or dispossessed outsider; an almost Manichean duality in the patterning of imagery and symbology, particularly of "shadow and light"; a

consideration of the artist's vocation and near-sacred function in the community; the place of illusion and dreams in otherwise thwarted lives; the relationship between madness and vision; an emphasis on repressed sexuality or neuroticism, and on the redemptive power of sexual love; the necessity for breaking free from the shell of self and responding compassionately to others; the need to accept human frailty without despair and move from guilt to expiation; a discussion of how societal mores and economic dependency constrict individual freedom; and a desire that civilization be feminized and humanized as a counter to masculine power and aggression. (Adler, *American* 132)

Cat on a Hot Tin Roof has most frequently prompted reconsiderations of Williams and homosexuality. Mark Royden Winchell contends that *Cat on a Hot Tin Roof* is a "scandalous, and ultimately subversive, play" because it "doubt[s] the 'innocence'" of a male-male relationship (701). Dean Shackelford sees, in *Cat on a Hot Tin Roof,* Williams's "courageous efforts to bring the subject [of homosexuality] 'out of the closet' in a repressive era of American history" (104). Like *Streetcar Named Desire* and *The Glass Menagerie, Cat on a Hot Tin Roof* has also prompted comparative character studies. Colby Kullman, for example, likens Big Daddy to tyrannical figures in George Orwell's *1984* and Joseph Heller's *Catch-22* (669). All three writers, Kullman contends, joined in "attacking the tyranny and bullyism of mind-controlling power structures" (669).

Although *Suddenly Last Summer* debuted with little fanfare in 1958, it has since provoked especially engaging critical attention, notably from Stephen Bruhm, who not only considers the "economics of desire" in the play but also usefully applies Lee Edelman's concept of "homographesis" to explicate the "queer meaning" of this complex drama.[21] Other remarkable commentaries include Andrew Sofer's discussion of the relationship between power and the body and Robert F. Gross's illuminating expedition beneath the surface of Williams's Gothic melodrama.[22] In that subterranean realm, Gross follows Williams's "most extensive exploration of the aesthetics of the Sublime" and considers the relationship of the Sublime to *Suddenly Last Summer*'s gay poetics (229). Together these commentaries point to a generally unnoticed complexity in Williams's drama and a depth in Williams's thinking that even Leverich, for all his comprehensiveness, neglects to probe.

In studies of other plays, Kevin Matthews draws upon manuscript drafts of *The Night of the Iguana* to show that Williams "constantly refined his attitudes toward his themes" (87). Of the late plays, *The Red Devil Battery Sign* has attracted attention as a drama in which Williams's political themes are overtly expressed.[23]

In other, more general considerations of Williams's work, the topics are as miscellaneous as Williams's plays are numerous. Representative subjects include: addiction, ambiguity, androgyny, flawed characters, heroines, unseen characters, saints and strangers, madonnas and studs, madness and dementia, the language of power, existentialist philosophy, and Tennessee Williams as a southern playwright.[24]

As advantageous as it would be to know the future direction of Tennessee Williams scholarship, only a magical muse could accurately predict. Although we might prescribe a course for scholarship, in so doing we would be assuming an authority comparable to that of the late Maria St. Just. At best, it seems reasonable to reflect upon what has been accomplished in recent years, to describe the paths that scholars have taken, and to profit from those who, like Williams, have the vision to lead us into the twenty-first century.

Williams's biographers as well as his editors provide valuable resources for the continuing reevaluation of Williams's life and work. Bibliographers and textual critics have likewise facilitated opportunities for research. Scholarly critics have set a standard for future studies of performance and the relationship between text and performance. Others have called for a much-deserved critical reassessment of the Williams canon in its entirety. "The torch has been passed to a new generation of Tennessee Williams scholars" (Kennedy 257). It remains for them to explain to a new millennium of readers and theater audiences the mystery of Tennessee Williams, the twentieth century's "magical muse."

Notes

1. Adler refers frequently to apocalyptic images in Williams; see *American Drama* 144 and 178, "Culture" 650, and "Tennessee Williams's 'Personal Lyricism'" 184. Fleche (*Mimetic* 22 and 93) and Savran (*Communists* 167) likewise mention Williams and apocalypse.

2. In her examination of "The Vengeance of Nitocris," Hitchcock maintains that this story is the keynote for much of Williams's later work (595–608), while Kolin concludes that "Big Black: A Mississippi Idyll" displays many of the distinctive features that mark Williams's later dramatic work ("No masterpiece has been overlooked" 27–34). For studies of the poetry, see Adler, "Tennessee Williams's Poetry" 63–72 and Tischler, "Tennessee" 73–79.

3. Hale has written extensively about Williams's life, education, and associations. See her "Accounting" 25–32, "Early Williams" 11–28, "Tennessee" 609–25, and "Tom Williams" 13–22.

4. See Bray's "Interview" 777–88. See also Dakin Williams and Shepherd Mead, *Tennessee Williams: An Intimate Biography.*

5. For essays about Williams's correspondence, see Devlin 23–31, Tischler, "Letters" 167–173, and Isaac 124–133.

6. Hale examines Mishima's influence in two essays; see "Noh and Kabuki" 37–41 and "The Secret Script" 363–75.

7. Hale considers Van Gogh's influence on Williams; see "Of Prostitutes" 33–45.

8. See Kolin, "The First Critical" 45–67.

9. Kolin describes premiere productions in Great Britain, in "Olivier" 143–57; in China, see Kolin and Shao; in Cuba, "Tennessee Williams's *A Streetcar*" 89–110; in Japan, "The Japanese Premier" 713–33; in Mexico, "The Mexican Premiere" 315–40; in Poland, "The First Polish" 67–88; in Spain, "'Cruelty'" 45–56; and in Sweden, "On a Trolley" 277–86.

10. See, for example, Kolin, "Black and Multi-Racial" 97–128.

11. Parker documents the manuscript records for *Suddenly Last Summer* in "Tentative" 303–36; for *The Rose Tattoo* in "Provisional" 279–94; for *Camino Real* in "Documentary" 41–52 and "Developmental" 331–41; and for *Cat on a Hot Tin Roof* in "Preliminary" 475–96.

12. See note 2 above for studies of the fiction and poetry. The most complete treatment of the late plays is Dorff, "Disfigured Stages."

13. See Kailo 199–236, Van Oostrum 117–27, and Hall, "'Gaudy Seed-Bearers'" 9–11. For other comparative studies, see Keller 2–3 and Kolin, "'Hello from Bertha'" 6–7.

14. Lant discusses the misogyny that "colors" Williams's play and the audience's response to it (225–38). For comparative studies, see Kolin, "Cleopatra" 25–27 and "Our Lady" 81–87, and Daniel 2–3.

15. Among the many commentaries on *A Streetcar Named Desire*, Kolin examines paper ontologies; see "'It's only'" 454–67. Kolin and Wolter consider character names (241–43). Cardullo explains "Belle Reve" in "The Meaning" 220–22 and also pinpoints the date of the final scene in *A Streetcar Named Desire;* see "Scene 11" 34–38. Monteiro comments on the significance of a prop, Blanche's seahorse pin (9), while Fleche traces Blanche's

"allegorical journey" through a nonrealistic world in which spatial distinctions are obliterated; see "The Space" 496–509. The conclusion of *A Streetcar Named Desire* is the focus of Toles 115–43 and Schlueter 96–106.

16. See McCraw 763–75. For reviews of the opera, see Ross 110–11, Teachout, "Brand-Name" 56–59, and Holland E1-E2.

17. Drewey Wayne Gunn first calls attention to a Chekhovian likeness in "'More than Just a Little Chekhovian'" 313–21. Bigsby draws a similar comparison in "Entering" 29–44. Savran also highlights Williams's indebtedness to Chekhov; see *Communists* 89–92. Harris points to the relevance of Williams's plays on the Filipino stage (163–74).

18. See Taylor 110–14 and Levy 529–37.

19. See Reynolds 522–27 and Crandell, "Cinematic" 1–11. Timpane's consideration of the "gaze" in Williams also acknowledges the influence of the cinema (751–61).

20. See Egan 61–98 and Adler, *American* 132.

21. See Bruhm, "Blackmailed" 528–37 and "Blond" 97–105. See also Edelman's *Homographesis*.

22. See Sofer 336–47 and Gross 229–51.

23. See Schlatter 93–101 and Grosch 119–24.

24. On addiction, see Plumb 178–83; on ambiguity, see Gronbeck-Tedesco 735–49; on androgyny, see Adler, "Tennessee Williams's 'Personal Lyricism'" 172–88; on flawed characters, see Taylor 110–14; on heroines, see Kataria; on unseen characters, see Koprince, 87–95; on saints and strangers, see Wolter 33–51; on madonnas and studs, see Hall, "The Stork and the Reaper" 677–700; on madness and dementia, see O'Connor; on the language of power, see Wilhelmi 217–26; on Williams and existentialist philosophy, see Colanzi 451–65; on Williams and the South, see Holditch 61–75, King 627–47, Inge 157–65, Evans 141–49, and Watson 174–91.

Works Cited

Adler, Thomas P. *American Drama, 1940–1960: A Critical History*. New York: Twayne, 1994.

——. "Culture, Power, and the (En)gendering of Community: Tennessee Williams and Politics." *Mississippi Quarterly* 48.4 (1995): 649–65.

——. *A Streetcar Named Desire: The Moth and the Lantern*. Boston: Twayne, 1990.

——. "Tennessee Williams's 'Personal Lyricism': Toward an Androgynous Form." In *Realism and the American Dramatic Tradition*, edited by William W. Demastes. Tuscaloosa: University of Alabama Press, 1996.

——. "Tennessee Williams's Poetry: Intertext and Metatext." *Tennessee Williams Annual Review* 1 (1998): 63–72.

Bak, John S. "From '10' to 'Quarter Past Eight Foot': Tennessee Williams and William Inge, 1957." *American Drama* 7.1 (1997): 18–29.

Bigsby, C. W. E. "Entering *The Glass Menagerie.*" In *The Cambridge Companion to Tennessee Williams,* edited by Matthew C. Roudané. Cambridge: Cambridge University Press, 1997.

———. "Tennessee Williams: The Theatricalising Self." In *Modern American Drama, 1945–1990.* Cambridge: Cambridge University Press, 1992.

Bray, Robert. "An Interview with Dakin Williams." *Mississippi Quarterly* 48.4 (1995): 777–88.

———. "*A Streetcar Named Desire:* The Political and Historical Subtext." In *Confronting Tennessee Williams's "A Streetcar Named Desire": Essays in Cultural Pluralism,* edited by Philip C. Kolin. Westport, Conn.: Greenwood Press, 1993.

Bruhm, Steven. "Blackmailed by Sex: Tennessee Williams and the Economics of Desire." *Modern Drama* 34 (1991): 528–37.

———. "Blond Ambition: Tennessee Williams's Homographesis." *Essays in Theatre* 14.2 (1996): 97–105.

Cardullo, Bert. "The Meaning of 'Belle Reve' in *A Streetcar Named Desire.*" *Language Quarterly* 32.3–4 (1994): 220–22.

———. "Scene 11 of *A Streetcar Named Desire.*" *American Notes and Queries* 10 (1997): 34–38.

Clum, John. *Acting Gay: Male Homosexuality in American Drama.* New York: Columbia University Press, 1992.

Cohn, Ruby. "Tennessee Williams: The Last Two Decades." In *The Cambridge Companion to Tennessee Williams,* edited by Matthew C. Roudané. Cambridge: Cambridge University Press, 1997.

Colanzi, Rita. "Caged Birds: Bad Faith in Tennessee Williams's Drama." *Modern Drama* 35 (1992): 451 65.

Crandell, George W. "The Cinematic Eye in Tennessee Williams's *The Glass Menagerie.*" *Tennessee Williams Annual Review* 1 (1998): 1–11.

———, ed. *The Critical Response to Tennessee Williams.* Westport, Conn.: Greenwood Press, 1996.

———. "Misrepresentation and Miscegenation: Reading the Racialized Discourse of Tennessee Williams's *A Streetcar Named Desire.*" *Modern Drama* 40 (1997): 337–46.

———. *Tennessee Williams: A Descriptive Bibliography.* Pittsburgh: University of Pittsburgh Press, 1995.

Daniel, LaNelle. "Mirrors and Curses: Blanche DuBois and the Lady of Shalott." *Notes on Contemporary Literature* 23.1 (1993): 2–3.

Devlin, Albert J. "*The Selected Letters of Tennessee Williams:* Prospects for Research." *Tennessee Williams Annual Review* 1 (1998): 23–31.

Devlin, Albert J., and Nancy M. Tischler. *The Selected Letters of Tennessee Williams.* Vol. 1. New York: New Directions, 2000.

Dorff, Linda. "Disfigured Stages: The Late Plays of Tennessee Williams, 1958–1983." Ph.D. dissertation, New York University, 1997.

Edelman, Lee. *Homographesis: Essays in Gay Literary and Cultural Theory.* New York: Routledge, 1994.

Egan, Rory B. "Orpheus Christus Mississippiensis: Tennessee Williams's Xavier in Hell." *Classical and Modern Literature* 14 (1993): 61–98.

Elam, Keir. *The Semiotics of Theatre and Drama.* London: Methuen, 1980.

Evans, Robley. "'Or else this were a savage spectacle': Eating and Troping Southern Culture." *Southern Quarterly* 30.2–3 (1992): 141–49.

Fisher, James. "'The Angels of Fructification': Tennessee Williams, Tony Kushner, and Images of Homosexuality on the American Stage." *Mississippi Quarterly* 49.1 (1995–1996): 13–32.

Fleche, Anne. *Mimetic Disillusion: Eugene O'Neill, Tennessee Williams, and U.S. Dramatic Realism.* Tuscaloosa: University of Alabama Press, 1997.

——. "The Space of Madness and Desire: Tennessee Williams and *Streetcar.*" *Modern Drama* 38 (1995): 496–509.

Griffin, Alice. *Understanding Tennessee Williams.* Columbia: University of South Carolina Press, 1995.

Gronbeck-Tedesco, John. "Ambiguity and Performance in the Plays of Tennessee Williams." *Mississippi Quarterly* 48.4 (1995): 735–49.

Grosch, Robert J. "Memory as Theme and Production Value in Tennessee Williams's *The Red Devil Battery Sign.*" *Tennessee Williams Annual Review* 1 (1998): 119–24.

Gross, Robert F. "Consuming Hart: Sublimity and Gay Poetics in *Suddenly Last Summer.*" *Theatre Journal* 47 (1995): 229–51.

Gunn, Drewey Wayne. "'More than Just a Little Chekhovian': *The Sea Gull* as a Source for the Characters in *The Glass Menagerie.*" *Modern Drama* 33 (1990): 313–21.

——. *Tennessee Williams: A Bibliography.* 2d ed. Metuchen, N.J.: Scarecrow Press, 1991.

Hale, Allean. "Accounting for Tennessee." *Black Mountain Review* 9 (1993): 25–32.

——. "Early Williams: The Making of a Playwright." In *The Cambridge Companion to Tennessee Williams,* edited by Matthew Roudané. Cambridge: Cambridge University Press, 1997.

——. "Noh and Kabuki in the Drama of Tennessee Williams." *Text & Presentation: The Journal of the Comparative Drama Conference.* 15 (1994): 37–41.

——. "Of Prostitutes, Artists, and Ears." *Southern Quarterly* 29.1 (1990): 33–45.

——. "The Secret Script of Tennessee Williams." *Southern Review* 27 (1991): 363–75.

——. "Tennessee Williams's St. Louis Blues." *Mississippi Quarterly* 48.4 (1995): 609–25.

———. "Tom Williams, Proletarian Playwright." *Tennessee Williams Annual Review* 1 (1998): 13–22.

Hall, Joan Wylie. "'Gaudy Seed-Bearers': Shakespeare, Pater, and *A Streetcar Named Desire*." *Notes on Contemporary Literature* 20.4 (1990): 9–11.

———. "The Stork and the Reaper, the Madonna and the Stud: Procreation and Mothering in Tennessee Williams's Plays." *Mississippi Quarterly* 48.4 (1995): 677–700.

Harris, Laurilyn J. "*Menagerie* in Manila and Other Cross-Cultural Affinities: The Relevance of the Plays of Tennessee Williams on the Filipino Stage." *Studies in American Drama, 1945–Present* 8.2 (1993): 163–74.

Hayman, Ronald. *Tennessee Williams: Everyone Else Is an Audience*. New Haven: Yale University Press, 1993.

Hitchcock, Francesca M. "Tennessee Williams's 'Vengeance of Nitocris': The Keynote to Future Works." *Mississippi Quarterly* 48.4 (1995): 595–608.

Holditch, W. Kenneth. "South Toward Freedom: Tennessee Williams." In *Literary New Orleans: Essays and Meditations,* edited by Richard S. Kennedy. Baton Rouge: Louisiana State University Press, 1992.

Holland, Bernard. "Pursuing the Soul of *Streetcar* in Opera." *New York Times* 21 September 1998: E1–E2.

Inge, M. Thomas. "The South, Tragedy, and Comedy in Tennessee Williams's *Cat on a Hot Tin Roof*." In *The United States South: Regionalism and Identity,* edited by Valeria Gennaro Lerda and Tjebbe Westendorp. Rome: Bulzoni, 1991.

Isaac, Dan. "Founding Father: O'Neill's Correspondence with Arthur Miller and Tennessee Williams." *Eugene O'Neill Review* 17.1–2 (1993): 124–33.

Kailo, Kaarina. "Blanche Dubois and Salomé as New Women: Old Lunatics in Modern Drama." *Madness in Drama*. Cambridge: Cambridge University Press, 1993.

Kataria, Gulshan Rai. *The Faces of Eve: A Study of Tennessee Williams's Heroines*. New Delhi: Sterling Publishers Private Limited, 1992.

Keller, James R. "A Fellowship of Madness: Williams' Blanche Dubois and Zindel's Anna Reardon." *Notes on Contemporary Literature* 23.5 (1993): 2–3.

Kennedy, John F. "Inaugural Address." In *The Speaker's Resource Book: An Anthology, Handbook, and Glossary,* edited by Carroll C. Arnold, Douglas Ehninger, and John C. Gerber. Chicago: Scott, Foresman, 1961.

King, Kimball. "Tennessee Williams: A Southern Writer." *Mississippi Quarterly* 48.4 (1995): 627–47.

Kolin, Philip C. "Black and Multi-Racial Productions of Tennessee Williams's *The Glass Menagerie*." *Journal of Dramatic Theory and Criticism* 9.2 (1995): 97–128.

———. "Civil Rights and the Black Presence in *Baby Doll*." *Literature and Film Quarterly* 24.1 (1996): 2–11.

——. "Cleopatra of the Nile and Blanche DuBois of the French Quarter: *Anthony and Cleopatra* and *A Streetcar Named Desire.*" *Shakespeare Bulletin: A Journal of Performance Criticism and Scholarship* 11.1 (1993): 25–27.

——, ed. *Confronting Tennessee Williams's "A Streetcar Named Desire": Essays in Critical Pluralism.* Westport, Conn.: Greenwood Press, 1993.

——. "'Cruelty . . . and Sweaty Intimacy': The Reception of the Spanish Premiere of *A Streetcar Named Desire.*" *Theatre Survey* 35.2 (1994): 45–56.

——. "The Existential Nightmare in Tennessee Williams's *The Chalky White Substance.*" *Notes on Contemporary Literature* 23.1 (1993): 8–10.

——. "The First Critical Assessments of *A Streetcar Named Desire:* The *Streetcar* Tryouts and the Reviewers." *Journal of Dramatic Theory and Criticism* 6.1 (1991): 45–67.

——. "The First Polish Productions of *A Streetcar Named Desire.*" *Theatre History Studies* 12 (1992): 67–88.

——. "'Hello from Bertha' as a Source for *A Streetcar Named Desire.*" *Notes on Contemporary Literature* 27.1 (1997): 6–7.

——. "'It's only a paper moon': The Paper Ontologies in Tennessee Williams's *A Streetcar Named Desire.*" *Modern Drama* 40 (1997): 454–67.

——. "The Japanese Premiere of *A Streetcar Named Desire.*" *Mississippi Quarterly* 48.4 (1995): 713–33.

——. "The Mexican Premiere of Tennessee Williams's *A Streetcar Named Desire.*" *Mexican Studies / Estudios Mexicanos* 10.2 (1994): 315–40.

——. "'No masterpiece has been overlooked': The Early Reception and Significance of Tennessee Williams's 'Big Black: A Mississippi Idyll.'" *American Notes and Queries* 8 (1995): 27–34.

——. "Olivier to Williams: An Introduction." *Missouri Review* 13.3 (1991): 143–57.

——. "On a Trolley to the Cinema: Ingmar Bergman and the First Swedish Production of *A Streetcar Named Desire.*" *South Carolina Review* 27.1–2 (1994–1995): 277–86.

——. "Our Lady of the Quarter: Blanche DuBois and the Feast of the Mater Dolorosa." *American Notes and Queries* 4 (1991): 81–87.

——. "Sleeping with Caliban: The Politics of Race in Tennessee Williams's *Kingdom of Earth.*" *Studies in American Drama, 1945–Present* 8.2 (1993) 140–62.

——, ed. *Tennessee Williams: A Guide to Research and Performance.* Westport, Conn.: Greenwood Press, 1998.

——. "Tennessee Williams' 'Big Black: A Mississippi Idyll' and Race Relations, 1932." *RE Arts and Letters* 202 (1995): 8–12.

——. "Tennessee Williams's *A Streetcar Named Desire* in Havana: Modesto Centeno's Cuban *Streetcars, 1948–1965.*" *South Atlantic Review* 60.4 (1995): 89–110.

Kolin, Philip C., and Jürgen Wolter. "Williams's *A Streetcar Named Desire.*" *Explicator* 49.4 (1991): 241–43.

Kolin, Philip C., and Sherry Shao. "The First Production of *A Streetcar Named Desire* in Mainland China." *Tennessee Williams Literary Journal* 2.1 (1990–1991): 19–31.

Koprince, Susan. "Tennessee Williams's Unseen Characters." *Southern Quarterly* 33.1 (1994): 87–95.

Kullman, Colby H. "Rule by Power: 'Big Daddyism' in the World of Tennessee Williams's Plays." *Mississippi Quarterly* 48.4 (1995): 667–76.

Kushner, Tony. *Angels in America: A Gay Fantasia on National Themes, Part One: Millennium Approaches.* New York: Theatre Communications Group, 1993.

Lahr, John. "The Lady and Tennessee." *New Yorker,* December 19, 1994, pp. 77–96.

Lant, Kathleen Margaret. "A Streetcar Named Misogyny." *Violence in Drama.* Cambridge: Cambridge University Press, 1991.

Leverich, Lyle. *Tom: The Unknown Tennessee Williams.* New York: Crown, 1995.

Levy, Eric P. "'Through Soundproof Glass': The Prism of Self-Consciousness in *The Glass Menagerie.*" *Modern Drama* 36 (1993): 529–37.

Lily, Mark. "Tennessee Williams: *The Glass Menagerie* and *A Streetcar Named Desire.*" In *Lesbian and Gay Writing: An Anthology of Critical Essays,* edited by Mark Lily. Philadelphia: Temple University Press, 1990.

McCann, John S. *The Critical Reputation of Tennessee Williams: A Reference Guide.* Boston: G. K. Hall, 1983.

McCraw, Harry W. "Tennessee Williams, Film, Music, Alex North: An Interview with Luigi Zaninelli." *Mississippi Quarterly* 48.4 (1995): 763–75.

Martin, Robert A., ed. *Critical Essays on Tennessee Williams.* New York: G. K. Hall, 1997.

Matthews, Kevin. "The Evolution of *The Night of the Iguana:* Three Symbols in the Manuscript Record. *Library Chronicle of the University of Texas* 25.2 (1994): 66–89.

Monteiro, George. "The Seahorse in *A Streetcar Named Desire.*" *Notes on Contemporary Literature* 23.3 (1993): 9.

Murphy, Brenda. *Tennessee Williams and Elia Kazan: A Collaboration in the Theatre.* Cambridge: Cambridge University Press, 1992.

Nelson, Benjamin. *Tennessee Williams: His Life and Work.* London: Peter Owen, 1961.

O'Connor, Jacqueline. *Dramatizing Dementia: Madness in the Plays of Tennessee Williams.* Bowling Green: Bowling Green State University Popular Press, 1997.

Parker, Brian. "A Developmental Stemma for Drafts and Revisions of Tennessee Williams's *Camino Real.*" *Modern Drama* 39 (1996): 331–41.

——. "Documentary Sources for *Camino Real.*" *Tennessee Williams Annual Review* 1 (1998): 41–52.

——. "A Preliminary Stemma for Drafts and Revisions of Tennessee Williams's *Cat on a Hot Tin Roof* (1955)." *Publications of the Bibliographical Society of America* 90.4 (1996): 475–96.

——. "A Provisional Stemma for Drafts, Alternatives, and Revisions of Tennessee Williams's *The Rose Tattoo* (1951)." *Modern Drama* 40 (1997): 279–94.

——. "A Tentative Stemma for Drafts and Revisions of *Suddenly Last Summer* (1958). *Modern Drama* 41 (1998): 303–26.

Plumb, David. "Finding the Click: Addiction and the Creative Spirit in Six Plays of Tennessee Williams." In *Beyond the Pleasure Dome: Writing and Addiction from the Romantics,* edited by Sue Vice, Matthew Campbell, and Tim Armstrong. Sheffield: Sheffield Academic Press, 1994.

Presley, Delma E. *The Glass Menagerie: An American Memory.* Boston: Twayne, 1990.

Price, Marian. "*Cat on a Hot Tin Roof:* The Uneasy Marriage of Success and Idealism." *Modern Drama* 38 (1995): 324–35.

Reynolds, James. "The Failure of Technology in *The Glass Menagerie.*" *Modern Drama* 34 (1991): 522–27.

Ross, Alex. "Off the Tracks: Previn Stumbles; Schoenberg Soars." *New Yorker,* October 5, 1998, pp. 110–11.

Roudané, Matthew C., ed. *The Cambridge Companion to Tennessee Williams.* Cambridge: Cambridge University Press, 1997.

Savran, David. *Communists, Cowboys, and Queers: The Politics of Masculinity in the Work of Arthur Miller and Tennessee Williams.* Minneapolis: University of Minnesota Press, 1992.

Schlatter, James. "*Red Devil Battery Sign:* An Approach to a Mytho-Political Theatre." *Tennessee Williams Annual Review* 1 (1998): 93–101.

Schlueter, June. "Reading Toward Closure: *A Streetcar Named Desire.*" In *Dramatic Closure: Reading the End.* Madison: Fairleigh Dickinson University Press, 1995.

Shackelford, Dean. "The Truth That Must Be Told: Gay Subjectivity, Homophobia, and Social History in *Cat on a Hot Tin Roof.*" *Tennessee Williams Annual Review* 1 (1998): 103–18.

Siebold, Thomas., ed. *Readings on The Glass Menagerie.* San Diego: Greenhaven Press, 1998.

Smith, William Jay. "Tom: The Making of *The Glass Menagerie.*" *New Criterion* 14.7 (1996): 72–77.

Sofer, Andrew. "Self-Consuming Artifacts: Power, Performance, and the Body in Tennessee Williams' *Suddenly Last Summer.*" *Modern Drama* 38 (1995): 336–47.

Spoto, Donald. *The Kindness of Strangers: The Life of Tennessee Williams.* Boston: Little, Brown, 1985.

Taylor, Jo Barbara. "Fragile and Flawed Female Characters in the Drama of Tennessee Williams." *Mount Olive Review: Images of Women in Literature* 6 (1992): 110–14.

Teachout, Terry. "Brand-Name Opera." *Commentary* 106.5 (1998): 56–59.

———. "Irregular Combinations." *National Review* 18 October 1985: 54–56.

Timpane, John. "Gaze and Resistance in the Plays of Tennessee Williams." *Mississippi Quarterly* 48.4 (1995): 751–61.

Tischler, Nancy M. "Letters to a Friend—Third Edition." *Mississippi Quarterly* 50.1 (1996–1997): 167–73.

———. "Tennessee Williams: Vagabond Poet." *Tennessee Williams Annual Review* 1 (1998): 73–79.

Toles, George. "Blanche DuBois and the Kindness of Endings." *Raritan* 14.4 (1995): 115–43.

Vanatta, Dennis. *Tennessee Williams: A Study of the Short Fiction.* Boston: Twayne, 1988.

Van Oostrum, Duco. "'Dear . . . I Have No objection to Anything': Constructing Identities in Apartment Buildings in New Orleans and San Francisco in Tennessee Williams's *A Streetcar Named Desire* and Armistead Maupin's *Tales of the City.*" In *"Writing" Nation and "Writing" Region in America,* edited by Johannes Willem Bertens and Hans Bertens. Amsterdam: Vrije University Press, 1996.

Watson, Charles S. *The History of Southern Drama.* Lexington: University Press of Kentucky, 1997.

Watts, Richard. "The Impact of Tennessee Williams." *New York Post,* March 25, 1955, p. 57.

Wilhemi, Nancy O. "The Language of Power and Powerlessness: Verbal Combat in the Plays of Tennessee Williams." In *The Text Beyond: Essays in Literary Linguistics,* edited by Cynthia Goldin Bernstein. Tuscaloosa: University of Alabama Press, 1994.

Williams, Dakin, and Shepherd Mead. *Tennessee Williams: An Intimate Biography.* New York: Arbor House, 1983.

Williams, Tennessee. "Beauty Is the Word." *Missouri Review* 7.3 (1984): 187–95.

———. "The Chalky White Substance." *Antaeus* 66 (1991): 467–73.

———. "Hot Milk at Three in the Morning." *Missouri Review* 7.3 (1984): 196–200.

———. *Not About Nightingales.* Edited by Allean Hale. New York: New Directions, 1997.

———. *The Notebook of Trigorin: A Free Adaptation of Anton Chekhov's "The Sea Gull."* Edited by Allean Hale. New York: New Directions, 1997.

———. *The Rose Tattoo*. The Theatre of Tennessee Williams. Vol. 2. New York: New Directions, 1971.

———. *Something Cloudy, Something Clear*. New York: New Directions, 1995.

———. *Spring Storm*. Edited by Dan Isaac. New York: New Directions, 1999.

———. *Stairs to the Roof*. Edited by Allean Hale. New York: New Directions, 2000.

———. *Sweet Bird of Youth*. The Theatre of Tennessee Williams. Vol. 4. New York: New Directions, 1972.

———. *Will Mr. Merriwether Return from Memphis? Missouri Review* 20.2 (1997): 79–131.

Winchell, Mark Royden. "Come Back to the Locker Room Ag'n, Brick Honey!" *Mississippi Quarterly* 48.4 (1995): 701–12.

Winer, Linda. "In *Cat* It's Kathleen's Show." In *New York Theatre Critics' Reviews,* edited by Joan Marlowe and Betty Blake. Vol. 51. New York: New York Theatre Reviews, 1990.

Wolter, Jürgen C. "Stranger on Williams's Stage." *Mississippi Quarterly* 49.1 (1995–1996): 33–51.

2

The Year 1939

Becoming Tennessee Williams

Albert J. Devlin

The instinct and taste of Tom Williams for higher education were found wanting at three institutions before he graduated from the University of Iowa in 1938. Free at last from academe, he went to Chicago, where he failed to find work on the Federal Theatre or Writers Project; then briefly to "the City of St. Pollution" (*Conversations* 180), where he fell under the yoke of his father, Cornelius; then on to Memphis, New Orleans, and points west. Soon it was 1939, a year in which both the United States and Tennessee Williams seemed to mark time before plunging, respectively, into World War II and a career on Broadway. Nancy Tischler and I have followed this story in editing volume 1 of *The Selected Letters of Tennessee Williams,* but I should like to elaborate upon this extraordinary year of preparation, especially upon two literary models that Williams considered in his travels. As the year progressed, he was still trying to answer the most basic questions of life, often posed in his journal with a kind of sophomoric splendor, and to deal with a new set of professional ones that came with his finally being a regarded author.

It was Williams who distinguished 1939 by signing himself "Tennessee" when he applied in the preceding December to a Group Theatre contest for young playwrights. The facts are few and sketchy, and I doubt that they solve the riddle of when Tom first became "Tennessee." If the memory of his mother, Edwina, can be trusted, Williams mailed at least one play from St. Louis before he left on (or about) December 26 to visit his grandparents in Memphis. From there he mailed additional plays, "in plenty of time" (*Selected Letters* 1: 141) to meet the contest deadline, as he informed Edwina on

January 2 from New Orleans. Contest rules limited the event to play-wrights under the age of twenty-five, a bar that the twenty-seven-year-old Williams easily ducked, the Memphis postmark and the in-digenous name a ruse, as he later revealed, to shield his deception from "'friends'" (*Selected Letters* 1: 163) in St. Louis who might oth-erwise expose him. Apparently no covering letter(s) exists to con-firm Williams's self-description, but when Molly Day Thacher, play-reader for the Group Theatre, wrote with news of a special award on March 20, 1939, she congratulated "Mr. Tennessee Williams" (March 20, 1939, HRC).

"Tennessee" replaced Thomas Lanier Williams, a name that smacked of belles lettres and ruefully reminded the subject of Wil-liam Lyon Phelps, a Yale brahmin of the 1920s and 1930s. ("Tennes-see," I should add, briefly gave way to "Valentine Xavier," as Wil-liams inscribed a typescript in New Orleans in January 1939, but the allusion to the Catholic roots of his father's family was canceled in favor of "Tennessee.") Immeasurable is the gulf between the venial motives that led Williams to rename himself and the iconic intui-tion from which the new name must have sprung. Something of this inspiration was recorded in his journal shortly after Williams ar-rived in New Orleans. He was "enchanted" by the "fabulous old town" and convinced that "here surely is the place that I was *made* for if any place on this funny old world" (December 28, 1938). The nagging final clause bespeaks the fear that pervades Williams's jour-nal, beginning as it does in March 1936. His estrangement from the world is one that is general and natural in origin rather than politi-cal or economic; it is often encoded by such grim cosmological im-agery as "Dead Planet, the Moon!"—a working title that he chose in January 1939 for the play *Vieux Carré;* and it is inherent, charged with the displacement of birth and realized in a lifetime that does not take place. Rose Williams modeled the pathological excess of this alienation, while her younger brother was stunted in "the active desires of loving and growing" (*Modern Tragedy* 108).

But in New Orleans, in early 1939, a peace and promise seemed to arise, as "Tennessee" Williams felt at home in the "funny old world." He wrote with uncharacteristic poise on January 14 that "things are impending in my life—of that I feel sure—& so I am reasonably content for the nonce—willing to wait & see what's up!" This auspicious moment led Williams to isolate the lyrical "something" (*Journal,* January 14, 1939) that had survived the stupefying treadmill days of St. Louis, days that had seemed "short" because they "repeat themselves so. . . . It was all one day over and over" (qtd. in *Tom* 482–83), he lamented in the journal. New Orleans, by contrast, promised an advancing plot, impending events, a personal equipoise. Two weeks later, an epoch in the whirling Williams psyche, he was still "sailing bravely into another week—not knowing what it may bring—wondering but not too daunted by those speculations" (*Journal,* January 29, 1939). "Silly old Tommy," as Williams described himself in the New Orleans journal, had assumed a Whitmanesque pose of waiting and watching, of absorbing, of seeing "what's up!"

The journal and letters both confirm and complicate the familiar view of Tennessee Williams as an unstable man. Physical weakness and strength, fear and resolution, ignorance and prophecy alternate like the rhythm of a song played "over and over" in the oppressive Williams household, where a radio did indeed often blare in the background. The career itself was subject to the same oscillation. Williams routinely despaired that his work was "smashed" and that he was "artistically defunct" (*Journal,* November 21, 1936, September 15, 1937). "Maybe I am not a poet but just a blooming idiot" (*Journal,* ca. June 20, 1937), he opined gloomily in June 1937, as he reflected upon his own enervation and the artist's general disadvantage in the modern world. Several months later, before leaving for the University of Iowa, he was buoyed by the near completion of *Fugitive Kind* and affirmed that "the next play is always the important play. The past, however satisfactory, is only a challenge to the future. I want to go on creating. I *will*!!!" (*Journal,* September 16, 1937). After a wasted year at Iowa, he caught the forward march once again in New Orleans and held it for much of 1939, largely oblivious to the growing disorder in the world and finely attuned to the prompting of his own career. In August he wrote from Taos to his friend and traveling companion Jim Parrott, whose dreams of an acting career would not be realized: "The nature of progress is a repercussion from tumbles, it seems to me. . . . It's a slow, slow, bulldog battle that we all have to fight—Good God, How many years have I been trying to write? Since I was eleven or twelve! And maybe five years from now I will begin to be known" (qtd. in "Tennessee Travels" 13). Precisely five years later, in August 1944, in another artistic enclave at Provincetown, Williams was typing a dramatic work—*The Glass Menagerie,* of course—that would soon be optioned by Broadway and that would make him "known" without a nagging "maybe."

The year 1939 was a watershed in the "bull-dog battle" of apprenticeship that Tennessee Williams waged. The periodic "tumbles" occasioned by his "crazy blue devil" of fear and depression, and the times, which threatened to reduce his generation to abstractions of economic and political history, were held in abeyance as Williams began his life as a traveler-artist. In "repercussions" of identity and prophecy, he named himself and foresaw the time of his success, and by year's end he had completed a draft of his first mature work—if *Battle of Angels* may be so described. This is the outer story, and naturally the acquisition of a powerful agent, Audrey Wood, in April 1939, is a critical chapter that must be addressed, but the inner story is the more interesting and elusive and the one that I should like to consider. Now that Williams had separated himself from St. Louis (although he would return after this and many other apparent breaks), had gained recognition by the Group Theatre as a promising young playwright, and had found an agent, how did he begin to construct a literary life that was commensurate with the outward circumstances of his career? Two models came to his attention in early 1939, and not surprisingly both were roving artists: Nicholas Vachel Lindsay and Richard Halliburton.

Vachel Lindsay (1879–1931) is remembered today, if at all, for the vivid imagery and syncopated rhythms of "General William Booth Enters into Heaven" (1913) and especially "The Congo" (1914), with its simulation of a pounding African cadence. These and several other poems (including ones devoted to his political heroes Abraham Lincoln and William Jennings Bryan) were immensely popular from 1913, when "General Booth" appeared in Harriet Monroe's *Poetry* magazine, to the mid-1920s, when Lindsay's fragile hold upon fame began to loosen. At his peak, he was the "inimitably original" (*A Poet's Life* 321) protégé of Harriet Monroe; for the (later) poet laureate John Masefield, he sang of America "as lustily as Whitman did"; and he was praised by William Dean Howells as an inspired singer, who "fills the empyrean from the expanses of the whole great West" (qtd. in *Vachel Lindsay* 290). Lindsay's evangelistic tramping and prolonged apprenticeship were redeemed, as it were, in 1914, when William Butler Yeats arrived in Chicago on a reading tour and paid tribute to the "strange beauty" (qtd. in *A Poet's Life* 337) of "General Booth." Lindsay responded by reciting "The Congo" at a banquet given in Yeats's honor by *Poetry* magazine. He did indeed "pound the table hard" (qtd. in *A Poet's Life* 333), as he had warned Harriet Monroe, in a performance that was a long-delayed triumph for the thirty-four-year-old poet from Springfield, Illinois.

How Tennessee Williams first became aware of Lindsay is a matter of speculation. Perhaps as a student chanting "The Congo," as did the Williams scholar Allean Hale in 1930: "Boomlay, boomlay, boomlay, Boom." Perhaps as a literary-minded St. Louisan who knew of Lindsay's courtship of the St. Louis–born poet Sara Teasdale. Williams's later friendship with the Filsinger sisters, nieces of Lindsay's rival and the man who finally married Teasdale in 1914, may have reinforced his knowledge of this awkward lover's address to a poet whose work he admired. Before Williams's first documented reference to Lindsay in June 1939, he may have shown his attention by the adage that "imitation is the sincerest form of flattery." In February 1939, Williams and Jim Parrott found themselves out of money and gas but not wits as they paused in El Paso before making a final push for California. Williams wrote a mock-serious letter to an unnamed "Editor" in which he tried to barter poems for gas:

> The author of these poems and his friend, Jimmy, a jobless musician, have run out of money and gas in El Paso, Texas. There is a terrific dust-storm raging and a sheriff named Fox who puts undesirable transients in the house of detention for thirty days. The author and the musician . . . Are not quite sure of their desirability and would like to continue westward to California where they understand that unemployed artists can make fifty cents an hour picking fruit. Their jalopy, running on kerosene or low-grade gas, could make Cal. on ten or fifteen dollars. If you like the poems an acceptance would aid materially in the author's survival. (*Selected Letters* 1: 150–51)

The itinerant Williams would soon remind his new agent, Audrey Wood, that Vachel Lindsay "was . . . for many years a tramp selling his poems for two cents—from door to door" (*Selected Letters* 1:

176). Both Lindsay and Williams were supremely restless and un-suited for any ordinary vocation or regularity in life. They tramped to keep their eccentricity intact and to stave off, as Lindsay put it, "the usual Middle West crucifixion of the artist" (qtd. in *Vachel Lindsay* 271).

Williams's first documented reference to Lindsay occurs in a let-ter written to Audrey Wood in June 1939 from Laguna Beach, Cali-fornia, where he and Jim Parrott had settled for the summer in a primitive cabin named "Airy Edges." To date, Miss Wood had re-ceived letters of thanks and introduction; with the latest correspon-dence, she began to see no doubt the far reach of Williams's imagina-tion and the dramaturgic problems that it would occasion. Williams had been reading Edgar Lee Masters's biography of Lindsay, which he thought filled with "a wealth of dramatic material." As he in-formed Wood, his biographical play about Vachel Lindsay

> would concern, in large, the whole problem of the poet or crea-tive artist in America or any other capitalistic state. . . . No-body with a desire to create has ever put up a braver, more pitiful struggle against the intellectual apathy and the eco-nomic tyranny of his times! . . . My play would center, I think, upon the closing chapter of his life—in Springfield, Illinois. . . . The play would terminate, of course, with Lindsay's suicide—that awful, grotesque crawling upstairs on hands and knees at midnight!—but would strike some positive, assertive note—I mean I would not want it to be just another futilitarian tragedy about a beaten-down artist. (*Selected Letters* 1: 176)

In reading Masters's biography, Williams could not have failed to notice the bold parallels between his own domestic history and Vachel Lindsay's. Both were the offspring of ill-matched parents; both were frail, bookish children, each more the mother's son than the father's. Both also had a complicated relation with nearby mid-western cities, Springfield and St. Louis, from which they derived much of their aesthetic energy and personal frustration. Lindsay dreamed of converting the cynical politicians and "climacteric women" (qtd. in *Vachel Lindsay* 335) of the capital city by preaching a "gospel of beauty." Williams held no such hope for "the City of St.

Pollution." All that remains (to my knowledge) of his enthusiasm for Lindsay are two undated, fragmentary typescripts in which he paid homage to "the last great poet in the troubadour tradition" (*Springfield, Illinois*). In the more substantial draft, entitled "Suitable Entrances to Springfield or Heaven," the scene is a Pullman car approaching Springfield, and the situation, the last homecoming of Lindsay in November 1931, a few days before his suicide. Also on the train are Luke and his wife Alice, a knife-throwing act whose sad but true story has Luke drinking heavily and Alice, his target, taking stage fright, as it were, with a transposed case of the shakes. Their presence is gratuitous unless it can be seen as Williams's attempt to echo Lindsay's theory of poetry as a "higher vaudeville" and his practice of this popular art form in the exuberant, capering stage recitals that he gave for years. Williams's script is feeble—by no means does it even approach the grandiose theme announced to Audrey Wood—but it is unerring in framing the vulnerability of the artist-performer and in suggesting the forces that work to destroy him. Of these Lindsay wrote astutely in 1929, in anticipation of Tennessee Williams's own "catastrophe of success":

> I begin to see how machinery closes in around the very topmost-seeming Americans. And how subtle is the appeal. It's a temptation and a complex of gathering forces no European ever faces, and hysterical shrieking against it keeps you right on the level with it, like Mencken, Lewis, *The Nation, The New Republic*. . . . So how would I define supremacy in America? Here it is: *to be above every single piece of machinery without shrieking against it. And yet to be completely effective as a traditional American.* (Qtd. in *The West-Going Heart* 390)

Williams wrote to Audrey Wood of his Lindsay play soon after he and Jim Parrott had settled for the summer in Laguna Beach, one of the many havens of artistic and sexual freedom that attracted Williams over the years. Earlier in May he corrected Edwina's "impression" that he planned to settle in Hollywood and assured her that he had not "been infected with the money-disease out here." He would keep his distance from that "putrid" atmosphere of "sham and corruption." "What I *want* to do," he continued, "is live out here this summer in a little beach colony for artists and writers which I have discovered on my bicycle tour. It is an indescribably beautiful place—Laguna Beach—lovelier than anything I saw in Europe" (*Selected Letters* 1: 168). By May 10 he and Jim Parrott had moved from Hawthorne, in south Los Angeles County, where Jim's aunt and uncle lived, and Williams wrote to his maternal grandmother—Rosina Otte Dakin, "Grand"—with further details of Santa Catalina Bay and the rugged mountains that surrounded Laguna Beach: "The water is a marvelous blue and the hills thickly wooded and covered with gorgeous wild flowers. The coast along here is very rocky but we have a beautiful sandy beach for swimming." For good measure, he added that "there are two beautiful twin girls we met in Los Angeles who entertain us frequently at their beautiful house on the beach—so we are ideally located" (*Selected Letters* 1: 173). Rarely in such dutiful correspondence did Williams violate the conventional expectations or values of his family. His allusion to girl-friends is doubly strategic, however, for in precisely a month's time his first known gay adventure would be recorded in the journal. He would also in the same letter to Grand make reference to the author-traveler Richard Halliburton, whose secret, now rendered profoundly academic, was in all probability the same as Tennessee Williams's.

Richard Halliburton (1900–1939) discovered Laguna Beach in 1930 and in 1937 completed the building of a "modernistic residence" overlooking the bay that he aptly named "Hangover House." Williams described both Halliburton and this curious edifice to his grandmother in the same letter of May 10:

> Richard Halliburton, who travelled all over the world, selected this place as his permanent home and has a big modernistic residence on one of the peaks overlooking the sea. Incidentally he has apparently met a tragic end in crossing the Pacific—I will enclose an article I just cut from the Laguna papers. I thought the sub-head about "County turns off water" added a rather grotesquely humorous touch. People around here say that Paul Mooney, mentioned as his collaborator, actually did most of his writing for him. They both went down in the junk—unless it all turns out to be a big publicity stunt. (*Selected Letters* 1: 173)

Williams probably mentioned Halliburton to his grandmother, and not to Edwina in a concurrent letter, because Halliburton's parents lived in Memphis, where the Dakins were retired. Halliburton had sailed from Hong Kong on March 4 in a Chinese junk bound for the Golden Gate Exposition in San Francisco. His arrival was timed for the opening of the fair and designed to create publicity for a national tour that would be the subject of his ninth book of travel. On March 24 radio contact with the *Sea Dragon* was broken and the woeful junk presumed lost in a typhoon in the western Pacific. Williams's surmise that this "tragic end" might be a "publicity stunt" echoed a general knowledge of Halliburton's genius for self-promotion and especially his history of filing premature reports of his own demise. But he and his companion Paul Mooney and a crew of twelve had indeed died at sea, and Halliburton was declared legally dead in October 1939.

Richard Halliburton was a restless youth who eagerly left Princeton after his graduation in 1921 to begin a life of tramping. There was, he told his father, a worried realtor, "something in turmoil inside me all the time. . . . The idea of leading a monotonous confined respectable life is horrible to me" (qtd. in *Halliburton's Royal Road* 52). Upon reaching his majority in 1921 he wistfully reflected: "I feel like Conrad in quest of his youth. Nine more years and I'll be thirty and the last vestige of youth will be gone. . . . I can look forward to no joy in life beyond thirty" (qtd. in *The Magnificent Myth* 57). He spent a frantic 600 days of travel doing research for his first book, *The Royal Road to Romance,* which was published in 1925 and became a national best-seller. It was followed quickly by a second, *The Glorious Adventure* (1927), in which Halliburton retraced the journey of Ulysses from Troy to Ithaca. This book was also "a *true* narrative," he said, "with buckets of bright paint flung over it," an image that he had used earlier to describe his mission as a writer: to "splash a little red paint" (qtd. in *Halliburton's Royal Road* 109, 8) over the commonplaceness of earth. By the mid-1930s, a Halliburton legend had been extruded from his headlong prose, dramatic photographs that showed him crossing the Alps on an elephant, posing in front of the Taj Mahal, consulting the oracle at Delphi, and embarking on a vast lecture tour in which he performed like "Apollo." The heroic pretension was no accident. If the commodification of the American literary career may be said to begin with Mark Twain, then Richard Halliburton, as well as Vachel Lindsay and Tennessee Williams, is a notable contributor to the process whereby art has come to be enfolded in fashion and publicity.

To my knowledge, Tennessee Williams made no further reference to Halliburton, nor is there any proof that he ever read his frothy prose. Their affinity, however, is pronounced and bears testimony to the power of the popular culture to sustain images that are used on many different levels. Williams and Halliburton were similar in defying fathers who offered conventional careers in shoes and real estate. They were also built along the same hypertensive lines and were given to depression, morbidity, and wide swings in mood. Halliburton used the conventional avenues of the media to exert a countervailing pressure upon the routines of life. More devoted to personal success than liberation, he was no exile or traveler in the way that Paul Bowles would later expound; but his projection of youthful dreams of escape onto the national culture was pervasive and compelling and may be said to have formed a background for Tennessee Williams's own similar plots of stagnation and defeat. In 1935, in his first produced play, in Halliburton's hometown of Memphis, a naive young sailor and his girlfriend intone "Cairo, Shanghai, Bombay!" with a reverence for the exotic and faraway that might have been learned from Halliburton. In *The Glass Menagerie,* Tom Wingfield "boils" in a hyperventilated speech that is sharply reminiscent of Halliburton's prose: "I know I seem dreamy, but inside—well, I'm boiling! Whenever I pick up a shoe, I shudder a little thinking how short life is and what I am doing!" (scene 6). When Tom leaves his "two-by-four" life in St. Louis, he goes as a merchant seaman, precisely the same way that Halliburton began his own travel on "The Royal Road to Romance."

A second and more delicate affinity between Williams and Halliburton is their sexual nature. The letter of May 10 to Grand, with its tale of beautiful girlfriends, is double-voiced in assuming normative airs shortly before Williams recorded his first homosexual experience. If not New Orleans, then Laguna Beach began in 1939 the arduous process of revealing to Williams his own complicated sexuality. "Getting a pack of neuroses on my heels," he wrote on June 11 after spending a "rather horrible night with a picked up acquaintance Doug whose amorous advance made me sick at the stomach." This foray quickly brought down the summer's idyll, "so marvelously calm and serene," so like one of Williams's favorite Gauguins, "'Nave Nave Mahana' The Careless Days." It was with "a feeling of spiritual nausea" (*Journal,* June 11, 14, 1939), he wrote, that he escaped briefly to Hawthorne, where Jim Parrott's family lived. An intuition of the spiritual dangers of Laguna Beach had also led Dick Halliburton's parents to object to the building of Hangover House and especially to the influence of Paul Mooney upon their son. They feared that the modernistic rectangle of glass and concrete, built sheer with a precipice of 600 feet, was not designed to soften their son's "unsociable nature" or to sanctify "the women situation," which seemed from afar to be one of profligacy and excess. He was not "morose" or "cynical," he answered in late 1936, and "the women situation is no cause for alarm. They play a very small part in my life, chiefly because their minds and natures bore me worse than men's." "Please," he concluded the letter, "don't be distressed because I'm the way I am. Just be grateful that I'm so much happier than most people and growing on a continually up-climbing curve" (qtd. in *Halliburton's Royal Road* 154). Did Williams in writing to his grandmother make a similar, if still more densely hedged, plea for understanding, with the strange conjunction of beautiful girls and a misogynous writer closeted high above the exotica of Laguna Beach? It was to Grand, of course, whom Williams went in life for understanding, and it was to her "transparent figure" (123) in "The Angel in the Alcove" that he turned for benediction upon his sexual difference. After his death, Halliburton quickly passed from view, but his rather prolonged vogue may have framed for a moment for Tennessee Williams the essential components of his own evolving career: art, celebrity, commerce, and a closeted sexuality, all grounded in the matrix of an equivocal family discourse.

Snapshots for the remaining months of 1939 show Tennessee Williams in August in Taos, New Mexico, where he met Frieda Lawrence and Dorothy Brett and began research at the Harwood Foundation for a play about D. H. Lawrence's life in America. Vachel Lindsay had given way to a much greater literary subject, whose love ethic Williams appropriated in an unpublished story written at Taos entitled "Why Did Desdemona Love the Moor?" It was also at Taos that "the foreign situation" finally broke into Williams's self-absorbed world and took, predictably, a theatrical turn. A now forgotten

Cleveland artist named William Eastman passed through Taos in the company of Hedvig Kraikow, a Polish baroness who was "very distraught" by the current German-Polish crisis. "To forget her troubles," Williams reported (in early-September 1939) in a letter to Grand, the baroness "gave a big dinner party" and "then went to a big casino" where she won "several hundred dollars at roulette! By the end of the evening she was quite unconcerned about the foreign situation" (*Selected Letters* 1: 202), and so too was Tennessee Williams. A brief "neurotic period" *(Journal,* September 17, 1939) in St. Louis, a month in New York observing the Broadway theater and meeting Audrey Wood, a return to St. Louis, the completion of a first draft of *Battle of Angels,* and the award of a Rockefeller Grant in late December brought 1939 to a conclusion that abruptly reversed Williams's growing conviction of his becoming "a decimated individual" *(Journal,* December 19, 1939) once again. Edwina "literally wept with joy" at the glad tidings from New York, while Williams was more restrained: "I have had to insulate my spirit against shocks in order to survive—result I'm dulled even to happiness" (*Journal,* December 21, 1939). Williams wrote these prescient lines well in advance of his own catastrophic success, but the example of Lindsay and Halliburton had left him with few vague guesses, if any, about the writer's life in America. It was, he knew, not "a peaceful profession" ("A Writer's Quest" 28).

It is no accident that Williams's chief interest or point of intersection with Vachel Lindsay and Richard Halliburton came with their premature deaths. Lindsay drank Lysol in 1931, while the journey of the *Sea Dragon* in 1939 was foolhardy, measured even by Dick Halliburton's wide standards of adventure, and may in retrospect seem suicidal. It is fair to say, I think, that each writer enjoyed a prolonged vogue rather than a career, with its phases and depth and maturation. They were far less gifted than Williams, but their very limitations seemed to expose them more directly to the national "machinery" of which Lindsay spoke in 1929, as "clos[ing] in around the very topmost-seeming Americans" and requiring that they trim their art to a mendacious popular culture. Even the dreamy Lindsay realized, as Williams once said, that it was "as hard to get rich on poetry as fat on vinegar" (letter to the Dakins, October 28, 1933, HRC); and so he developed a highly expressive, interactive platform style that drew admiring audiences to his "higher vaudeville." He boasted that his publisher, Macmillan, had lent him "the whole weight of their advertising and punch and prestige. You will see me rolling across the literary asphalt" (qtd. in *The West-Going Heart* 236). It proved, however, an exhausting and demeaning circuit that he trod before untold civic, educational, and literary groups. In 1925 a sympathetic reviewer saw not the "boyish poet who pranced across the stage" but a man "weary, worn and inexpressibly sad" and lacking "the old spirit of comradeship" (qtd. in *The West-Going Heart* 353) with his now dwindling audience. On his last tour, in 1931, he refused to recite "The Congo" and wrote in explanation to his young wife, Elizabeth: "You will have to wait till you are all of 51 before you know what it means to be doomed to sit in the attic with your dustiest poetry and feel your creative force thwarted every day. . . . I will *not* be a *slave* to my yesterdays. I will not. I was born a *creator* not a parrot" (qtd. in *The West-Going Heart* 411–12). Richard Halliburton followed precisely the same arc of ambition, exuberant performance, and diminishing spiritual returns. By 1936 it was clear to him that his book sales and lecture draw were down and that "much of the joyous wonder" had gone out of his writing. "It would have gone out anyway," he wrote to his mother in October, "because I am older and less astonished and amused by what I see" (qtd. in *Halliburton's Royal Road* 152). Still, he too was haunted by his "yesterdays" and driven to top these exploits with a final daring raid. The local news story that Williams sent to his grandmother with the subhead "County turns off water" was indeed grotesquely humorous and wholly in keeping with the cartoon persona that Halliburton had succeeded in creating.

The truest line that Williams wrote in homage to Lindsay was the poet's valediction to his wife Elizabeth: "A poet dies two deaths. He dies the death of his genius: that's the hard one, the hard one comes first" ("Suitable Entrances" 11). Williams certainly knew this truth at the end of his own life, when the "whomped up" myth of Tennessee Williams had lost its power to protect him from the "machinery" of Broadway. But he also knew it at the outset, in 1939, when he magically wrote "Tennessee Williams" and indentured himself to a "bull-dog battle" with his own "crazy blue devil" and with those of the culture. He could not have failed to see that Lindsay and Halliburton had endured a demeaning exposure in marketing their books and in holding the attention of a capricious mass audience.

No literary text, their consecutive experience seemed to say, could pretend to claim authority. Their words instead required incessant annotation, with "trick entrances and exits," and in Halliburton's case, simulations of death through deeds of mock valor. Williams endured precisely the same exposure, and although he would mildly echo Artaud in describing the "benevolent anarchy" ("Something Wild" 8) of art, he too was often a complaisant performer in the marketplace of signs. I am still intrigued by a prognostic hypothetical scene in which Tennessee Williams, "sun-drenched and serene" at Laguna Beach, and feeling himself "a perfect young animal" (*Journal*, May 25, 1939), saw the concrete box high above the bay and intuitively adopted it as a defensive emblem of his own career. A year later he reverted to a similar constructional metaphor in a letter to his friend Joe Hazan:

> We are clutching at hard, firm things that will hold us up, the few eternal values which we are able to grasp in this welter of broken pieces, wreckage, that floats on the surface of life. Yes, it is possible, I think, to surround one's self with stone pillars that hold the roof off your head. It takes time to build them, time and careful selection of materials, infinite patience, endurance. We must make a religion of that last thing—endurance. (*Selected Letters* 1: 274)

Bibliographical Note

Quotations from Williams's published correspondence follow the text of volume 1 of *The Selected Letters of Tennessee Williams*. Unpublished letters are identified parenthetically by date and provenance (HRC = Humanities Research Center, University of Texas at Austin). Quotations from the unpublished journal are also dated and identified parenthetically in the text. The journal is forthcoming from Yale University Press under the editorship of Margaret Thornton.

Works Cited

Cortese, James. *Richard Halliburton's Royal Road*. Memphis, Tenn.: White Rose Press, 1989.

Leverich, Lyle. *Tom: The Unknown Tennessee Williams*. New York: Crown Publishers, 1995.

Masters, Edgar Lee. *Vachel Lindsay: A Poet in America*. New York: Charles Scribner's Sons, 1935.

Monroe, Harriet. *A Poet's Life: Seventy Years in a Changing World*. New York: Macmillan, 1938.

Parrott, Jim. "Tennessee Travels to Taos." *Tennessee Williams Literary Journal* 1 (1989): 9–13.

Root, Jonathan. *Halliburton: The Magnificent Myth*. New York: Coward-McCann, 1965.

Ruggles, Eleanor. *The West-Going Heart: A Life of Vachel Lindsay*. New York: W. W. Norton, 1959.

Williams, Raymond. *Modern Tragedy*. Stanford, Calif.: Stanford University Press, 1966.

Williams, Tennessee. "The Angel in the Alcove" (1948). In *Collected Stories*. New York: New Directions, 1985.

———. "Cairo, Shanghai, Bombay!" (n.d.). Typescript. Harry Ransom Humanities Research Center, University of Texas at Austin.

———. *Conversations with Tennessee Williams*. Edited by Albert J. Devlin. Jackson: University Press of Mississippi, 1986.

———. *The Glass Menagerie* (1945). In *The Theatre of Tennessee Williams*, vol. 1. New York: New Directions, 1971.

———. *The Selected Letters of Tennessee Williams*. Edited by Albert J. Devlin and Nancy M. Tischler. Vol. 1. New York: New Directions, 2000.

———. "Something Wild" (1949). *Where I Live: Selected Essays*. Edited by Christine Day and Bob Woods. New York: New Directions, 1978.

———. *Springfield, Illinois* (n.d.). Typescript. Harry Ransom Humanities Research Center, University of Texas at Austin.

———. "Suitable Entrances to Springfield or Heaven" (n.d.). Typescript. University of Delaware Library, Newark.

———. "Why Did Desdemona Love the Moor?" (August 1939). Typescript. Harry Ransom Humanities Research Center, University of Texas at Austin.

———. "A Writer's Quest for Parnassus" (1950). In *Where I Live: Selected Essays*, edited by Christine Day and Bob Woods. New York: New Directions, 1978.

3

"Tiger—Tiger!"

Blanche's Rape on Screen

Nancy M. Tischler

Tiger! Tiger! burning bright
In the forests of the night,
What immortal hand or eye
Could frame thy fearful symmetry?
                    —William Blake, 1794

When will the sleeping tiger stir
among the jungles of the heart?
I seem to hear the sound of her
gentle breathing in the dark.

O you that are deceived by this
apparent innocence, take care!
You know that storms are presaged by
such trembling stillness in the air.

And all that breathe have in their breast
capacity for certain flame.
Domesticated cats are merely
beasts pretending to be tame.

Not for the pelt but for the passion
would I track that tiger down,
to dwell with her more dangerously
beyond the lighted streets of town!
                    —Tennessee Williams, Acapulco, September 1940

"Tiger—tiger!" These are Stanley's words of recognition when Blanche challenges him to a brawl by breaking a bottle and threatening to twist the broken end in his face. Her practiced gesture validates his judgment of her as a temptress with round heels all too happy to be brought down off those legendary columns at Belle Reve. This scene, the foreplay for the rape, has an inevitability signaled by Stanley's words: "We've had this date with each other from the beginning!" (Williams, *Theatre* 402)

The preceding scenes foreshadow this moment in Blanche's invitations to sexual violence and in Stanley's brutal actions, gestures, words, and tone. When we first meet him, he throws a bloody package at Stella; later he bangs drawers and doors, smashes the radio, shouts at everyone, and demands repeatedly to be respected as the alpha male of this tribe. When Blanche laughs at him, spraying him with perfume, teasing him, treating him as a little boy, he responds with irritation and rising anger. She is flirting with him, a southern sexual ritual that he rejects: "I don't go in for that stuff," he asserts— perhaps without recognizing his own growing interest (Williams 278). As Elia Kazan has explained, "Nothing is more erotic and arousing to him than 'airs'. . . . she thinks she's better than me. . . . I'll show her" (Qtd. in Cole 377). Stanley senses in this woman a challenge to his authority and to his family. He must be rid of this meddlesome woman but finally realizes that he can be rid of her only by destroying her himself. Their fearful symmetry is at the core of the drama.

Audiences watching this play or film today accept the inevitability without contemplating the difficulties involved in articulating it some fifty years ago, when women were considered less sexual; onstage lasciviousness and rape were forbidden, and a man capable of violating a woman was expected to be punished. The 1930 Motion Picture Production Code, which was still in effect at the time of the film, stated that there were to be no rape, no prostitution, no homosexuality, and no unpunished crimes. In dramatizing this powerful climax and the subsequent denouement in *A Streetcar Named Desire,* which he himself had revised over and over, Tennessee Williams was challenging the censors and the morality of the era. This first "adult" film to come out of Hollywood presented a number of challenges to the code of the Motion Picture Association of America. These two final scenes were to become the crux of the conflict involving numerous individuals and organizations, from producers, directors, and advisers to the Hays office and the Roman Catholic Church.

In our era of open sexuality and violence-ridden entertainment, we are inclined to forget that halfway through the twentieth century, even Rhett Butler's famous final line in *Gone with the Wind* was a real shocker. In 1939, the producer of *Gone with the Wind* had to seek special permission from the Hays office for a breach of the Production Code in order for Rhett to say to Scarlett, "Frankly, my dear, I don't give a damn!" On the other hand, another sequence was apparently not contested—the conjugal rape scene, in which Rhett sweeps a protesting Scarlett into his arms and carries her up the grand staircase to unspoken delights of powerful sexuality. The following morning finds him chastened and her fulfilled but both unable to express their feelings openly. The scene was allowed because the couple were married, the language was not explicitly violent or sexual, and the action was off-camera.

This remarkable sequence lingered in the viewers' imaginations long after the actual plot line had dissipated. Molly Haskell (214) believes that Scarlett must remain silent to keep her power over Rhett. As a "superwoman" who seeks to adopt male characteristics in order to survive, she is obliged to refuse to acknowledge her bliss to this overpowering male, preferring the weak, unavailable, and easily dominated Ashley (166). Haskell, who apparently finds Scarlett's type of woman repellent, says, "She is a diabolically strong woman—deceptively so, in the manner of the southern belle—and she fears the loss of her strength and selfhood that a total 'animal' relationship with Rhett would entail" (167). Whatever the actual motivation, Scarlett's evident pleasure at the make-believe rape and the suggestive morning-after scene were in conformity with the rules of the Production Code.

When an older and more complex Vivien Leigh signed the contract to play the older and more complex Blanche DuBois in the film version of *Streetcar,* she once again assumed the role of a woman who sought control over a weak man (Mitch) while lusting after a strong, sexual brute (Stanley). Thus the rape scene and its aftermath in *A Streetcar Named Desire* retained an unspoken resonance of the earlier film. This time, implicit taboos intensify the conflict: the pair are in-laws, and Blanche's sister, Stella, is in the hospital having Stanley's child.

Both Tennessee Williams and Elia Kazan knew what they were doing here; they were also well aware of the spoken and unspoken rules of the theater and the cinema. Williams, who repeatedly demonstrated his taste for rough sex in his own life, was forced by theater conventions of the time to moderate his portrayal of sexual violence. Kazan, who relished the notion that sex for Stanley is a need to dominate, felt he should retain the hint of violent sexual battle in order to be faithful to the inner spirit of Williams's story. According to Michel Ciment, Kazan identified Blanche with Williams himself—"an ambivalent figure who is attracted to the harshness and vulgarity around him at the same time he fears it, because it threatens his life" (Ciment 71).

As Kazan said,

Blanche Dubois [*sic*] comes into a house where someone is going to murder her. The interesting part of it is that Blanche Dubois-Williams is *attracted* to the person who's going to murder her. That's what makes the play deep. . . . So you can understand a woman *playing* affectionately with an animal that's going to kill her. So she at once wants him to rape her, and knows he will kill her. She protests how vulgar and corrupted he is, but she also finds that vulgarity and corruption attractive. (Qtd. in Ciment 71)

While Harold Clurman, who later directed the road version of the play, thought this conflict symbolic of a dying culture in America, Kazan thought it more explicitly autobiographical. This possibility is reinforced by Williams's own comment that he conceived Blanche as a very sexual woman: "In a small southern town like Laurel, Mississippi, to live such a life is totally revolutionary and totally honest. She was over-sexed, [and] dared to live it without harming anybody" (qtd. in Isaac 26).

For the play and the film, Kazan and Williams chose Marlon Brando for the role of Stanley as a debased Rhett, coaxing his wife down the rambling staircase rather than carrying her up the elegant one. When Kazan selected Vivien Leigh to play the role of Blanche, she was the only major actor replaced in the film version, taking the role created by Jessica Tandy. He made the choice partly because of her greater fame (derived largely from the earlier role), probably also because of recent gossip about her private life, and finally because of her proven experience: she had already played Blanche in the London production of *Streetcar,* under the direction of her husband, Sir Laurence Olivier. She struck Kazan as the ideal person for the part in the film, and according to Maurice Yacowar, the producers insisted on at least one box-office name (15).

The script itself was a larger problem for everyone concerned. The play had been a success from the moment it opened on Broadway at the Barrymore Theater on December 3, 1947. As was usually the case when Tennessee Williams had a hit, his agent, Audrey Wood, immediately began to negotiate film contracts. Murray Schumach describes some of the preliminary exchange:

> Torn between the desire to produce a money-making and artistic movie and fear of offending powerful pressure groups, interested studios and producers sought the advice of [Joseph] Breen, who had not yet retired as administrator of the industry's self-censoring body. His responses were discouraging. Thus, he told Paramount that, if it tried to make *Streetcar* into a movie, the homosexuality and rape would have to be eliminated. More significant was his letter to Irene Selznick, who had produced the play and was interested in the movie prospects. "You will have in mind," Breen wrote to Mrs. Selznick,

> > that the provisions of the Production Code are quite patently set down in the knowledge that motion pictures, unlike stage plays, appeal to mass audiences; to the mature and the immature; the young and the not-so-young.
> >
> > Because these motion pictures are exhibited rather indiscriminately among all kinds of classes of audiences, there is a frank acknowledgment on the part of the industry, of a peculiar responsibility to this conglomeration of patrons. Material which may be perfectly valid for dramatization and treatment on the stage may be questionable, or even completely unacceptable, when presented in a motion picture. (Schumach 73)

Here, clearly stated by the leading authority on movie censorship at that time, was a variation of the philosophy that movies are suited to the mentality of twelve-year-olds. Here was the conviction that some material is not for the American screen, regardless of its artistic merit or the taste shown in making the movie. The subject itself was censurable, regardless of the film's beauty or sensitivity. The concept of the adult movie was, obviously, not yet acknowledged by Hollywood's chief censor in 1950 (Schumach 73).

Before the purchase by Warner, Selznick had tried another strategy. After receiving the quoted message from Breen, she wrote Williams on July 1, 1949, that she was negotiating the deal for the film rights. She added this note to her letter:

> Very, very confidentially, I have laid my hands on the Hays office report which is the factor, aside from generally poor business prospects, which has most seriously damaged us. The worst of it says, "The element of sex perversion would have to be omitted entirely. The rape scene is also unacceptable . . . but most specifically because in the play this particularly revolting rape goes unpunished. The element of the lead's prostitution should not be discussed in so much detail. (Selznick to Williams, n.p., July 1, 1949, 3 pp., typed letter, Boston University)

The censors also worried about the toilet gags, the other vulgarities, and so forth. Selznick admonished Williams to keep this quiet until after the property was sold. And then she added, "In any case, I think most objections can be met, others compromised, and withal, the flavor, essence and story retained."

As a possible solution, she says that she took a

> bold step . . . , a personal gamble I feel justified. I engaged a writer to come here for discussion, conjecture and to work on a treatment. I chose someone with knowledge and feeling for the South and a writer with the most respect for your work and the greatest esteem for the play. I'll spare you further detail lest you expire meanwhile and advise you immediately that it is Lillian Hellman.

Selznick goes on to explain that Hellman is a "skilled scenario craftsman," one "resourceful at managing to meet the Code and yet not lose substance." She continues:

Lillian arrives here July 7th and will stay with me for the two weeks for which she has committed herself as I am just across the street, fortunately, from Willie Wyler who has agreed to sit in and work with Hellman. Willie has agreed to contribute his time, even though "on spec" because of his passion for the property and because the screenplays of three of his most successful pictures have been done by Lillian. If things work out on our two-week venture, then Lillian will agree to do the shooting script, and it is our hope that we can sell a shooting script to Paramount. . . .

Lillian has stated her position fully last night: she won't contribute anything of which you would not approve, she has no intention of distorting the play in any way, she is not going to superimpose her stamp, AND she wants very much to know, as does Wyler, your thinking in terms of screenplay. . . . I *cannot* tell you how valuable any ideas you have will be, both in regard to preserving content while meeting the Code as well as added material to compensate for losses which will be inevitable. (Selznick to Williams 2–3)

There must have been a flurry of activity at this point—probably telephone calls, delivery of bits of manuscript previously cut, and so forth. The other important document that I found in the Selznick file to testify to the fascinating work in these preliminary arrangements in anticipation of the sale of the "property" is a six-page, typed, double-spaced document that is unsigned. I assume it is the result of the work of Hellman and Wyler those two weeks in July and bears the unmistakable mark of Hellman—her clear view of human character, her disdain for fragile southern belles, and her firm judgments.

The Hellman typescript begins with what she labels the "FIRST PROBLEM: Blanche tells Mitch of her marriage to a homosexual."[1] The author then marches staunchly on to the SECOND PROBLEM: The Rape Scene. She acknowledges that any approach can prove "foolish and tricky." "It is the most common of Hollywood delusions that if a writer can describe a good scene he can also write a good scene. It is impossible to tell what will fit until you come to fit it; impossible to see a part without knowing the whole. The solutions put down here are practical and possible. It is hardly necessary to say that their worth—their "literary" worth can only be proved by a full and final script." This is the way she saw the problem at hand, and her solutions, neatly numbered:

> One: The beginning of scene ten, as is. Scene ten opens as Stanley comes back from the hospital to find Blanche drunk and in a mood of hysterical exhilaration. Blanche flirts with Stanley. He is part tempted, part maliciously amused. But he decides not to sleep with her. Maybe he gets bored with her fancy talk and falls asleep from it, the beer and the heat. He did want her and would have taken her but her intensity, her high-flautin [*sic*] attempt to make the seduction into something else, is as alien to him as it must have been alien to many men from whom she had begged pretty decoration for sexual intercourse. (I have always seen her reading poetry in bed to a bewildered travelling [*sic*] salesman from Memphis, Tenn.) His refusal of her is horrible to her: she pretends to herself that *he* wanted her, that *she* is shocked, that she is frightened of him, that she cannot stay in the house with him, etc. The scene ends in a violent fight between them. She has now so twisted and turned that an already sick mind believes he did try to rape her. And by morning is convinced that she must tell Stella of Stanley's villainy. This is not a lie: it is a delusion. But the delusion-stage set long before—years before the play begins. (From Hellman typescript 2ff.)

This scenario, cast in Hellman's ironic voice, makes Blanche a more lascivious version of her own character Birdie, from *The Little Foxes* and *Another Part of the Forest*. But in actuality, Blanche has some of the strength of Regina as well. She, like Scarlett, enjoys both sex and romance. Her love of poetry is more important to Williams than simply class reinforcement. She peppers her speech with poetic allusions, as did he. She wants the romance of "Rosenkavalier" as part of her relationships; she sees herself as Camille, as he saw himself as Byron. I think it unfair to call this hunger a "high-falutin attempt to make seduction into something else" or "pretty decoration." It is more than a superficial ploy but rather the mark of a hunger for a deeper meaning to sexuality, the difference between animalistic coupling and romantic love.

Not only does this Hellman typescript scenario caricature the romantic nature of our heroine but it also diminishes her truth-telling. If this be delusion, then much of the remainder of the story is also problematic. This interpretation calls into doubt the whole of Blanche's judgments and narratives, an enormous price to pay for audience comfort.[2] Thus the climactic scene of the play is eviscerated, the ambiguities are eliminated, and the play is reduced to the unwelcome visit of a delusional sister-in-law.

Suspecting that this scenario may not prove satisfactory, the writer, who sounds more and more like Lillian Hellman, continues:

> Two: The beginning of scene ten, as is. Blanche is closer to the edge of mental breakdown, perhaps because all through the script we bring her nearer to the edge. Perhaps because of Mitch's refusal to marry her. Stanley does try to sleep with her. She becomes hysterical, runs from the house. (Stanley doesn't give a damn: he falls asleep.) Blanche wanders around the district trying to find somebody to talk to, occasionally buying a drink or asking for one. The wandering becomes a nightmare: the streets are confused with Belle Reve; a passing young man with his girl fade into an image of herself and her husband; the music of a Quarter honky-tonk becomes "her" song; men at bars are men with whom she slept in Laurel, Miss.; an open window looking into a cheap Quarter bedroom fades into the bedroom she had as a child. She finds, at a bar, a bewildered man to tell about the cruel rape that did not happen; a bewildered woman to whom she explains that she never had anything to do with Stanley, that he is unworthy of her sister, etc. I think we could do an extremely effective night of the increasing darkness of a woman's mind: her lostness, her loneliness, her desire to go back to Stanley and her guilt in wanting to go to him. Perhaps she does return to the house expecting Stanley to be waiting for her, only to find that he is sleeping. She tries to wake him, tries to make him listen to her, realizes that he is bored, and cruel, in the face of her misery. And runs to Stella. (Hellman typescript 3–4)

Stanley sounds increasingly like Dashiell Hammett in this version, though Blanche sounds not at all like Lillian Hellman. The last sentences elaborating on the cinematography of the mad scene testifies to Hellman's infatuation with this variation. She is expanding the play into a film, using the medium's possibilities of space and shading in ways denied the stage-bound playwright. Curiously, Williams is the one generally accused of diffusion and Hellman is praised for her efficiency, but this is an example of Williams accomplishing a host of outcomes in a handful of gestures and phrases while Hellman embroiders a whole series of gratuitous scenes.

The point at issue is still the same: to satisfy filming's constraints, the rape did not happen and Blanche is delusionary. In this ironic scenario, Stanley displays passing interest but is less sexy or violent than sleepy and bored. Hellman has reduced his brutality, has ameliorated his cruelty and his will to power, and has demonstrated her continuing disdain for weak-minded southern belles. For her, this forest of the night contains no powerful mystery worthy of exploration.

Hellman then tries a couple of shorter scenarios, building on ideas she has previously elaborated:

> Three: The beginning of scene ten, as is. Stanley has no interest in Blanche, and wishes only to be rid of her. She identifies Stanley's rejection of her with the bridegroom's rejection. He goes to bed. Blanche wants him, knows she does, feels intense guilt, begins to drink by herself, tries to wake Stanley on various foolish excuses, and grows more desperate and more frightened as the night wears on, and the drinks take effect. (I would also like to include in this plan the night-wandering which I have previously described.) By morning—the crack-up has come—she believes that he did rape her. And she runs to Stella. (Hellman typescript 4)

This version turns Blanche into a lusty dipsomaniac who is pestering poor Stanley; he, in turn, sleeps the sleep of the innocent. (Note that Hellman is still enamored of her earlier mad scene.) She must have realized that this scenario has slight hope of finding acceptance, for she moves quickly to the final solution: "Four: Beginning of scene ten, as is, very much as is. But an outside force interferes as the rape is about to take place. Maybe by Mitch reappearing, maybe by Eunice appearing. So that all intent, and all effect, is the same as in the play. Except the censor's forbidden act of rape. I don't like this solution but it could be done, and I put it down here because it is one of the ways" (Hellman typescript 4).

The deus ex machina is no solution for this troubled trio. Hellman had used the surprise and improbable intervention at times in her own plays, but they were well-made plays in which the scene could be neatly foreshadowed. *Streetcar,* unlike *The Little Foxes,* is a play of passion in which the tragedy moves inexorably toward the meeting of Blanche and Stanley. There must be a rape. The play demands it.

Hellman remains uncomfortable with all the solutions, realizing that "in so good a play the elements are so well blended that the choice [of the most important motives and the most important emotions] must be delicate and careful." She believes that Blanche has been headed for a mental collapse for years and that it could come at any time. "If this is true, then the sleeping with Stanley is of as much importance, and as little, as the desertion of the boy in Laurel, Miss. Stanley is guilty of his own act, he precipitates destruction of Blanche, but the actual destruction began years before he ever knew her name" (Hellman typescript 5). This puzzling statement would appear to make Stanley guilty with or without the rape, which seems to suggest that he is a symbol of those forces that will inevitably destroy the fragile and beautiful. This strikes me as more nearly true of her "little foxes" than of this more complex all-American Kilroy figure, who is trying to make a life for himself and his family. He may have no background, but Stanley Kowalski is certainly striving for a future. The writer acknowledges her own ambivalence about Stanley, attributing it to Williams and/or Kazan. This meditation on Stanley and evil is worth quoting more fully, inasmuch as the censors demanded that Stanley be punished for the rape, if the rape is to remain in any form:

> There is a very interesting difference between Stanley in the book and on the stage. And because of this difference I know now why the last scene in the play always worried me. (It seemed hurried, as if a trick were being played on the mind and eye.) I think somebody—Kazan or Williams—was conscious of an unsolved problem. Was it this problem? What is Stanley, how "good" or "bad" is he meant to be, how responsi-

ble, how simple? Is he the victory of the low-down over the sensitive? Or is he like everybody else, no better no worse? (That is not possible because it would be a sentimental untruth.) Stanley cannot allow Blanche to be sent to an insane asylum if he thinks he alone caused the breakdown. This would make him a villain too large for life or art and I thus conclude that I am right in thinking the act of rape was only the shove over the dangerous mountain: the end act of what had begun years before, and the fall inevitable, whatever the nature of the shove.

If this is a true conclusion then the omission of the actual act of rape need not fundamentally change this play. (Hellman typescript 5)

The Hellman typescript may be referring to the way Marlon Brando played Stanley, with humor and irony, in accordance with Kazan's view of the character as a virile man who seeks to protect his family from the threats of Blanche and all she represents. Hellman is clearly distressed by the ambivalence that Williams frequently felt about his "villains" and his "heroes." He frequently blends inevitability with guilt, a complex theological mix not unlike Blake's recognition of beauty in danger, a common creator for both the tiger and the lamb. Nothing is ever as straightforward for Williams as for Hellman.

Williams must have been dismayed by this set of ideas. From his earliest letter to Audrey Wood, March 23, 1945, where he had set out the idea for "The Moth," "The Poker Night," "The Primary Colors," or "Blanche"s Chair in the Moon"—all early versions of the play— he had affirmed that the attraction/revulsion between Blanche and "Ralph" (a.k.a. Stanley) is a "strong sex situation": "Ralph and Blanche being completely antipathetic types, he challenges and is angered by her delicacy, she repelled and fascinated by his coarse strength." This line of action moves along until Ralph/Stanley unconsciously falls in love with Blanche, uncovers her background and the scandalous reputation, and exposes them to his wife and Mitch. Having lost Mitch, Blanche sits alone in the flat (two rooms by the freight yards). Ralph enters. "There is a violent scene at the end of which he takes her by force." As Williams outlined the three possible endings, the madness is not inevitable but just one option:

"One, Blanche simply leaves—with no destination. Two, goes mad. Three, throws herself in front of a train in the freight-yards, the roar of which has been an ominous under-tone throughout the play" (TW letter to Audrey Wood, n.p., March 23, 1945, 2 pp., typed letter signed, Boston University).

Evidence that Brando is playing the role much as Williams had expected/hoped comes from his letter to Audrey, in which he says, "I know this is very heavy stuff and am writing it with as much lyrical and comedy relief as possible while preserving the essentially tragic atmosphere. The comedy comes mostly from Ralph's friends, and the sex theme dignified and relieved by a poignant character-ization of Blanche."

In one early version of the play, called *The Passion of a Moth*, Stanley and Blanche are shown the morning after the rape, both admitting that it was the best sex they had ever had. Then comes word that Stella has had a baby girl. So Blanche prepares to leave, apparently to "get her lily white hooks" into someone else some-where else, and Stanley takes the streetcar to the hospital.[3]

Dan Isaac (*Louisiana Literature* 10) describes a related scenario in an early draft that he convincingly dates as September 1946, in which Blanche and Stanley wake up together, discuss their sexual encounter, and describe Stanley's igniting of Blanche's violent sexu-ality as "putting dynamite under a teapot." "She depicts the sexual act as a contest—literally an agon, a wrestling match," which Blanche has won. Blanche plans to leave, and Stanley threatens to follow, "because I won't be able to help myself." The resulting child, because of the nature of their passion, will be an "angelic monster" (11).

Brenda Murphy also discusses *The Passion of a Moth* in her ex-tended study *Tennessee Williams and Elia Kazan: A Collaboration in the Theatre* (21.) She mentions that the anticipated son will "wash them all clean."

On the other hand, in *The Poker Night*, another version, Blanche becomes a victim, catatonic at the end of the play, crouching in a grotesque twisted position, screaming in a straitjacket. In what Mur-phy calls the "August version" of the play, the rape is emphasized; Stella subsequently discovers Stanley's pajama top "ripped to shreds," his shoulders and back covered with scratches.

Tennessee Williams was always ambivalent about his monsters. They are rarely clearly good or evil. Stanley was never intended to be a stereotypical villain. He is a combination of Williams's "Kilroy" figure, the red-blooded American boy in *Camino Real,* and "One Arm," the gay sexual fantasy figure. Molly Haskell spoke of his flexing and posturing as an example of homosexual pornography aimed at a "repressed or 'closet' seductee."

> The feelings expressed by . . . Vivien Leigh . . . for the studs played by . . . Brando . . . are of lust, not love, a desire not for souls but for beautiful bodies; but it is lust pierced with bitterer emotions—with the pathos and vulnerability and the self-exposure of the woman/homosexual past her/his prime. The other undercurrent in these tortured relationships is the ambivalence, even self-hatred, of the cultured homosexual who is bound to be spurned by the mindless young stud he is compelled, often masochistically and against his "taste" to love. (Haskell 249)

Some of the correspondence appears to be missing at this point. There was apparently a great deal of negotiation, perhaps much of it by telephone. According to Schumach, *A Streetcar Named Desire* was to become Hollywood's first "adult" movie, primarily because of Charles K. Feldman. While others were clearly frightened of the censorship battles that such a film would invite, Feldman, a leading talent agent, persuaded Warner Brothers to join him in the project, with a screenplay to be done by Tennessee Williams and direction by Elia Kazan.

We assume that Williams contacted Selznick to reject most of these proposed changes to his play but without offering to write the film script himself. He knew from experience that he must maintain artistic control. Warren French describes the intricate process of negotiations this way:

> Tennessee Williams refused to write the script, but insisted on approving any changes. When Kazan took Oscar Saul's script to Joseph Breen's office, which administered Code, Thomas Pauly reports that he learned that to get the seal of approval that most exhibitors required, 68 changes, including major omissions of any references to homosexuality, nymphomania, or the rape—the principal causes of Blanche's downfall, would have to be made. The first two big no-nos were handled by

glossing over them with euphemistic references to "nervous tendencies" that many viewers already understood from widespread discussion of the play. Kazan insisted, however, that the rape was essential. Breen acquiesced, so long as there was no evidence of evil intention on Stanley's part, as leeringly suggested by the line in the play, "We've had this date with each other for a long time [*sic*]," and by merely suggesting what will transpire as Stanley advances on the terrified Blanche, brandishing a beer bottle which he smashes into a mirror. Since the Code also demanded that crimes could not be exonerated, Breen insisted that Stella must make it clear that she would not return to Stanley, even though many viewers would realize that in the still patriarchal South a woman with a baby might have no alternative. (French 966)

In his study of film censorship, Schumach notes that when he heard that the Hays office wanted the rape removed, "Williams, who had reluctantly agreed to other changes, decided he would not permit his play to be shattered or branded as smut. Williams wrote to Breen:

"Streetcar" is an extremely and peculiarly moral play, in the deepest and truest sense of the term. . . . The rape of Blanche by Stanley is a pivotal, integral truth in the play, without which the play loses its meaning, which is the ravishment of the tender, the sensitive, the delicate, by the savage and brutal forces of modern society. It is a poetic plea for comprehension. . . . Please remember, also, that we have already made great concessions which we felt were dangerous, to attitudes which we thought were narrow. In the middle of preparations for a new play, I came out to Hollywood to rewrite certain sequences to suit the demands of your office. No one involved in this screen production has failed to show you the co-operation, even the deference that has been called for. (Qtd. in Schumach 75–76)[4]

Maurice Yacowar says that Williams himself finally wrote the screenplay for the film with Elia Kazan. In their collaborative effort, "the film moves even more inexorably than the play toward the clash between Blanche's romantic illusions and Kowalski's brutish, though affable, realism." (Yacowar is convinced that Kazan's sympathy with Stanley's overbearing masculinity altered the relationship, making him somewhat more sympathetic. His notebook would seem to justify this conclusion.) Thus the rape itself is "Kowalski's physical triumph over Blanche's fragile dreams" (Yacowar 15–16).

Elia Kazan searched for means to make the play more cinematic but worried about weakening the drama in the process. He reports that he experimented with a process of "opening out" the script but finally discarded the idea as inferior to the original. Basically, Kazan decided to film the play rather than try for a radically different approach.[5]

Given the concern with the Hays office and the problems of making the rape scene conform to the Production Code, Kazan undertook interesting filmic strategies. He shot the struggle between Blanche and Stanley in reflection through a large, oval mirror: "Blanche's last defense, a broken bottle, shatters the mirror. The solid object (bottle, Kowalski) shatters the fragile image (mirror, Blanche). The mirror is an image of Blanche's shattered composure and self-respect. There is also a horror in the shot, as if it were too powerful to be viewed directly and needed to be deflected" (Yacowar 20).

The second shot Yacowar calls a visual pun: it is a fire hose that sprays the garbage off the street. As he explains, the image has been set up by Eunice's earlier line to Stanley: "I hope they do haul you in and turn the fire hose on you, same as last time." (20) Any close observer understands that this is a phallic image; it is so obvious that it usually elicits a gasp and a laugh. Yacowar explains the "multiple perspectives" of the pun:

> As bawdry, it tempts us into Stanley's view, that the affected Blanche is trash, which needs to be washed away by his purifying, direct force. This sense agrees with the "raffish charm" that the screenplay . . . described in Kowalski's furnishings. From Blanche's perspective, however, the shot expresses her shame and the blow to her self-respect caused by the rape and then Stella's disbelief. Eunice's line gives the image yet another meaning: it suggests that Stanley, formerly a victim of the hose and treated as trash by the regularizing forces in society, is

now enjoying a kind of revenge by bringing Blanche down to his level. Finally, the image relates to the succeeding scene, where we see the Kowalski baby in his carriage. From this perspective, the characters are washing aside the embarrassing past in order to begin life anew. At whatever cost to Blanche, of course. (Yacowar 20)

The other, related concern of the Hays office, as mentioned before, was the punishment of the rapist. By this time, the Catholic Legion of Decency had also entered the picture and was making further demands before the play could be cleared. Apparently, this body sought once again to remove the rape and change the ending.

Yacowar reports that Williams and Kazan labored to find an acceptable compromise while refusing to remove the rape scene, which they argued was "the crux of the action" (22). They finally agreed that the rape would remain but that the rapist would not go unpunished. Thus the film ends with Stella rejecting Stanley ("Don't you touch me. Don't you ever touch me again.") and assuring her baby, "We're not going back in there. Not this time. We're never going back. Never, never back, never back again." Although Kazan and Williams thought this sufficient to clear the film, Warner Brothers—without informing either the author or the director—made another twelve cuts to appease the Legion (22).

Apparently Kazan heard that cuts had been made during his absence and threatened to remove his name from the picture. A draft letter Williams apparently wrote to Charles Feldman ends with this plea: "I also feel grave mistake to exceed cuts we all agreed upon in New York. A great picture can be botched by injudicious cutting. Don't let them spoil a great picture" (TW to "Charlie" n.p., n.d., 1 p., autograph letter, Columbia University). His emotional request was apparently ignored.

The cuts, which have been restored in the most recent release of the film, create a conclusion for the film that reverses the conclusion of the play. The play had ended with Blanche destroyed and Stella lying to herself. Yacowar describes this painfully realistic ending:

Stella collapses into Stanley's arms "with inhuman abandon".
. . . As the curtain falls, Stanley unbuttons Stella's blouse and

his brutish friends play on ("seven card stud," aptly enough). But the film ends with Stanley isolated and rejected—at least for the time being. Even his card cronies turn against him. Blanche, then, would seem to have won, for she has exposed Stanley and kept Stella from "hanging back with the brutes." As Blanche is driven away, against the silhouette of the cathedral, we hear the bells that she earlier called "the only clean thing in the quarter." Where in the play it seems that Stanley has won, in the film Blanche seems triumphant. (22–23)

Yacowar acknowledges that the film's conclusion, which reverses the "externals of the play," does not change the "bleak vision beneath. To the questioning viewer, the film ends as negatively as did the play" (23). He attributes this compromise ending to Kazan, who believed that life can be sustained by a lie. Kazan rejected Williams's proposed ending with Stella crying. This action reflects his preference for truth-tellers, unlike Williams's sympathy for romantic dreamers.

All of these struggles with the censors, both secular and religious, the producer, the director, and a host of other people helped determine the actual product that we see as a completed work of art. The finished film—a "collaboration," according to Williams—stands along with *Gone with the Wind* as a screen masterpiece.

The artistic triumph is in no small measure the result of Tennessee Williams's constant insistence on the integrity of his own vision. In retrospect, we can see how intricate and nuanced his characterizations, how inextricably entangled his relationships and actions. Like the blues music that underscores the entire play, it is full of passion, laughter, brutality, and lyricism. And like Blake's tiger, Blanche and Stanley both stand before a backdrop that is dark and mysterious, not easily understood or domesticated, splendid and dangerous, the creations of an imagination that loved both tigers and lambs.

Notes

1. In an earlier paper, I covered this issue. See Nancy M. Tischler, "Sanitizing the Streetcar," *Louisiana Literature* 14.2 (Fall 1997): 48–56.

2. Dan Isaac has written at length on the significance of "truth-telling" as a factor in the tragic structure of the play. See "No Past" 8.

3. In a conversation in 1995, Allean Hale noted this scenario that she discovered in the Williams file at the Harry Ransom Humanities Research Center. It parallels one of the variant scenarios described by Vivienne Dickson 164, which she identifies as *The Primary Colors*.

4. Rev. Gene D. Phillips, S.J., also quotes extensively from this letter in *The Films of Tennessee Williams,* 81ff.

5. See his interview with Elia Kazan, reported in Gene D. Phillips's article, included in the Kolin collection, *Confronting Tennessee Williams's "A Streetcar Named Desire,"* 225.

Works Cited

Ciment, Michel. *Kazan on Kazan.* New York: Viking Press, 1974.

Cole, Toby. *Directors on Directing.* New York: Bobbs-Merrill, 1953.

Dickson, Vivienne. "*A Streetcar Named Desire:* Its Development through the Manuscripts." In *Tennessee Williams: A Tribute,* edited by Jac Tharpe. Jackson: University Press of Mississippi, 1977.

French, Warren. "*A Streetcar Named Desire.*" In *International Dictionary of Films and Filmmakers,* vol. 1, edited by Nicholas Thomas. Chicago: St. James Press, 1994.

Haskell, Molly. *From Reverence to Rape: The Treatment of Women in the Movies.* Harmondsworth: Penguin Books, 1974.

Hellman, Lillian (?). 6 pp. Typescript, Irene Selznick file, Boston University Library.

Isaac, Dan. "No Past to Think in: Who Wins in *A Streetcar Named Desire?*" *Louisiana Literature* 14 (Fall 1997): 8.

Kolin, Philip C., ed. *Confronting Tennessee Williams's "A Streetcar Named Desire."* Westport, Conn.: Greenwood Press, 1993.

Murphy, Brenda. *Tennessee Williams and Elia Kazan: A Collaboration in the Theatre.* Cambridge: Cambridge University Press, 1992.

Phillips, Gene. *Films of Tennessee Williams.* Philadelphia: Art Alliance Press, 1980.

Schumach, Murray. *The Face on the Cutting Room Floor: The Story of Movie and Television Censorship.* New York: William Morrow, 1964.

Selznick, Irene, to Tennessee Williams, n.p., July 1, 1949, 3 pp., typed letter, Boston University Library.

Tischler, Nancy M. "Sanitizing the Streetcar." *Louisiana Literature* 14 (Fall 1997): 48–56.

Williams, Tennessee. Tennessee Williams to Audrey Wood, March 23, 1945, 2 pp., typed letter signed, Boston University.

——. Tennessee Williams to "Charlie," draft, n.p., n.d., 1 p. autograph letter signed, Columbia University.

——. *The Theatre of Tennessee Williams*. Vol. 1. New York: New Directions, 1971.

Yacowar, Maurice. *Tennessee Williams and Film*. New York: Frederick Ungar, 1977.

4

The Escape That Failed

Tennessee and Rose Williams

Michael Paller

I

If one reads *The Glass Menagerie,* an encyclopedia entry about Tennessee Williams, or any of the biographies or memoirs of him prior to Lyle Leverich's landmark *Tom,* one is likely to come away with a particular impression of his sister Rose and of Williams's feelings for her. The reader will have learned that Williams loved his sister very much, that he felt closer to her than he did to any other person in his life, and that, famously, he based Laura in *The Glass Menagerie* on her. But Williams felt a number of other things about his sister besides love, and these various feelings dictated the shape, content, and effectiveness of much of his work from the very beginning of his career until its end.

While I'm not going to suggest that there is only one way in which to view the career of Tennessee Williams, I do propose that it *can* be seen as a long dialogue with his sister. It is a dialogue full not only of love but of regret for her terrible fate. It is also full of anger over certain acts that may or may not have actually taken place. One, especially, surfaces again and again in the course of a career that spanned seventy-odd plays and more than forty years. I would like to examine some images in his work that repeat themselves, sometimes to the point of obsession and beyond. New ones arrived to take the place of old ones or moved in alongside them, reflecting Williams's conflicting feelings toward Rose. These feelings are, at first, ones of love, and they never altogether vanish from the plays. But Williams's feelings were complex as well as lifelong. There is no discernible, neat pattern to the way the feelings occur from play to play; they are too volatile and too human for that. In this sense, his career was a continuous dialogue with himself, in which Williams insisted he felt one way about his sister while many plays make clear that he felt differently.

First, some background. Rose Williams was born on November 19, 1909; Tom, as Tennessee was christened, followed on March 26, 1911. Although they were separated by sixteen months, the two were often mistaken for twins. So alike were they that their nurse called them "The Couple." They were unusually close, and Tom idolized his older sister. Until 1918, they lived a sheltered, idyllic existence, first in their maternal grandfather's rectory in Clarksdale, Mississippi, and later in one he took over in Nashville, Tennessee.

In 1918, their father exchanged the traveling salesman's life he loved for a supervisory desk job at the St. Louis headquarters of his employers, the International Shoe Company. Almost every aspect of their new lives frightened the children, from the noisy, dirty city to the strange neighbors to the atmosphere in their home. From the beginning, their parents, Cornelius Coffin Williams and Edwina Rose Dakin, were a dreadful mismatch: she was the neurotically puritanical daughter of an Episcopal minister; he, a hard-drinking, profane veteran of the Spanish-American War. The children were spared Cornelius's domineering presence for much of their early life, as he was usually on the road selling men's clothing. But this absence ended in St. Louis. Cornelius was frustrated by his desk job, disdainful of the "sissy" way in which he thought Edwina was raising their son, and furious with a wife he could dominate neither intellectually nor sexually. Life at the Williams home was a constant round of arguing, smoldering silences and sexual tension. In self-defense, Rose and Tom clung together all the more fiercely.

As Rose approached adolescence, her personality began to change. She became increasingly distant and aloof; her habitual good spirits slowly became a kind of hysteria. She fell in love with a series of young men, but nothing worked out, in part because Edwina had done such an excellent job of passing along to her children her monolithic hatred of sex.

The family's rage, anxiety, and neuroses—together with a history of mental illness on both sides—affected Tom and Rose differently. Tom was discovering his talent for writing, and it became both his escape from family pressures and an outlet for stresses he felt internally. But Rose had no such escape. She turned her growing psychological pressures inward. By 1928, she was experiencing severe depressions and suspected that she was being poisoned. She began retreating into fantasies, wandering the house in a nightgown, and talking of imaginary gentleman callers. In 1937, after years of living as a virtual shut-in, Rose was committed by the family to the state hospital in Farmington, Missouri. It was stated on her admission report that Rose had "delusions of sexual immorality by members of the family." Diagnosed with dementia praecox (schizophrenia), she was subjected to a series of insulin treatments, which failed to improve her condition. In 1943, after six years of confinement and no improvement, Rose underwent a prefrontal lobotomy. At this time, more than 100 such operations had been performed in America, and although medical opinion was sharply divided over their efficacy, the popular belief was that lobotomy was a cure for the previously incurably insane. The operation made her calmer and seemingly happier but doomed her to a shadow life of dependency and institutionalization (Leverich 224, 480).

When Edwina informed Tennessee of the surgery, he wrote in his journal:

A chord breaking.
1000 miles away.
Rose. Her head cut open.
A knife thrust in her brain.
Me. Here. Smoking.
My father, mean as a
devil, snoring—1000 miles
away. (Leverich 482)

II

The Glass Menagerie is the one Williams play with an image of Rose that most people are familiar with—although it is by no means the most representative.

We think of *The Glass Menagerie* as a lovely memory play. It is seen through a gauze-covered lens, brimming with nostalgia, its characters gentle, lost people. This is also the view many of us have of Laura: sweet, introverted, helpless before the world. Not only is this not an especially representative image of Rose in Williams's work, however, it is not even an accurate view of Laura any more than the way I've just described the play is an accurate depiction of what the play is really like. Reading Williams's description of the set of *The Glass Menagerie* carefully, as an important clue to the world of the play, one discovers that the world its characters inhabit is one defined by desperation:

> The Wingfield apartment is in the rear of the building, one of those vast, hive-like conglomerations of cellular living-units that flower as warty growths in overcrowded urban centers of lower middle-class population and are symptomatic of the impulse of this largest and fundamentally enslaved section of American society to avoid fluidity and differentiation and to exist and function as one interfused mass of automatism.
>
> The apartment faces an alley and is entered by a fire escape, a structure whose name is a touch of accidental poetic truth, for all of these huge buildings are always burning with the slow and implacable fires of human desperation. (*Theatre* 1:143)

Each of the play's characters is desperate to achieve a particular goal. Amanda wants to keep her children safe from the ravages of a dangerous world; Tom, to escape the prison of his life at home and at work. Laura seeks refuge in her own private world. To do this requires more will and resolve than Laura is usually given credit for. After all, she successfully thwarts each of her mother's plans for her—an education, a job, a husband. For all her occasional foolishness, Amanda is a resilient woman who knows exactly how the world treats those not strong enough to stand up to it. She is not easily thwarted. If we are to form an accurate picture of Laura, we must understand just how much of her mother's strength she has inherited.

In her quiet way, Laura is quite as indomitable as Amanda. Laura may be fragile, but she is no weakling. She defies her mother as effectively as her brother does. Tom's battle of wills with Amanda is, except for the question of where he spends his nights, straightforward and open. Laura's is quieter and sly. Daily, for six weeks, while Amanda has thought her daughter has been learning typing and shorthand at business school, Laura has been wandering the city, resolutely avoiding the vocational education that Amanda believes is so necessary if she's to survive. Indeed, Laura could have continued the deception indefinitely, had Amanda not made an unscheduled stop at the school on her way to her installation as an officer in the Daughters of the American Revolution. Just as Tom has his secret life, Laura has hers, and it provides her with not only a place to escape but also a source of strength. The cocoon she has woven around herself is made of steel, not silk. One way or another, one senses, she will have her way in the end, and the final image of her in the play, being cared for and comforted by her mother, is the way things will always be for her, because she wants them that way.

We think of Laura as something of an innocent, and in this, despite her successful battle against her mother's wishes, we are correct. Her victory in her war of wills with Amanda leaves her with little knowledge of the way the world works. Certainly, she knows little or nothing of sex. This is, as I've said, the popular image we have of Rose Williams. But it is by no means the only image of her in Williams's work. It's not even the first image.

I want to turn to a play that Williams wrote before *The Glass Menagerie*. *The Long Good-Bye* was written in 1940. In many ways, it is the progenitor of *The Glass Menagerie,* and it contains the seeds of material Williams would use over and over again for the next forty years. *The Long Good-Bye* is also a memory play, set in "a tenement apartment situated in the washed-out middle of a large mid-western American city" (6: 203). A young writer named Joe is waiting for movers to empty the apartment; he is moving on. His mother is dead, his father long since skipped the light fantastic out of town, and his older sister is gone, too. What's most interesting about this play is how the positions of brother and sister reverse those in *The Glass Menagerie:* the brother, Joe, is the innocent stay-at-home, while his sister Myra is out every night with a different man. Joe is prim and proper and can't bear to hear his sister talk about her dates, while Myra breaks every rule that propriety throws in her path. As Laura would do for Tom in *The Glass Menagerie,* Joe waits up late one night for Myra to come home after a date:

JOE: I used to have hopes for you, Myra. But not any more. You're goin' down the toboggan like a greased pig. Take a look at yourself in the mirror. Why did Silva look at you that way? Why did the newsboy whistle when you walked past him last night? Why? 'Cause you looked like a whore—like a cheap one, Myra, one he could get for six!

MYRA: You never would have said a thing to me like that—when Mother was living.

JOE: No. When Mother was living, you wouldn't have been like this. And stayed on here in the house.

MYRA: The house? This isn't a house. It's five rooms and a bath and I'm getting out as quick as I can and I mean it! (6: 224)

And she does.

At the end of this one act, when Myra is gone and Joe finally leaves the apartment, Williams describes a strange thing. Joe picks up his suitcase, gives the room a "mocking salute," and exits. But he leaves four items behind: Myra's glass bottles of perfume, a chair, a table, and, on that table, most crucially, his typewriter. Joe, the devoted young writer, cannot go far without that typewriter. He'll have to come back for it. And neither, over the next forty-three years, did Williams go far from home. He returned to these characters in a place like this, in various guises, again and again. Tennessee Williams, who led a life of constant travel, imaginatively and geographically, was in many ways trying to escape the memory of his damaged sister. But his repeated attempts at escape only landed him closer to home. His good-bye to his sister was long because it didn't suffice, and things between them were never finished.

III

In *The Long Good-Bye*, the writer's sister takes on a persona that is sexual, worldly, and knowing. Something more startling occurs in *The Purification*, another one-act play that Williams wrote in 1940 (and the only published play that he wrote in verse).

The play takes place in a small New Mexico town after a murder has been committed. Something called "an informal trial" is taking place, in which the events that led to the murder are recounted—this, too, is a memory play. It seems that a rather coarse rancher from Casa Rojo has killed his young wife, Elena, who hails from nearby Casa Blanca. In life, Elena had a rather ambiguous reputation. Williams refers to her both as the Desert Elena and Elena of the Springs. Her servant, Luisa, says repeatedly, as if reciting from a liturgy, "The tainted spring—is bubbling" (6: 43). In one extended speech, she elaborates:

> You have heard the dead lady compared to mountain water.
> A very good comparison, I think.
> I once led goats through the mountains;
> we stopped to drink.
> It seemed the purest of fountains.
> Five of the goat herd died. . . .
> The water was crystal—but it was fouled at the source.
> The water was—tainted water! (6: 47)

Interestingly, the figure at the center of this "informal trial" is not The Rancher, who murdered Elena, but Elena's brother, identified in the play as The Son. His name is Rosalio; he is only the first of a very long line of male and female characters named, if not exactly in honor of Rose Williams, then at least in remembrance of her. When the judge asks Rosalio to describe his sister, the play grows even more curious. He speaks of the late, murdered Elena less reverently than cautiously, as if she'd been a force to be feared:

> Her eyes were always
> excessively clear in the morning.
> Transparency is a bad omen
> in very young girls!
> It makes flight
>   necessary
>   sometimes! (6: 44)

This is the first time in one of his plays that Tennessee Williams mentions the need to flee from a young woman. Luisa the servant had seen Rosalio come to visit his sister at night at her new home, Casa Rojo:

> I did not trouble the master, he was sleeping,
> but went alone through the meadow:
> the grasses were chill: I shivered:

I bore no lantern—the starlight proved sufficient.
I had not come to the barn
when suddenly through the window of the loft,
that was lit with the wavering radiance of a candle,—
two naked figures appeared in a kind of—dance. (6: 49)

We learn, in the rest of *The Purification*, that Rosalio and Elena, brother and sister, had sex more than once in her husband's barn. He discovers them there and, in a fury, kills Elena with an axe. He testifies that, while Elena might have been like a spring to others, to him she was a desert. She spurned his advances, preferring the naked company of her brother at night in the barn.

The court passes no judgment on The Rancher, whom it deems wronged. Rather, a silent judgment of guilt is passed on The Son, who carries out his own execution, stabbing himself to death with his own knife.

Now clearly, it seems as if I am leading up to a charge of incest between Williams and his sister, Rose. This is not a new idea. It was one familiar enough to Williams himself for him to have addressed it in his *Memoirs:*

> I may have inadvertently omitted a good deal of material about the unusually close relations between Rose and me. Some perceptive critic of the theatre made the observation that the true theme of my work is "incest." My sister and I had a close relationship, quite unsullied by any carnal knowledge. As a matter of fact, we were rather shy of each other, physically, there was no casual intimacy of the sort that one observes among the Mediterranean people in their family relations. And yet our love was, and is, the deepest in our lives and was, perhaps, very pertinent to our withdrawal from extrafamilial attachments. (*Memoirs*, 119–20)

Though Williams was not always the most reliable reporter when it came to the details of his own life, there is no evidence to make us doubt his word on this point. What is more interesting is the fact that over the course of more than forty years, such images as those I've noted in *The Purification* crop up in play after play after play.

At about the time Williams wrote *The Purification*, he wrote another one-act play, *This Property Is Condemned*. The images here are still sexual but less cataclysmic than they are in *The Purification*. The play takes place on the railroad tracks outside a small Mississippi town. It has only two characters, and its world feels very small and intimate, as if the two people on these tracks under a milky white sky are the only people in the world—much the same way that, as children, Tom and Rose felt about each other. We see a young girl named Willie, thirteen years old, walking precariously along the tracks, high on a embankment. She is not dressed as a thirteen-year-old, however: her face is rouged and lipsticked; she has adorned herself in dime-store jewelry and a long blue velvet party dress. She is playing at being a woman of the world, much like her late sister Alva, who, we learn, had, "a wonderful popularity with the railroad men" (6: 251).

At the moment, tottering down the tracks, she is concentrating very hard on keeping her balance—or, to put it another way, on not becoming unbalanced. Her exertions amuse the other character, a boy named Tom, who is slightly older. Now, Tom is one of the first characters, if not the first, Williams ever named directly after himself, and this Tom is not interested in getting to know Willie on merely a social basis. He asks her to take her clothes off for him, the way she reportedly did for his friend Frank Walters.

Willie's response is to tell him about the doll dangling from her arms. The doll's name is Crazy Doll.

> WILLIE: Oh, Crazy Doll's hair needs washing. I'm scared to wash it though 'cause her head might come unglued where she had that compound fracture of the skull. I think that most of her brains spilled out. She's been acting silly ever since. Saying an' doing the most outrageous things. (6: 256)

In the end, Willie doesn't disrobe for Tom. Instead, she disappears along the tracks, in Williams's words, "weaving grotesquely." Although Willie is trying to emulate her prostitute sister, there is a childlike sweetness to both her and Tom. Willie's description of Crazy Doll's condition is an equally childlike description of Rose at the time that Williams wrote the play. But with Willie's and Tom's childlike sweetness comes an unseemly desire: she wishes to be like her sister, and Tom wants to see her naked. Edwina Williams had

Rose committed in part because Rose was saying and doing the most outrageous things. At some point during her time in the state hospital at Farmington, according to Donald Spoto, one Williams biographer, she accused her father of trying to rape her (66). No one else, as far as we know, recalled that Rose made this specific charge, although delusions of persecutions and an obscenity-laced babble were among her symptoms (Leverich 335). It's also worth noting that the house where Willie lived with her sister and her mother (who ran off with one of the railroad men) is now boarded up, decaying, and condemned. But Willie lives there still. Characters lingering in a house where traumatic events occurred, unable or unwilling to leave, constitute another image from which Williams could never quite shake himself loose.

IV

After her incarnation in *The Glass Menagerie* in 1944, Rose turns up again in *The Unsatisfactory Supper,* a one-act play from 1946. But now she is almost unrecognizable. She is not the young woman, either sexually precocious or withdrawn, whom we have already met. Williams has transformed her into an old relation, a jabbering spinster shuffled from sibling to sibling to sibling, unwelcome and unwanted. Williams describes her as an eighty-five-year-old woman who "resembles a delicate white-headed monkey. . . . She has a continual fluttering in her chest which makes her laugh in a witless manner" (6: 301).

Her name is now Aunt Rose. For the moment, Aunt Rose is living with her niece Baby Doll and Baby Doll's husband, Archie Lee. They are none too pleased to have the old woman around. They put up with Aunt Rose's constant babbling as long as she pulls her weight with the household chores. On this particular night, however, she has forgotten to light the stove and has ruined dinner. This is the last straw: in the morning, Archie decrees, Aunt Rose will pack her bags and be driven to whichever relative will take her—or to a run-down old-age home in the country. At the end of the play, Aunt Rose finds herself locked out of the house, with a terrible storm coming up.

There is another image of Rose in *The Unsatisfactory Supper.* In the yard grows a rose bush. Williams describes it as "a very large rose bush, the beauty of which is somehow sinister looking" (6: 299). It is one of the few blossoming things in an otherwise barren locale. Aunt Rose trims the bush and offers the blooms to Baby Doll and Archie Lee, who could not care less. And as much as Aunt Rose cuts it back, the bush keeps growing: the large, unruly plant stubbornly refuses to die. The image of Rose Williams has here been transmuted from that of a damaged, lost girl into a chattering, unwanted nuisance, and a sinister beauty who won't go away. It seems that Williams has begun to grow impatient with his sister's memory, which refuses to let him go.

At the same time, however, it's important to note that Williams's sympathies, and most likely an audience's, lie with Aunt Rose, not with the indolent Baby Doll nor with the demanding Archie Lee. We may recoil from the old, annoying, forgetful spinster, but we recoil further from the indifference and cruelty of her relations. Williams's images of Rose were never unequivocal, but from now on they will more and more often mix love and loyalty with a certain fear and resentment, even an anger at the lifelong torment that he would feel over her condition and over his implication in it, real or imagined.

V

The Rose Tattoo, which opened on Broadway early in 1951, occupies an unusual place among Williams's works: it has a happy ending. Or rather, it seems to have a happy ending. The play's primary relationship, between Serafina Della Rose and the truck driver Alvaro Mangiacavallo, ends well. He brings love back into her life when she thinks it is gone forever, and then, unlike most of Williams's other objects of female desire, he stays. Another story, however, ends more ominously. Serafina's daughter, Rosa Della Rose, who is fifteen, falls in love with a sailor named Jack. When her mother locks Rosa in the house and takes away her clothes so that she can't escape to see this inappropriate suitor again, she tries to slit her wrists. In act 1, scene 6, when the boy and girl are alone, Rosa is clearly the aggressor. "She rains kisses on him," says one stage direction, "till he forcibly removes her face from his" (2: 318). Earlier, on the dance floor at the high school gym, threatened by this young girl's sensuality, he tells her, "Honey, you're dancing too close" (2: 318). He doesn't run away yet; he likes Rosa and is eager to have her. But by act 3 it's also clear

that Rosa and Jack have very different visions of the future. He intends to light out on his own; she intends not to let him get away.
Here, as we saw in *The Purification,* and as we will see more and
more in the works to come, Williams presents a man (or occasionally, a woman) fleeing some kind of illicit heterosexual sex.

Rosa is not above a little emotional blackmail if that's what it
takes to hang onto Jack. When he says he has to go, she clasps him
"fiercely," as the stage direction reads, saying, "You'd have to break
my arms to!" (2: 399). "You want me to scream?" she says and
throws herself between Jack and the door. "I know, I know!" she
moans. "You don't want me! No, no, you don't want me!" (2: 400).
Apparently, they didn't have sex—but that, Jack insists, was no
thanks to Rosa:

> JACK: Now you listen to me! You almost got into trouble today
> . . . ! You almost did, but not quite!—But it didn't quite happen
> and no harm is done and you can just—forget it. . . .
> ROSA: It's the only thing in my life that I want to remember!
> (2: 400)

Jack admits to her that before he boards his waiting ship he intends
to check into a fleabag hotel and get loaded.

> ROSA: Do me a little favor. Before you get loaded and before
> you—before you—
> JACK: Huh?
> ROSA: Look in the waiting room at the Greyhound bus station,
> please. At twelve o'clock, noon!
> JACK: Why?
> ROSA: You might find me there, waiting for you. . . .
> JACK: What—what good would that do?
> ROSA: I never been to a hotel but I know they have numbers on
> doors and sometimes—numbers are—lucky.—Aren't they?—
> Sometimes?—Lucky?
> JACK: You want to buy me a ten-year stretch in the brig?
> ROSA: I want you to give me that little gold ring in your ear to
> put on my finger.—I want to give you my heart to keep forever!
> And ever! And ever! Look for me! I will be there!

JACK: In all my life I never felt nothing so sweet as the feel of your little warm body in my arms.

And then the crucial stage direction reads: "He breaks away and runs toward the road. From the foot of the steps he glares fiercely back at her like a tiger through the bars of a cage. She clings to the two porch pillars, her body leaning way out." Rosa cries, "Look for me! I will be there!" And Jack runs from the house (2: 403–04).

But we don't know that he'll get away. As the play ends, Serafina sends Rosa after him, and breathlessly she goes. She is coming after him, whether he wants her or not. If she finds him, will she get him, her tiger in his cage? This ending, unlike Serafina's, is not necessarily happy. One can imagine another Williams play in which a sailor named Jack turns up, fleeing a determined fifteen-year-old girl. Indeed, we'll see something very much like that in 1961 in *The Night of the Iguana.*

Earlier in *The Rose Tattoo,* in act 1, scene 6, Serafina subjects Jack to an inquisition: where did he take her daughter, what did he do with her? He insists that nothing has happened between them and says: "Whatever story she told you, it ain't my fault!" (2: 328) "It's not my fault!" will become a watchword uttered by a constellation of Williams's male characters when accused of a sexual impropriety. Williams seemed to need to find himself guiltless of incest, an event that probably never occurred—except in his imagination.

The Rose Tattoo also marks the beginning of a habit that over the years would come to mar more and more of his work. At every turn, the images of roses threaten to overwhelm the play. Not only the characters' names—Serafina Della Rose and Rosa Della Rose—but the Rose Tattoo itself, that emblem that appears mysteriously on characters' chests when they are in love and/or pregnant. In Serafina's house, images of roses run riot: there is rose-patterned wallpaper and a rose-colored carpet. There is rose-colored silk, more than one bouquet of roses, a rose in a young girl's hair; Alvaro wears rose oil in his hair; roses sprout all through the dialogue like an untamable bush. As the years went by, roses would proliferate in Williams's plays, a habit he seemed increasingly helpless to avoid, as if a hand were reaching from the past, insisting that he remember something that he'd rather forget.

In an essay called "The Timeless World of a Play," which serves as an introduction to many editions of *The Rose Tattoo,* Williams wrote, "We love and betray each other, not quite in the same breath, but in two breaths that occur in fairly close sequence" (*Theatre of Tennessee Williams* 2: 261). A betrayal takes two. Increasingly, his plays became episodes in a private conflict between two imperatives: "It's the one thing in my life that I want to remember!" versus "It's not my fault!"

VI

In the 1950s, new images began appearing in Williams's writing. His plays had always been melodramatic; he admitted a weakness for melodrama even as a child when, in his grandfather's library in Clarksdale, he preferred *Titus Andronicus* to *Hamlet.* In the fifties, however, his imagery became increasingly violent. Some of this change, no doubt, was due to the analysis he began undergoing, first, disastrously, under one Dr. Lawrence Kubie (who, according to Williams, suggested he give up both writing and homosexuality, because it would be good for him). There are images of traumatic, catastrophic surgeries, brutally performed and involuntarily undergone. What's striking here is, again, not only the repetition of such images but also the kind of melodramatic relish with which they are detailed. Specificity is all to the good in playwriting, but one senses something more at work beneath mere fidelity to detail. One wonders about the theatrical panache with which Williams tosses these characters, men and women, under the knife, the gun, the rope, and the blowtorch. None of the good is rescued at the last moment, which is a principal difference between Williams's sense of melodrama and that of the tradition he inherited. Is he furious at a world in which such things actually do occur? Or is he, in some way, getting back something of his own, from a force, an image, that will never let him be, slashing at it, shooting at it, burning it up?

The most famous example of mutilation in his work, perhaps, is the endlessly intriguing *Suddenly Last Summer,* produced in 1958— one of the first plays produced Off Broadway. Catharine Holley is a young woman who has been locked up in a mental institution by her aunt, the fearsome Mrs. Venable, because she has dared speak the truth of a terrible event, a circumstance redolent with sexual overtones. At a resort called Cabeza del Lobo, Catharine witnessed the murder by cannibalism of her cousin, the poet Sebastian Venable. The grotesque manner of his death is the revenge by the island's poor boys for Sebastian's sexual predation. Back home, in the Garden District of New Orleans, no one wants to believe Catharine's horrible tale: not Mrs. Venable, Sebastian's wealthy, powerful mother, nor Catharine's mother and brother, who depend on the kindness of Mrs. Venable. The old woman has decided that if Catharine insists on repeating her story, she will be taken to Lion's Head, a state mental institution, and subjected to an operation in which a needle-thin knife will be inserted into her head to relieve her of this terrible story—and, incidentally, of her personality as well. As the plot unfolds, Catharine repeats her story in awful detail while under the influence of a truth serum. Because the drug makes her tell the truth, we must assume that the story is true. Nonetheless—or because of this fact—Mrs. Venable cries out, "Lion's View! State asylum, cut this hideous story out of her brain!" (3: 423). It seems likely that lobotomy will indeed be Catharine's fate.

It's interesting to note the striking intensity with which this play is written. It contains some of Williams's most concentrated and effective writing. His sympathies are clearly with Catharine—who is both storyteller, like Tennessee, and lobotomy victim, like Rose. But we are also likely to be taken, I think, with the evil Mrs. Venable, mesmerizing and charismatic, who will go to any length to suppress the horrible truth and silence the one living reminder of the awful event that just couldn't have taken place in Cabeza del Lobo. The energy and power with which Williams invests Mrs. Venable suggests that he, too, takes great theatrical enjoyment in her determination to shut this young woman up.

In the late 1960s, Williams began working on a play that he considered his best in many years—a judgment few would share. He called it *The Two-Character Play,* then *Out Cry* and then *The Two-Character Play* again. It was under that name that it briefly played on Broadway in 1973. It shows, perhaps more than Williams intended, a playwright in extremis. It is complicated, craggy, and, in every sense, difficult.

It is a play within a play. The outer play concerns Felice, a playwright and actor, and his sister Clare, an actress. They have been touring together for a very long time—much longer than either expected—in Felice's drama called *The Two-Character Play.* The play within a play concerns a brother and sister, also named Felice and Clare, who have lived all their lives in a Victorian house somewhere in the South. They are trapped inside, wanting to leave but unable to do so. In their childhood, the home was the scene of a dreadful crime: their father murdered their mother and then himself. Or perhaps it was their mother who killed their father before committing suicide. Or perhaps Clare and Felice killed them both. It is never made clear.

The play as a whole entity reflects Williams's creative and emotional fatigue and contains his darkest portrait of Rose. Clare will, in Williams's words, alternate between a grand theater manner and startling coarseness. When we and Felice first hear her cry his name offstage, Felice's response is also startling in its savagery:

> You can't, you must never catch hold of and cry out to a person, loved or needed as deeply as if loved—"Take care of me, I'm frightened, don't know the next step!" The one so loved and needed would hold you in contempt. In the heart of this person—him-her—is a little automatic sound apparatus, and it whispers, "Demand! Blackmail! Despicable! Reject it!" (5: 310).

Clare is drunk when we first see her, exhausted by years of touring with her demanding brother. Like a child, she asks, "When are we going home?" His answer, meant to supply some comfort, is really rather chilling: "Our home is a theatre anywhere that there is one" (5: 315).

Neither can go on without the other, and neither can bear to go on with the other. As both partner and muse, Clare is used up. She refuses to perform, although the audience is gathering. The temperamental playwright loses his temper and screams at his sister: "You— castrating bitch, you—drunk—slut! Yes, I did call you that, I don't look at you onstage because I can't bear the sight of your—eyes, they're eyes of an—old demented—whore! Yes, a water-front whore! Lewd, degenerate, leering!" (5: 324). With this, Felice raises the curtain and they begin to perform *The Two-Character Play*.

But strong-willed Clare won't say all of her lines. When they come to a passage to which she objects or a passage that she can't bear to face, she strikes a C-sharp on the piano. For example, Felice places an opal ring on her finger. The stage direction reads, "He turns the ring on her finger—a sort of lovemaking. She strikes the piano key" (5: 328). They constantly interrupt the inner play to quarrel. During the intermission they come to blows. They have reached what seems to be a permanent stalemate. Now we are in Beckett country: "I can't go on. I'll go on."

They go on. In the play within the play, they struggle to leave the house, but they fail. Felice addresses the audience:

> I stand here—move not a step further. Impossible without her. No, I can't leave her alone . . . And behind me I feel the house. It seems to be breathing a faint, warm breath on my back. I feel it the way you feel a loved person standing close behind you. Yes, I'm already defeated. . . . [The house] seems to be whispering to me, "You can't go away. Give up. Come in and stay." Such a gentle command! What do I do? Naturally, I obey. I come back into the house, very quietly. I don't look at my sister.
> CLARE: We're ashamed to look at each other. (5: 353)

The play within a play ends. Brother and sister find that the audience has left long ago and that the two of them are locked in the theater. Clare asks, "Do you hate me, Felice?" Felice answers, Of course I do, if I love you, and I think that I do" (5: 363). She picks up their father's pistol and tries to kill her brother. "Do it while you can!" he urges. She cries out, "I can't! Can you?" (369–70).

The answer is no. As the lights fade, they reach toward each other, trapped together forever. Although Williams has traveled a great distance indeed from Laura Wingfield, it seems that, after all these years, he is rehearsing the last lines of *The Glass Menagerie*. "Oh, Laura, Laura! I tried to leave you behind me, but I am more faithful than I intended to be."

It is hard to say which is more striking or more poignant: Williams's unquenchable desire, still, to blow Laura's candles out or his increasing inability to create a work of art that might allow him finally to do so. The play is, almost literally, artless: everything that should be beneath the surface and subtextual is stated directly, baldly. There is almost no creative buffer between the extremity of Williams's emotional state and the words, actions, and images that are meant to act as theatrical metaphors. Rather than providing a painting based on his inner life, the play is an X-ray of an increasingly unmanageable neurosis.

Williams's last play to be performed on Broadway in his lifetime was *Clothes for a Summer Hotel,* produced in 1981. Not surprisingly, it imagines a meeting, late in life, between a famous writer, now down on his luck, and his unstable female muse. Zelda Fitzgerald has been incarcerated in Highland Hospital, a mental asylum in North Carolina, where she is shortly to die in a fire. She is visited there by her husband, F. Scott, novelist, story writer, screenwriter, drunk. Williams calls the piece a ghost play, and Scott may already have died before making this ghostly, gentlemanly call. The couple have a kind of showdown, and Williams provides this image of Rose with some new feelings about her brother. Scott has come penitently, wanting to make up for past offenses. Zelda will have none of it. "Is that really you, Scott?" she greets him. "Are you my lawful husband, the celebrated F. Scott Fitzgerald, author of my life?" They exchange a perfunctory kiss (8: 213).

> ZELDA: Good. So what is the program for us now? Shall we make a run for it and fall into a ditch to satisfy our carnal longings, Scott?
> SCOTT: That was never the really important thing between us, beautiful, yes, but less important than—
> ZELDA: *What was important to you was to absorb and devour!* (8: 215)

Zelda is furious that no one will ever know her version of her own story. She will be known only through the filter of her husband's books. To this charge, Scott has no answer. He is, after all, a writer. She is his material. To him, that is the way it sadly is. To her, it is the theft of her life.

This becomes the play's principal conflict: Zelda's fury at her husband for turning her into mere material and Scott's bewildered defensiveness: turning family members into material is what writers do. The conflict is not resolved here any more than it would be in Williams's life. At the end of the play, when Scott implores her to accept a second wedding ring as a renewed covenant between them, she says, again in strongest italics: "I'm not your book! Anymore! I can't be your book anymore! Write yourself a new book!" (8: 280). The muse who was exhausted and perhaps insane in *The Two-Char-*

acter Play is now, after a lifetime, asserting her rights. The last words are given to Scott: "The ring, please take it, the covenant with the past—still always present, Zelda" (8: 280).

In *Clothes for a Summer Hotel,* Zelda and her grievance are in the ascendancy. She is a powerful figure, more appealing than the somewhat pathetic, if still charming, Scott. Scott may have the last word, but it is a pleading word, and it goes unheeded.

But if, through Zelda, Rose has the upper hand with language, Williams still reserves to himself the primacy of images. In *Clothes for a Summer Hotel,* he gives us a telling image of what a sister is. The Highland Hospital is portrayed as a Catholic institution, overseen by nuns. Here the sisters are jailers—Zelda's and Williams's. The past and Rose have become Williams's jailers, have been his jailers for a long time. More than ever, Tom Wingfield is trying to leave Laura behind, but now he is no longer afraid to display his dark feelings about being jailed by her—or perhaps he is no longer able to conceal them. For Williams, who was of several minds about his sister, perhaps it was only fair: Rose, who had been incarcerated for such a very long time, had turned around and incarcerated him.

Williams would have one last go at this lifelong subject. The final play of his to be produced in New York before his death, *Something Cloudy, Something Clear,* was produced at the Off Off Broadway Jean Cocteau Repertory in 1981. In this autumnal play, which has about it an aura of grace and acceptance, Williams does finally effect some small escapes. While the play is suffused with a sense of regret for innocence lost, it contains a remarkably small amount of guilt. Certainly there is no sexual guilt. The play's central figure, a struggling young playwright named August, is Williams himself in the summer of 1940 on the beach in Provincetown, Massachusetts. August receives a visit from his childhood friend Hazel (also Williams's real-life childhood friend). When she confesses to him that she loves women, he says simply, "You loved. You loved! That's all that matters, Hazel. I know that now." Such "illicit" sex, such "transgressions," no longer call for guilt (*Something Cloudy* 21).

Williams drops real characters from his life into the play, sometimes (as with Hazel and Frank Merlo) using their real names. Indeed, there is only one character who seems wholly or even mostly fictional. Her name is Clare. She claims to be the sister of Kip, a dancer with whom August the playwright falls in love (another figure taken directly from Williams's life, including the name). Eventually, Clare confesses to August that she and Kip are not really brother and sister; they are more like lovers, except that they are not exactly lovers, because with her, Kip is impotent. This has not stopped her, however, from attempting to physically consummate their relationship. They share a bed because, she says, "we like to be with each other, I mean we're like brother and sister with each other with absolutely no incest, except I sometimes, well, I reach out to see if he wants me and he—well, he doesn't want me" (*Something Cloudy* 28). Kip and Clare conspire to be cared for by August, because both are terminally ill: Kip with a brain tumor and Clare with diabetes. Sensing, however, that August may be willing to care for Kip but not her, Clare comes between them, denouncing August as little more than a savage who makes sexual demands on her brother/lover. She begs Kip to run away with her, away from August.

What really happened in the summer of 1940 in Provincetown, as Williams was revising *Battle of Angels* for its doomed Boston production, was a very intense, brief relationship between Williams and Kip Kiernan, a Canadian dancer (who did in fact die of a brain tumor a few years later). A woman friend of Kip's convinced him that Williams was trying to turn him into a homosexual. Kip withdrew. Furious at the meddlesome woman, Williams hurled a boot at her head and then spent several months recovering not only from Kip's rejection but from the startling intensity of his own feelings for the young man (Leverich 365).

In *Something Cloudy, Something Clear* Williams assigns to Clare and Kip the protective, loving relationship that was part of the truth of his feelings for Rose. At the same time, he makes Clare into the woman who destroys any possibility of a loving relationship between the young playwright and the dancer. At August's expense, Clare won't be parted from Kip. And then Williams erases any clear line between brother/sister and lovers. The distinction becomes as mutable as a line drawn in sand. These images of Rose—as the loved and loving sister, as lover, and as the crippling jailer—now exist side by side in the open. Having one image allowed Williams to have the others.

If Williams was, finally, unable to escape the long shadow of Rose, it seems that in this, his seventieth play, he manages to attain at least some measure of peace with his condition. One hopes, anyway, that

Williams believed August's words to Hazel: "You loved. You loved! That's all that matters. I know that now."

There are many ironies in this story of Tennessee and Rose. His very deep love acquired shades of resentment and even hatred, which, through guilt, bound him ever closer to Rose, until escape became impossible. His web of feelings for her inspired some of his best plays and was responsible for some of his worst. The more the years went by, the less distance there seemed to be between them, between his present and his past, until everything seemed to occur all at one time: until the young Tom who longed to make voyages stands beside the old Tom, who never left home, and Rose stands watch over both.

Works Cited

Leverich, Lyle. *Tom: The Unknown Tennessee Williams.* New York: Crown, 1995.

Spoto, Donald. *The Kindness of Strangers: The Life of Tennessee Williams.* New York: Ballantine Books, 1986.

Williams, Tennessee. *Memoirs.* New York: Anchor Press/Doubleday, 1975.

———. *Something Cloudy, Something Clear.* New York: New Directions, 1995.

———. *The Theatre of Tennessee Williams.* 8 vols. New York: New Directions, 1971–92.

5

Four Characters in Search of a Company

Williams, Pirandello, and the
Cat on a Hot Tin Roof Manuscripts

Jeffrey B. Loomis

While discussing Friedrich Nietzsche's *The Birth of Tragedy*, Michael Hinden wrote: "Tragedy incarnates pain, annihilates structure, threatens hope, and yet . . . also has the power to sweep us up in the tow of powerful personalities whose grand passions and embellished language draw us into solidarity with—what?—dream images, really: towering characters who are at bottom insubstantial and subject to dissolution before our eyes, uniting us in collective emotion" (Hinden 113). Hinden's words remind me of how, in *Six Characters in Search of an Author*, Pirandello portrays a grand ensemble of "towering characters"—huge-spirited beings who do, nonetheless, eventually "dissol[ve]" into "collective emotion." Pirandello also reveals to us the author's terror in dealing with some of these characters: those who will not cooperatively *join* the collective ensemble but instead assert their will to dominate over the other characters, and the constellation of themes, and the total scheme of the plot, and the stagecraft devices, and all else.

I was reminded again of this Pirandellian perspective when reading, during recent summers, more than twenty draft versions of Tennessee Williams's *Cat on a Hot Tin Roof*, besides other related Williams documents, at five different U.S. research libraries. There I saw how twenty-four years of work on the *Cat* writing project caused Williams at times to be plagued by would-be dominator characters (who sometimes had living human allies, chiefly Elia Kazan, to abet them in their quest for primacy over other characters within the cast). By contrast, the 1975 final revision of *Cat* has, I think, achieved a wonderfully balanced ensemble of the various characters—one that Kazan sometimes helped to evoke, by urging Williams to develop Maggie and Big Mama as characters more completely, but also a balance that Kazan for a long time apparently contravened, through insisting that the character of Brick needed to make personality-altering, and evidently somewhat noisy, onstage transformations. To a degree, the character of Big Daddy also sometimes threatened to overdominate the *Cat* ensemble in certain versions of the play text—whether this threat also came about solely as a result of Kazan's ardent interest in Big Daddy or whether it perhaps resulted from Williams's taunting of Kazan's zeal to magnify this character.

But in any case, the drafts of *Cat* do reveal several directions in which this script could have gone and sometimes *did* go—all of which might, indeed, prove intriguing to deconstructionist, would-be revisionist readers of the text. Like such a deconstructionist reader, I can find *other* Williams plays—especially *The Rose Tattoo*—inviting me to treat draft variants of the play often as really "playable" alternatives to the published drama. Contrariwise, though, in the case of the *Cat* manuscripts, many drafted alternatives seem only chaotic approximations of the ultimately polished American Shakespeare Festival production version published by New Directions in 1975. Such drafts' qualities of chaos resemble the inanity that the Pirandellian *Six Characters* at times nearly impose upon the Author character in that play. Therefore, I cannot but be *conservatively* minded toward the manuscript history of *Cat on a Hot Tin Roof.* I find the entire manuscript progress toward the 1975 *Cat* altogether necessary—and would never be able to laud most of the earlier assaults that were made on the playwright from, or on behalf of, overly "towering" characters.

Williams first created the Pollitt family of characters in "Three Players of a Summer Game," a short story he began in Venice in 1951 and revised many times before the Pollitts found their way to the stage in *Cat.* The story occurs in the 1920s, so the character known there as Brick (and at first as Brick *Bishop*, not *Pollitt*) would have had a fictively historical birth date less like that of the later-to-be-dramatized Brick than like that of the play's Big Daddy. The short story's characters also have rather different fictive biographies from the playscript cast, and in the story it is a rather masculine, perhaps even lesbian Maggie who refuses to have sex with Brick (Texas 1— Subfolder 7: 3,7).

Such details, however, do not seem most important about the "Three Players" short story in its many drafts. What does stand out in the oft-revised tale is its constant Pirandellian sense of life's inherent theatrics: for example, "Mr. Brick Bishop had bought the corner lot to use as a stage to put on . . . his brave play [at adulterous courtship of another woman] . . . mainly in defiance of the wife who never came to see it" (Texas 1—Subfolder 8: 3). On at least one occasion, too, Williams (like Pirandello?) enunciates a clear belief that the writing process alone is what makes literary characters thrive: "and of course there has . . . been time enough, now, for Mary Louise's thin pretty mother [Brick's fictional adulterous paramour] to become no more than the shadow that she is here [on the page]" (Subfolder 8: 6).

In a fairly early revision of the dramatized full-length *Cat* (the Texas 11 manuscript, on which green-inked comments by the play's stage director Elia Kazan appear), Williams demonstrates that he shares Pirandello's understanding (as defined by Della Terza 29, 31 and Brustein 107-108) of *umorismo*: that inborn, darkly comic matrix of a life where one must struggle between obvious self-division and the social roles one is forced to play. In the Texas 11 manuscript, Maggie declares, very near the drama's final moments, "If I looked in the mirror right now, I'd say 'Who're you?' and yet, at the same time, know more about myself than I've ever known" (Texas 11; addendum, 4). Perhaps Williams was here sketching a direct or indirect response to Kazan's observation, after reading earlier versions of the script, that Maggie is "heartbreaking," "tender and dear and desperate and funny and so touching!" "a wonderful, loyal, single-loving girl who has no defenses, leaves herself wide open to hurt" (Harvard 4/1: 11). And Williams himself became more and more convinced that Maggie was complicated, not just a brazenly sex-driven wife. To be sure, she did, in the very early Texas 10 manuscript, taunt a standoffish, maddeningly prudish, Brick with the hot-blooded words, "I'll be sleepless tonight while you slumber peacefully on the shores of Echo Spring. And just my luck, the moon will fall over the sofa that you sleep on. Oh, I could teach the Chinese a trick or two about torture!" (Texas 10: 33). Granted, even in the Texas 10 manuscript, Williams was giving Maggie words that defined perspectives other than the merely sexual: "You'll discover that I'm not unkind, not really. I'm only a bitch because I long to be loved by someone who doesn't love me" (Texas 10: 41); "The only comfort is love, the only protection is love, the only refuge is love" (40). Yet even in the Texas 11 revision, Williams hasn't seen as much complexity as he gives her in the 1975 final version, where her ultimate statements tell Brick that "what [he] want[s] is someone to— . . . take *hold* of [him]" (*Cat* 1975: 173; emphasis mine); in Texas 11 she remains more clearly manipulative by nature, declaring to Brick, "What you want is someone to . . . take *control* of you" (Texas 11: addendum, 4; emphasis mine).

Williams obviously had doubts in these manuscript treatments about deemphasizing Maggie's sexual self-flaunting—although he eventually did so. Kazan repeatedly told him (Harvard 4/1: 1: 5A, Texas 11/1: 14) to drop an early revision schema in which Maggie and Brick both wear pajamas, hers translucent. At one point, Williams may specifically have used Maggie's revealing costume in order to help signify that Brick retained some heterosexual tendencies; for example, Texas 15's act 1 revision declares that Brick looks at her in the pajamas and "is probably not aware that [he] is licking his lips and twisting them at the same time, into a grimace of—*what?*" An alternate presentation of the same episode, however, collected on the same page of the same manuscript, has Brick react to Maggie's sheer apparel with more "twist" than "lick" of lips (Texas 15/2: 2). Yet Mae, Brick's sister-in-law, who intrudes upon the couple's paired pajamas scene, still finds it "sexy" (Texas 15/2: 5). It was in the script as late as December 9, 1954, the date clearly ascribed to the Columbia 1 manuscript, where the double-pajamaed party is mentioned (Rewrite, beginning of act 2: 2).

Also, Maggie's "kneeling at [Big Daddy's] feet to claim she is pregnant," in the Texas 15 and Texas 21 manuscripts (Parker 485, 487), is fairly torridly enacted and is thus called "a little indecent" by the Gooper, Brick's brother (Texas 15—Subfolder 4: 2). Her sensuous histrionics lead to the point where "Big Daddy explicitly feels Margaret's body before affirming that she has 'life' in her" (Parker 487), and Brick declares, when he and Maggie are alone at the end of the play, "You fell on your knees and begged for some of his money, you made a strong bid for it, without pretendin' you didn't know he was goin'" (Texas 15/4: 6). More energetically yet, he says, in a later variant, "—Life is a damn fire in you, you know that, don't you? Big Daddy felt that[;] it must have burned his fingers when he ran his old dyin' hand down over your body" (Texas 26/3: 40). Still, Maggie does change; she does not *talk* nearly as frankly and constantly about sex in any later version as she does in the very earliest.

Transformations that Williams made in Maggie's character probably resulted mostly from his attempts to please Elia Kazan. Williams tells us, in a "Note of Explanation" from the 1955 published edition of *Cat*, that, "while [Kazan] understood that [Williams] sympathized with her and liked her [him]self," Kazan felt that she "should be, if possible, more clearly sympathetic to an audience" (*Cat* 1955: 124–25). Kazan also "felt that the character of Brick should undergo some apparent mutation as a result of the virtual vivisection that he undergoes in his interview with his father in Act Two" (*Cat* 1955: 124). In some of the stabs Williams made at incorporating Brick into the play differently from the way he had appeared in the earliest versions, or from the way he would appear in the very latest, the New Directions publication of 1975, the playwright turned him into a surprisingly articulate near-rationalist or into a sort of gushily sweet, shame-ridden child. These portraits of Brick do not fit him into the character ensemble nearly as well as do the earliest and very latest (both quite similar) delineations of his personality—for, as Williams himself declared in the famed 1955 "Note of Explanation," "The moral paralysis of Brick was a root thing in his tragedy, and to show a dramatic progression would obscure the meaning of that tragedy . . . [as well as the fact that] a conversation, however revelatory, [n]ever effects so immediate a change in the heart or even conduct of a person in Brick's state of spiritual despair" (*Cat* 1955: 125).

In some versions of the antecedent work that gives rise eventually to *Cat*, the 1951–1952 short story "Three Players of a Summer Game," Brick demonstrates a wild sort of compassion fused with anger, much like the oxymoronic amalgamation of behaviors that we encounter in the Big Daddy of *Cat on a Hot Tin Roof*. When Mary Louise, the daughter of his extramarital girlfriend Isabel, is taunted by neighborhood girls, Brick defends her, yelling for a hose to be turned on these youngsters, whom he meanwhile calls (with no very great show of compassion) "a bunch of little bitches, the same as their mothers, a bunch of mean little bitches" (Texas 4—Subfolder 4: 3). Brick is hardly admirable and allusively Christlike in his response—as is, by contrast, Mary Louise's mother Isabel, when she tells the bratty children (Subfolder 4: 4), "You're just children, you don't know what you're doing, you don't understand anything, you don't understand what you're doing!" This early narrative version of Brick, not very different from the dramatis personae version of "A Place of Stone" or of the 1975 final *Cat,* has some tendency to kindheartedness but does not demonstrate this kindheartedness without simultaneously revealing some markedly unpleasant wrath.

The "moral[ly] paraly[tic]" Brick, as he is defined by Williams in his 1955 "Note of Explanation," is thus already foreshadowed in the Brick of the earlier short story "Three Players of a Summer Game." He is, like plenty of other characters in twentieth-century American literature, a stereotypically drink-obsessed male southerner—and as debilitated as any by his boozing. According to the manuscript writer Williams, the "Defiance" that Brick wanted to emphasize as the theme of his life's "play" was "somehow invalidated" by his tippling, which left him in a frequent mental fog (Texas 1—Subfolder 3: 2).

In this narrated musing of 1951, as in the earliest version of the *Cat* playscript (Texas 10—Subfolder 1: 3; Subfolder 4: 10), Williams describes a character, appropriately named Brick, with red hair and alabaster skin, though most actors who have played Brick have not had these physical traits. On the other hand, we find this Brick's somber character traits familiar—even though Williams's short story manuscripts sometimes have him dance on a publicly viewed croquet lawn in giddy near-nakedness, dressed only in necktie and undershorts, spraying himself with a garden hose (Texas 4—Subfolder 3: 9). By contrast with such actions, Brick is in general already a demoralized, existentially dread-ridden gloomster not very prepared to make quick alterations in his behavior, whatever the quickening motivation might be. Hence Williams's attempts to please Kazan, by repeatedly refocusing Brick, eventually provide not focus but a blur.

Having myself acted the role of Big Daddy, in two 1982 mountings of *Cat on a Hot Tin Roof* at West Virginia's University of Charleston, I can testify that act 2 can become emotionally wrenching in performance. I will never forget the shock of seeing Terry Wetmore, the actor who played Brick in both Charleston productions, suddenly break into tears after having grasped the intense kinship that Brick and Big Daddy might feel after completing a long sequence of confessions and revelations. Terry broke into tears only once, though, and I sense that any Brick would only rarely let loose the floodgates of interpersonal sympathy. Yet at the same time, Terry did, albeit on only one occasion, reveal a potential for profoundly self-scouring catharsis in Brick.

A Brick stammering toward change would, however, I think, do so mostly through visceral behaviors, rather than through analytical preachments. Therefore, I believe that Williams's best tentative (albeit eventually unused) alterations in Brick's portrait occur in the Texas 21 and Texas 26 manuscripts.

In the first of these, Brick utters guiltily, after having spitefully revealed to his father that the old patriarch is dying, "I've done it!" "—done it" (Texas 21/3: 3). Brick soon afterward cries out, according to the Texas 21 manuscript (3: 3), "I see him out in the yard" (3: 3), and he calls out, to "a figure dimly visible," "Big Daddy" (3: 3C). At about the same place as these Texas 21 stammerings, in the Texas 26 revision of Texas 21, he tells Maggie, who was shocked to find him standing on his broken ankle without the support of his crutch, "*Experiencing pain!*—is part of—life" (Texas 26/3: 16). Again, he seems to be viscerally shrieking out his anguished guilt, in a way that seems fairly plausible to expect from a son who has just undergone an hour of bitter intergenerational epiphanies.

Also in the Texas 26 variant, though, Williams has Brick shout at Maggie, "Maggie, don't give me that crutch! I nearly killed you with it for a crime I committed!" (3: 16). This outburst, like so many of the revisions Williams tended to give to Brick for Kazan's sake, reflects more apparent rationality of tone than one would expect from a man who has lived for a long while in grief for Skipper, a very close friend, and in general besotted misery. Other such passages manifest themselves in Texas 21: "Gooper, I got violent in this room a while back and I struck hard at somebody with this crutch and I'm not responsible if this, this, this!" (3: 33). "[He halts, stammering, with a semantically incomplete utterance.] —I am—false! Broken.— Fell off the goddam roof [Maggie's] still scrambling up . . . Truth is something desperate, and she's got it!" (3: 34). Even his remark about possibly being "impotent," at the point of capitulating to Maggie's scheme for putting the two of them once again into bed together (Texas 21/3: 35), seems to me to rest on the borderline of a pseudorationality inappropriate to his character. To many, Brick will seem falsely rationalistic when he stumbles into bed with Maggie while also loudly pronouncing his fears of "impotence" (Texas 21/3: 35). And besides, in some revised drafts, Brick voices supposed deep repentance but mostly by mere echoing of his father:

> Look, look. I don't want anything that I'm not fit for, and I'm fit for nothing, **nothing but rot and corruption.** A goddam **fool on the bottle** is not worth subsidizing, as Big Daddy put it[;] I'm not worth endowing. False! Broken! I **dug my old friend's grave and kicked him in it!** A while ago I almost killed my wife for a crime that I had committed! **I hung up!** Said nothing, **I just hung up!** Hell, I'd been taught by all of your kind all my life that the thing to do is hang up when somebody makes a desperate call for something that *shocks*, or *disturbs* you, even! I want nothing! All I ask about whatever arrangement you come to is what you'll grow on **twenty-eight thousand acres of the richest land of the valley Nile,** what will grow on it, but a crop of lies? **Twenty-eight thousand acres** of lies and lies and more lies? That's all I—(Texas 26/3: 21; Big Daddy's act 2 words in bold)

When I read this particular manuscript speech at a gathering of scholars, Jon Rossini, of Texas Technological University, wondered whether Brick's sincerity would not actually seem to increase when he repeats as his own so many of Big Daddy's words from their powerful act 2 confrontation. The issue, of course, may be not so much our desire for Brick's sincerity as our wish for an aesthetically attractive array of speeches, not overly repetitive. Perhaps, to be sure, Williams did not intend Brick to be repeating Big Daddy's words. At times, after all, in the massive collection of *Cat on a Hot Tin Roof* drafts, Williams will assign a familiar speech from the play to a character who does not utter it in any version of *Cat* that we commonly know. In the example I have quoted here, though, he appears fairly clearly to announce that Brick is repeating verbal material that we have very recently heard Big Daddy relay to *him* (for Brick directly announces that he speaks "as Big Daddy put it"). And so it seems to me that to have Brick echo Big Daddy so much detracts from the play's aesthetic shimmer, while also making his speech sound potentially "canned" in its emotions.

Another, although somewhat opposite, way in which Williams dealt with Brick, in the course of revising his play's original drafts, was to portray him as a creature whose grace (of physique, and, supposedly, of spirit) caused him to inspire much love in others and simultaneously to inspire envy in some love-*deprived* creatures—like his plain-visaged, and very plain-spirited brother, Gooper, as well as his own wife, Maggie, who cannot ever forget her torment-filled childhood, with its emotional and monetary deprivation. An extensive passage, which I have dubbed Maggie's *envy disquisition,* appears in quite a few extant manuscripts of *Cat* (Texas 15 and 21, NYPL 2, Harvard 2) and includes the following declarations by Maggie:

(*Taking center stage, panting with vehemence*)—Yes, [Gooper,] I did say envy, I said envy. You admitted!—You admitted as much when you said you'd always resented Big Daddy's partiality to Brick. That was truthful, understandable, excusable. I respected you for it; —you noticed I held my tongue, which is something I don't often hold? It isn't easy, it's far from bein' easy, to live in someone's shadow, a husband's, a brother's shadow, because he's blessed by nature with somethin' you have to *sweat* for, and still can't get. . . .

It's love, it's bein' loved, Gooper! You've never been loved, Little Daddy. Don't you know that you have never been loved, in spite of all your—your lively behavior, your sociable, affable nature, you've just—never been loved, Little Daddy. But Brick had something about him, he had a light about him, a, a, a— natural grace!—about him that made him . . . loved, much loved, by many! many! I know. I lived in his shadow. (I was eclipsed by his beauty!) And I envied him, too. But now he's sick, he's wounded,—(winged by the huntress Diana!). So now, I beg you, don't vent your envy on Brick, try to contain your envy or—vent it on me, yes, vent your envy on me, I'm tough, *real* tough, I—(Texas 15—Subfolder 3: 2; second paragraph actually rewritten, somewhat less compactly, in Subfolder 3: 3)

Williams probably wrote this text not so much in order to prove Brick noble as to show Maggie expressing more emotional commitment to her husband than we might always have felt from her. Intriguingly, Williams thus makes Maggie seem *less* "tough" even as she claims for herself a particularly hidebound toughness. But the passage makes Brick sound more wimpish than ever would appear appropriate—more like Blanche's victimized homosexual poet-husband Allan, in *A Streetcar Named Desire,* than like the sexually ambiguous but still often boisterously rebellious Brick. Granted, even the final 1975 version of *Cat* retains some echo of this *envy disquisition,* for Maggie declares, in that inscribed text, that Gooper and his wife Mae are "venting . . . malice and envy on [Brick,] a sick boy" (*Cat* 1975: 157). She seems to be using medical terminology there, however, mostly as a rhetorical flourish.

One more means by which Williams made Brick seem to respond to Big Daddy was to have Brick, during Big Daddy's act 3 reappearance, speak to, and physically touch, his father with affection. Some of the mildly affectionate speeches are still in the 1975 ultimate script, where the two men interchange some comments about Big Daddy's ribald elephant joke and then (with even more unity of spirit) castigate the "obnoxious odor" of "mendacity" that permeates the room (*Cat* 1975: 164–66). The physical touches, however, manifest themselves only in earlier texts—such as Harvard 1 (2: 44), where Brick's head, for example, "drops" to Big Daddy's shoulder in act 2, just after he has blurted out the truth about Big Daddy's cancer; or in Harvard 2 (3: 30), where the stage directions record, first, that "Brick moves across room on crutch, sits beside Big Daddy on table and rests one hand lightly on his father's shoulder. The OLD MAN does not glance at him: blinks just once: his wry smile increases." Similarly, on the same page, we read, "He chuckles. BRICK chuckles with him, staring steadily at his father's profile with a soft, vague smile of affection." Besides, in the New York Public Library's manuscript called NYPL 2, Brick expresses affection with his hand on his father's shoulder and then "laughs hugely" at the elephant story (3: 29–30). The manuscript called NYPL 4, which became the basis for the 1975 published version of *Cat,* by contrast has Big Daddy remark, "You didn't laugh at that story, Brick" (3: 25). Brian Parker, the scholar who has done the most extensive work of cataloging the various *Cat on a Hot Tin Roof* drafts, proclaims as uncharacteristically "sycophantic" Brick's occasionally recorded jovialities and shoulder slappings with Big Daddy during the elephant joke episode

(Parker 487–88). I do not believe that Brick's motivation needs to be read as sycophantic. But I do think that Williams probably eventually realized that the physical touching was something that Big Daddy and Brick would never have practiced very regularly, so that it would be an unlikely sudden addition to their interpersonal repertoire of behavior, even at this crucial juncture in their lives. Williams must also have eventually judged that Brick would *not* laugh at the elephant joke, even if he believed it perfectly legitimate for Big Daddy to tell it, since its subject is an elephant with a noticeable erection, and Brick fears, or already frequently experiences, impotence.

It is obvious that Kazan's agenda for revising *Cat* in a certain way did affect Williams greatly as he treated Brick's character in successive drafts. Few of the revisions that Williams tried out, concerning Brick, look like much more than means for making Brick's personality even more dominant than it already was in the play (and in fashions that were more than somewhat confusing to the stage action, since the would-be revisions were guided by the goal of appeasing Kazan's somewhat overly schematic attitude toward character development).

On the other hand, Big Mama is the character who may have been most valuably aided by Kazan's suggestions to Williams. Kazan inked the following notations onto a historically early manuscript now at Harvard: "[Big Mama is] terribly touching here. She's still completely and helplessly adoring of BIG DADDY and still wants him badly" (1: 17); "Couldn't we *see* a bit of Big Mama's 'TAKING OVER'[?]" (2: 9; emphasis mine).

It thus seems fitting that the one episode that proves both the ardor of Big Mama's love for her mate and her personal acumen for tough-minded businesswomanlike dealings is the scene where Big Mama refuses to let Gooper talk any further about the "Basis! Plan! Preliminary! Design!" that he has created for dividing the Pollitt estate (*Cat* 1955: 147; *Cat* 1975: 159–60). By shouting a Big Daddy–like "CRAP!" to such sneaky business shenanigans (1955: 147; 1975: 160), Big Mama appears to prove her likely ability to run all the business affairs of the plantation. She may also thus prove that, if she did seem to take over that activity, during the years when Big Daddy first became dreadfully sick with cancer, she most likely did so rather fully out of love and not out of any strong desire for power. But her

AMERICAN RIVER COLLEGE

scene of blunt retort to Gooper is not in the Harvard 4 manuscript, the textualization of her story that Kazan probably first read, nor does it appear in the equally early Texas 10. It has, however, found its way into the script by the time of Texas 15 (Subfolder 3: 5). This is surely one of the most beneficial additions ever made to the play.

Kazan also had commented, on the Harvard 4 manuscript leaves (1: 19), that Big Mama "always laughs like hell at herself." It seems no wonder that she does so, in terms of one of the play's most idealistic constellations of themes—for she provides a "funny" (both quirky and smile-producing) answer to Big Daddy's question (already in the early text of Texas 10: 61 and still in *Cat* 1975: 80) "Wouldn't it be funny if [love] was true[?]." He asks this as Big Mama protests that she really did love him during all their years together, especially perhaps during the period when his disease—as he naturally, even according to himself, "let things go" (Texas 10: 74)—led him to deep insecurities, and indeed to a near-paranoia, about her supposed seizing of total control.

Cat does not finally assert that love is always enduring, or beneficent, or perfectly sound. Brick's and Maggie's marital troubles will not very likely end in a "happily ever after" following the play's final curtain. And even Big Mama's love has some dangerous tendencies to codependent support of a very difficult man, one who is at least verbally abusive to those who care for him. Still, Big Mama's love at least looks to be rather firmly "true" and to deserve the beautiful culminating expression it receives in a speech that Williams vividly revised from an earlier and more prosaic specimen of the statements:

> Oh, time goes by so fast, it goes so fast you don't know where it's gone to. . . . We all got to love each other, we all got to love and stay close as we can to each other. . . . Specially now that death has moved[—]into this place! (Texas 10: 131; Harvard 2/3: 22 [with bracketed dash]; Delaware 1)
>
> Time goes by so fast. Nothin' can outrun it. Death commences too early—almost before you're half-acquainted with life—you meet the other. . . . Oh, you know we just got to love each other, an' stay together[,] all of us, just as close as we can, [e]specially now that such a *black* thing has come and moved into this place without invitation. (1955: 148–49; 1975: 161–62 [with bracketing])

I have admired both this speech's expression and its sentiments for many years. Nonetheless, the speech, and the entire role of Big Mama, may carry (as a binary opposition?) incipient hints of a characterization focused more upon cloying sentimentalism than upon stalwart love. And it is noticeable that Amanda Wingfield, in Williams's *The Glass Menagerie,* whose stalwart love can easily become obfuscated by her cloying sentiments, does sigh, and berate her son Tom, with the words "We have to do all that we can to build ourselves up. In these trying times we live in, all that we have to cling to is—each other" (Williams, *The Glass Menagerie* 171). On the other hand (perhaps because of actresses who have so convincingly enacted the vigor of Big Mama's personality), I share what was evidently long ago Elia Kazan's primal instinct: enthusiasm for her character.

She is not, however, the only character who makes the Texas 15 manuscript intriguing. Williams, in this folder, appears to have been testing methods by which to satisfy Kazan's demands that Big Daddy reappear onstage in act 3, rather than vanishing completely after his act 2 dominance. I am not certain that some of these draftings are not intentionally excessive so as to mock Kazan's entire push for textual changes. The revisionary sketches involved are, all the same, highly striking to encounter.

In Texas 15, first of all, Williams does try out Big Daddy's return to recount the risqué elephant tale. He tests that option here much as, in Texas 29 (3: 24), he will later examine the viability of having the old man come back on in order to harrumph, along with Brick, about the "obnoxious odor" produced by "mendacity" in Gooper's would-be manipulation of the family's future fortunes. Both the elephant joke and the condemnation of an "obnoxious odor" are finally combined in the 1975 edition of the ultimately revised play (163–66).

But the Texas 15 materials also include a fascinating, albeit also grotesquely overwrought, scene in which Big Daddy, actually starting at the very end of act 2 but continuing into act 3,

removes a hunting rifle or shot-gun from a glass case or cabinet in the room, loads it, and instead of going out the hall door, goes out upon the gallery. At this point the curtain rises for the first time to the full height of the proscenium, exposing the roof of the house and the belvedere, a white-fenced square at the center of the roof, open to the night sky, dappled by leaf-shadows from trees as tall as the house. Big Daddy mounts a flight of stairs from the gallery to the roof, the back wall of the set becoming transparent at this point to show his ascension. He speaks the last line of the act on the belvedere, the moon on his face. . . .

ACT THREE

Curtain remains all the way up. In his seat on the belvedere Big Daddy remains dimly visible throughout Act Three, but light and shadow, alternating with clouds' passage under the moon, sweep his lonely figure up there like spasmodic waves of pain in his body. When the spasm grips his bowels, he rises from the wood bench and his hands clench fiercely on the white balustrade of the belvedere and through his clenched teeth, each time, he says to himself and the sky: "A pig squeals: a man keeps a tight mouth about it."—This seems to be the last thing left in his heart, the ultimate dictum by which he has chosen to die, and it serves him well, for even though he bites his lips till they bleed, he never cries out in his anguish. He is not yet dying up there, but "the pain has struck" and he suffers "without the needle." He's probably suffered before, but never before with the certain knowledge of doom, which is going to be unmercifully slow, in the belvedere or below. Did he take the gun up to kill himself or to defend his position away from, above, all liars? He probably doesn't know which: it doesn't matter. There's nothing in him but rage and hate and pride to the end of the play. (Subfolder 5: 3)

Williams, evidently immediately upon writing some of this material, balks at it enough to call it "a bit corny" (Subfolder 5: 3). He, indeed, also crosses out a huge portion of drafted paragraphing, in which, among other draft ideas, he had included Big Daddy's addressing of the moon, first, with the "mocking" comment of "Hello, moon!" but "then, the grin turning fiercer, add[ing] . . . 'You filthy bitch!'—distorting his face up at it like a grey stone gargoyle" (Subfolder 5: 3). Here he also plucks a magnolia blossom—playing the guessing game, with a gradual depletion of plucked blossoms, "God loves me!—he loves me not." Finally, and surprisingly or even shockingly, he asks, "Who loved me? Big Mama and Peter Ochello!—

Ha ha ha ha ha ha!—Big Mama and—Peter—Ochello, that ole—
bitch . . . dead now! Hunh!—Sup with him in Hell or—Heaven. . . .
(Wherever good old aunties go!) Brick? No. Brick loves his liquor!—
Oh, well. Big Daddy has 28,000 acres of the richest land this side of
the Valley Nile! What's anyone's love?" (Subfolder 5: 3).

These virulently cynical lines Williams did, I repeat, excise from
even the draft copy. He did not, by contrast, censor the following
passage, quite opposite in content and tone to any obsessive concern
with 28,000 acres of real estate reminiscent of the Nile Valley: "[He
behaves n]ot always mockingly, sometimes with a lingering pride of
possession, but sometimes as if he would like to seize it between his
two clenched hands and crush it like a rotten pulp between them,
as if he identified this prodigious growth of property with the ma-
lignancy in his flesh" (Subfolder 5: 4).

I find it keenly relevant that Williams would seem to be validat-
ing this passage, in which Big Daddy appears to equate materialism
with disease, but that he would simultaneously use his editing pencil to repudiate a segment of words wherein Big Daddy deemed materialism to be the sum total of life. For as much as Williams finds
the materialistic, and particularly the sexual, part of life to be unde-
niable, I think he may still find spirit more ultimately intriguing.

To be sure, this assertion does not deny that, for example, more
places exist in the *Cat* script where Williams subtly tantalizes us
with hints about Big Daddy's ambiguous materialism of the body.
More than once, certainly, he implies that Big Daddy had been
loved—somehow, ambiguously—by Peter Ochello (the homosexual
former landowner of what is now Big Daddy Pollitt's plantation). In
the Texas 10 version of the early *Cat* manuscript "A Place of Stone,"
Maggie (30) speculates that Big Daddy "must have had [Brick's]
looks" in order ever to gain a job with Ochello and his lover and
plantation partner Jack Straw. Recent examiners of *Cat*, like John
Clum (170–71), have been willing to read some possible actual confession of homosexual activity into Big Daddy's admission that he
had "knocked around," "bummed this country," "slept in hobo jungles and railroad Y's and flophouses in all cities" (*Cat* 1955: 85–86;
Cat 1975: 117). There is also Williams's cannily ambiguous use of
the word "coupled," in the following familiar stage directions from
both published editions of *Cat:* "[Big Mama reviews the history of
her forty-five years with Big Daddy, her great, almost embarrassingly

true-hearted and simple-minded devotion to Big Daddy, who must have had something Brick has, who made himself loved so much by the 'simple expedient' of not loving enough to disturb his charming detachment, also once *coupled,* like Brick, with virile beauty.]" (*Cat* 1955: 103; *Cat* 1975: 144; emphasis mine).

All this textual data, implying sexual ambiguity on Big Daddy's part, was most likely material about which Williams deliberated in multivalent ways. I suspect that he probably did wish to encode a subtext, for Big Daddy as much as for Brick, that would make his two main male characters' sexual preferences somewhat uncertain. But he also encoded, in the portraits of both men (and of their female mates, too—even the money-desperate Maggie) subtexts that repulse the notion that any kind of materialism, including sex, is ultimately the most important human value.

According to a passage that has remained constant in Brick's act 2 discussion with Big Daddy, Brick paradoxically seems to find every college football player filled with "disgust and confusion"; he makes this judgment even though he proclaims himself "[un]fit for" such "contests" any longer (Texas 10: 102). In the very early Texas 10 manuscript (10: 102—as also in Delaware 1/2: 44), Brick goes on to discuss how he had taken private showers, in a separate cubicle away from his university football team, in order to wash off [his] naked body all the sweat and disgust and confusion," "all contact and all disgust that comes from contact." These latter references would suggest his potential questioning of his sexual preferences, and yet he surely is not meanwhile judging every football player in the world to be a bisexual. Instead, he seems to imply principally that American competitive life causes people to lose their spiritual bearings among daily competitive "mendacity," which he elsewhere, probably in every textual variant of *Cat,* condemns as a source of "disgust" (*Cat* 1955: 79; *Cat* 1975: 108).

Big Daddy, like Brick, is disgusted, definitely, with a lie-crowded world. Numerous worldlings, like Gooper and Mae, seem to dedicate themselves to trafficking in lies, and they thus produce a Dionysian tragic "stawm," one that particularly weathers the Pollitt plantation during act 3 (1955: 149–50; 1975: 163). Yet a hyperventilating Dionysian colossus of a Big Daddy, bulked against the panorama of his plantation while threatening all around with a rifle, was not, I think, what this play most needed. It needed, instead, the antithesis to such bluster that was already also present in the play: the Big Daddy who had tenuously learned, in act 2 with Brick, that "being friends is telling each other the truth" (1955: 94; 1975: 130). Two often-alienated kinfolk there realized that it would be best, if not necessarily funny, for love to *tell* true.

Therefore, Williams may principally have created Big Daddy's rage on the belvedere scene so as to *defy* Kazan—very *cagily* defying him, by creating a too much "towering" Dionysian character, one who would not fit any more comfortably into a full plot and ensemble cast than does The Father in Pirandello's *Six Characters*. Such a character, at least (in the alternate Big Daddy reappearance scene that Williams was preparing at the same time), might tell an off-color elephant joke and thus, by displeasing the censors, perhaps destroy Kazan's plans for featuring Big Daddy in act 3 at all.

But Williams, it appears, kept musing (over a long, long period) on this drama. Hence he eventually revised *Cat* as much as Pirandello revised *Six Characters*—with a keen "artistic instinct," one that protected the play against the "molestation" of inappropriate transformations (Moestrup 185). The elephant joke (along with audience attitudes toward ribaldry) evolved, so that the joke became more workable in the script. Eventually, Big Daddy's dramatized character no longer exposed what Pirandello labeled as his inner, tormented, chaotic psychological "face"; instead, his act 3 reappearances represented him behind the guise of what Pirandello deemed a sly social "mask," one that could successfully dupe even the daily-dominoed Gooper and Mae (Oliver 12). The old Mississippi patriarch, indeed, came skillfully to copractice metatheatrical role-playing along with Maggie, supporting her beneficent lie about being pregnant and thus perhaps vanquishing the ugly nonbeneficent lies of Mae's and Gooper's greed (1955: 153; 1975: 167–68).

Meanwhile Brick, especially by the time of *Cat*'s 1975 final revision, has returned to being a figure who dwells primarily in the Pirandellian realm of inner psychological "face" rather than negotiating busy social interactions as a rationalistically masked man. Oddly enough, Brick's characterizations did not work any better in the play ensemble when he wore gregarious but false social masks, for Kazan's sake, than Big Daddy's characterization worked, with full effectiveness, as he fulminated with fustian from his rooftop belvedere. Hence (even though he was not writing about *Cat on a Hot Tin Roof*) the critic Jorn Moestrup may well be correct in surmising that there exists some wondrous (albeit highly arcane) "artistic instinct" that can, luckily, free an oppressed art work from assaultingly wrongheaded strategies of modification.

Perhaps it is aesthetically appropriate, then, that in the belvedere scene draft filed with the manuscript called Texas 15, Williams combined Big Daddy's tortuous spasms of pain with Brick's and Maggie's bedroom fadeout by "the rose-silk lamp" (Texas 15—Subfolder 5: 4). He declared, in addition, that "the play says only one [fully] affirmative thing about 'man's fate': that he has it, still in his power, not to squeal like a pig but to keep a tight mouth about it" (Texas 15—Subfolder 5: 4). On the same page, nonetheless, Williams judged love . . . *possible;* not proven or disproven, but *possible.*"

Works Cited

Brustein, Robert. "Pirandello's Drama of Revolt." In *Pirandello: A Collection of Critical Essays,* edited by Glauco Cambon. Englewood Cliffs, N.J.: Prentice-Hall, 1967.

Clum, John. *"Something Cloudy, Something Clear:* Homophobic Discourse in Tennessee Williams." *South Atlantic Quarterly* 88.1 (Winter 1989): 161–79.

Della Terze, Dante. "On Pirandello's Humorism." In *Modern Critical Views: Luigi Pirandello,* edited by Harold Bloom. New York: Chelsea House, 1989.

Hinden, Michael. "The Five Voices of *The Birth of Tragedy." Comparative Drama* 22.2 (Summer 1988): 97–113.

Moestrup, Jorn. *The Structural Pattern of Pirandello's Work.* Odense: University of Odense Press, 1972.

Murphy, Brenda. *Tennessee Williams and Elia Kazan: A Collaboration in the Theatre.* Cambridge: Cambridge University Press, 1992.

Oliver, Roger W. *Dreams of Passion: The Theatre of Luigi Pirandello.* New York: New York University Press, 1979.

Parker, Brian. "A Preliminary Stemma for Drafts and Revisions of Tennessee Williams's *Cat on a Hot Tin Roof." Publications of the Bibliographical Society of America* 90.4 (December 1996): 475–96. (Parker provided the labeling numbers that I am including for all the *Cat* manuscripts; I have added the label Harvard 4 for a manuscript evidently acquired after he visited that Boston site. These Parker/Loomis numbers are not, however, used at any of the research collections; the additional catalog data I here provide will help collection users find specific drafts.)

Pirandello, Luigi. *Six Characters in Search of an Author.* [*Sei personnagi in cerca d'autore*]. 1922. Translated by Edward Storer. Mineola, N.Y.: Dover, 1998.

Williams, Tennessee. *Cat on a Hot Tin Roof.* New York: Signet/New American Library, 1955.

———. *Cat on a Hot Tin Roof.* New York: New Directions, 1975.

———. (Columbia 1) Manuscript Collection Tennessee Williams/23 pp. of rewrites (dated December 9, 1954), probably typed by TW. Tennessee Williams Papers, Rare Book and Manuscript Library, Columbia University, New York City.

———. (Delaware 1) Manuscript 115, Tennessee Williams/Box 1, F9/ *Cat on a Hot Tin Roof; or, A Place of Stone* (a play) n.d./typescript, 118 pp./bound in blue folder. Special Collections, University Library, University of Delaware, Newark, Delaware.

———. (Harvard 1) Manuscript 91.3/*Cat on a Hot Tin Roof*/manuscript (mimeographed) (New York and Key West 1955). Harvard Theatre Collection, Pusey Library, Harvard University, Cambridge, Massachusetts. (Copy 21 of the playing script revised by the author/lacks act 3)

———. (Harvard 2) Manuscript 91.1/*Cat on a Hot Tin Roof*/typescript unsigned/(Key West 1955)/additions and revisions by Tennessee Williams. Harvard Theatre Collection, Pusey Library, Harvard University, Cambridge, Massachusetts

———. (Harvard 4) *Cat on a Hot Tin Roof.* 152 leaves/typescript (carbon) with cuts and annotations throughout, in pencil by T. Williams and in green ink by "EK" (Elia Kazan) and some typescript. Harvard Theatre Collection, Pusey Library, Harvard University, Cambridge, Massachusetts. (I myself have assigned the manuscript number and have declared the green ink markings Kazan's [on the basis that green inkings by Kazan also appear in Texas 10 and because the initials "EK" actually appear in marginal notations within Harvard 4]. There exists another Harvard manuscript of *Cat* that Parker names Harvard 3, so that Harvard 4 seems a natural numbering for the additional manuscript.)

———. (NYPL 2) NCOF+/93-7995/*Cat on a Hot Tin Roof*/121 pp., mimeograph on bond by Hart Stenographic Bureau/gift of Roger Stevens/1955? Billy Rose Theatre Collection, New York Public Library, New York City.

———. (NYPL 4) NCOF/93-77961/119 leaves mimeographed by Studio Duplicating Service, Inc./title page has "property of: American Shakespeare Theatre, Stanford, Connecticut"/ANTA Theatre, New York, 1975? Billy Rose Theatre Collection, New York Public Library, New York City.

———. (Texas 1) Manuscript (Williams, Tennessee) Works/"Three Players of a Summer Game"/Typed ms./drafts/incomplete with autograph revisions and autograph note [78 pp.]/1951 (Venice). Harry Ransom Humanities Research Center, University of Texas, Austin.

———. (Texas 4) Manuscript file (Williams, Tennessee) Works/"Three players of a summer game" (short story)/Typed carbon copy manuscript (33 pp.) with typed insert [9 pp.] and autograph emendations on 10 pp./1952 April/insert dated May 9, 1952, by Audrey Wood. Harry Ransom Humanities Research Center, University of Texas, Austin.

———. (Texas 10) Manuscript file (Williams, Tennessee) Works/*"A Cat on a [Hot] Tin Roof"; or, "A Place of Stone."* Typed ms./early version with heavy revisions, inscribed to Andreas Brown on back of "Characters" page. Harry Ransom Humanities Center, University of Texas, Austin.

———. (Texas 11) Manuscript file (Williams, Tennessee) (A play)/Typed carbon copy ms. [31 pp.]/inc. with autograph emendations on 2 pp. and autograph notes by Elia Kazan on 14 pp./n.d. Harry Ransom Humanities Center, University of Texas, Austin.

———. (Texas 15) Manuscript file (Williams, Tennessee) Works/*Cat on a [hot] tin roof*/Composite typed ms./incomplete [33 pp.] with typed carbon copy inserts [13 pp.] and autograph emendations on 22 pp./n.d. Harry Ransom Humanities Center, University of Texas, Austin.

———. (Texas 21) Manuscript (Downing, R.)/Misc./Typed and autograph/ *Cat on a Hot Tin Roof*/mimeograph/stage manager's script with typed inserts and autograph notes and revisions [169 pp.]/n.d./includes two versions of act 3. Harry Ransom Humanities Center, University of Texas, Austin.

———. (Texas 26) (the second, revised version of act 3 in Texas 21 above). Harry Ransom Humanities Center, University of Texas, Austin.

———. (Texas 29) Manuscript (Downing, R.)/Misc./Typed and autograph/ *Cat on a Hot Tin Roof*/Typed ms./Stage manager's copy with T. inserts and A. notes [121 pp.]/n.d./Bound in hard notebook cover. Harry Ransom Humanities Center, University of Texas, Austin.

———. "The Glass Menagerie." *The Theatre of Tennessee Williams.* Vol. 1. New York: New Directions, 1971.

6

The Metaphysics of Tennessee Williams

Robert Siegel

From Parmenides' insistence that language instead of empiricism could lead us to immutable truths, to Plato's form of a cat as the ideal rather than any living cat, to Descartes's distrust of an evil genie who deceives his senses, and to Kant's sense of isolation, the human being trapped in his body without ever knowing what another body thinks and feels, Western rationality has regarded the flesh as an impediment and an impostor, a troublemaker thwarting the mind's awareness of the self and the world. Nowhere in modern theater is this split examined and evaluated as it is in the work of Tennessee Williams. What has often been regarded as a critique of the remnants of Victorian repression in the South (Falk 70–71) is in fact a running dialogue, a much deeper ambivalence about whether the mind and body can communicate or even coexist. That the battleground for this apprehension is often sexual transgression, at least as defined by the last decade's standards, should not mislead readers into thinking that Williams is solely a moralist. He is also a metaphysician searching for a connection between seemingly different entities. This duality has been mentioned in passing by Nada Zeineddine (*Because It Is My Name* 136) in a section on *The Night of the Iguana* and has been analyzed in more depth with regard to *Summer and Smoke* by Alice Griffin (*Understanding Tennessee Williams* 81–103), although only in a one-sided manner with respect to Alma. Dualistic approaches to Williams's work have, instead, focused on gender, geography, power relations between weak and strong or gentle and violent, illusion and reality, good and bad faith (using Sartre's sense of the term), the self and other, and, more recently, heterosexual/homosexual schisms in his work. While these approaches certainly speak to the playwright's concerns, a mind-body analysis can amplify and perhaps integrate these other dualities.

The argument between mind and body is spoken in vastly different contexts by characters with vastly different motives, and yet the conflicts are almost identical. When Amanda confronts Tom for wanting to leave his job at the warehouse in *The Glass Menagerie*, Tom defends his need for adventure by claiming that man is by instinct a lover, a hunter, and a fighter; and Amanda's rebuke is that instinct belongs to animals, that Christians desire the mind and spirit, and that surely Tom's aims are higher than those of pigs and monkeys. His answer has the cadence of a punch line: "I reckon they're not" (*Glass* 30). The clash becomes more caustic and the dichotomy blunter in Blanche's famous monologue as she pleads with her sister to leave the lowly Stanley, to choose art and tender feelings over the Neanderthal brutes (*Streetcar* 72). If instead of Stanley Big Daddy were eavesdropping, his rejoinder would plainly assert that man is no different from fish, bird, or reptile, just a lot more complicated and more trouble (*Cat* 75).

These exchanges resemble the Shavian arguments between the realist and the idealist in *Arms and the Man, Major Barbara,* and *St. Joan*. And as with Shaw, Williams's plays often create archetypes, in his case for the flesh and the spirit, that seek, test, and do battle with each other.

As mentioned, Griffin explores the spirit-flesh conflict in *Summer and Smoke,* but mainly in the context of Alma's awakening to her own body. She sees John's awakening to the spirit as a "sudden turnabout" that needs to be made credible through acting technique (*Understanding* 89). Though John's is described by Williams as Promethean, and flesh, here, is clearly more aware of its nature than spirit, John's isolation and discontent are as palpable as Alma's. John admits that he can offer little comfort to his dying patients: "I'm made for the science of medicine but not for the practice of it" (*Four Plays* 171). John diagnoses Alma's "condition" as a doppelgänger, the earthy double that Alma's chaste spirit yearns for, but John, too, has a doppelgänger and seeks out Alma in her element, the sterile, intellectual social club. Once there, he is quickly bored by the pompous squabbling, and he satisfies his curiosity with a more familiar pleasure, Rosa Gonzales, the sensual queen of the local gambling casino. But body is not content with just another body and is still drawn to spirit. In the following scene, John tells Alma, "You know I like you and I think you're worth a lot of consideration . . . because you have a lot of feeling in your heart and that's a rare thing" (*Four Plays* 191). John tries to resolve his doppelgänger by bringing Alma into his world, a date at the gambling casino. This is not just a seduction as portrayed by Griffin (88) using the duality of the sensualist and the repressed. John confirms this in a later exchange when he confesses that he wouldn't have made love to her even if she consented, because "I'm more afraid of your soul than you're afraid of my body" (*Four Plays* 210). In fact, in the subsequent scene, with the connection broken, body and mind retreat to their respective worlds, Alma to her antiseptic social club and John to drunken sex with Rosa next door in his house. We hear John, however, not delighting in passion but rather reveling in his corruption: "Has anyone slid downhill as fast as I have this summer? Like a greased pig!" (*Four Plays* 204). If the nexus of the duality is sex, then why isn't John satisfied? The key to John's awakening, the recognition of the spirit by the body, comes only after a confrontation with death. What he has run from as a child, his mother's death, John finally faces after his father's killing and after he is summoned to fight an epidemic. The recognition of the body by the spirit comes after Alma's breakdown, a death from which she, too, can no longer run.

Williams has been criticized for not depicting Alma's breakdown on stage. It occurs between acts. So much of her pathology has been dramatized, however, that the transformation is credible. We don't have to be in bed with Martha and Nick between acts in *Who's Afraid of Virginia Woolf* to understand Martha's reversal at the opening of act 3, the sudden hostility toward her stud and the newfound concern for her missing husband. John and Alma have been also characterized as abstractions rather than realistic characters. Griffin defers to Benjamin Nelson and the short story "Yellow Bird," from which the play was developed, concluding that William's intention is allegorical (*Understanding* 82). As Eric Bentley has observed about Brecht, however, "the disproof of Brecht's theory is Brecht's practice" (*Bentley on Brecht* 47). Allegorical abstractions do not yearn for their "other half," engage in the push-pull of attraction-aversion, and reverse roles credibly. Griffin credits Geraldine Page's brilliant performance for wider acceptance of the play (100–101), but her performance doesn't explain why John's evolution also works. The resolution for William's pair of doppelgängers is also credible—acceptance but not union. John will marry Nellie, a bright, more temperate representative of spirit, and Alma will go on a date with a young salesman to the Moon Lake Casino. Both have faced their demon, and yet there is an unresolved loneliness in each. When John is asked whether he's happy, he says that he's settled for life on acceptable terms, and that "it's best not to ask for too much" (*Four Plays* 220). In their last meeting, Alma reflects that she and John have become like "two people exchanging a call on each other at the same time, and each one finding the other has gone out, the door locked against him and no one to answer the bell" (*Four Plays* 223–24).

This sadness, this rift between spirit and flesh, erupts into emotional and physical violence in Williams plays such as *A Streetcar Named Desire,* and *Suddenly Last Summer.* Williams seems to reserve his harshest judgment when body masquerades as spirit, although Blanche is treated with much more compassion for her pretense and self-deception than is Sebastian for his predatory hypocrisy.

That Blanche is a woman whose mind and body are at war with each other almost seems besides the point. Her overwrought reactions and coquettish narcissism are thrust center stage as we watch a remnant of a privileged class unravel. Mary Ann Corrigan, in *Modern Drama,* writes that "the conflict between Blanche and Stanley is an externalization of the conflict that goes on within Blanche between illusion and reality" (392), the illusion being the Southern Belle and the reality being the lonely, hungry woman. Her revulsion toward Stanley, the sensualist, however, is first and foremost a result of his seeing through her pose immediately, self-hatred through *his* eyes, what William Kleb, citing Foucault, calls the Other (*Confronting Tennessee* 27–41). A quick review of the article might shed new light on the illusion-reality duality so often mentioned in William's plays.

Kleb is critical of the propensity to view Blanche as "simply a prostitute, a nymphomaniac, or both. Ironically, such a reading at the sexual limits, has serious limits of its own. . . . it can obscure . . . the power relations . . . in Williams's play" (*Confronting Tennessee* 30). Kleb introduces Foucault's concept of the Other, the sick, the criminal, and the mad who helped define the historical boundaries for social norms and political power by their position outside those norms. He places Blanche as the Other, the destitute sister connected to a past of sickness, dying and epic fornications—in opposition, by the end of the poker night—to Stella and Stanley (*Confronting* 32). Kleb then turns his attention to Mitch as her only ally. Kleb is right in noting that even before Blanche's assessment of Mitch as different, Mitch establishes the difference by emphatically opting out of the poker game because of his sick mother. Kleb makes the link: "Mitch, it turns out, is linked to Blanche by a kinship of temperament" (33). But here his analysis shifts; Mitch's temperament puts his manhood in question, and Kleb returns to the sexual nexus he previously eschewed:

> unmanly sensitivity, disease, arrested adolescence, even sexual confusion, have all symbolically transplanted their seeds in Mitch; Blanche's presence threatens to make these seeds grow. . . . there are actually two major questions dominating the Blanche-Mitch movement of Williams's play; [one is marriage,] the other, whether Mitch will escape the sexual fate she represents, with its connections, finally, to madness and death. (35–36)

Mitch, however, is anything but relieved at having escaped this "fate." His rancor in the final scene toward Stanley is loud and clear; his loss is not the least bit hidden. Foucault's model of the Other is striking in juxtaposition to Blanche and the Kowalskis; but as a paradigm based on sickness, sexual deviance, and madness, it doesn't explain Mitch's "Sameness" with Blanche.

The kinship of temperament makes more sense. She and Mitch are not just linked by the death of those they loved in the past. The mutual attraction is genuinely present, based on a shared sensitivity of spirit. When spirit is also grounded in the necessity of the body, such as Mitch's simple but eloquent statement that they need each other (*Streetcar* 96), stability and happiness are real possibilities. But Blanche toys with Mitch. Part of the deception is her fear of losing him after sleeping with him. None of her numerous sexual encounters back in Laurel led to a relationship. To a large extent, Blanche's spirit, driven by shame and panic, has been devastated by the time she appears on Stella's doorstep. Blanche's marriage to a man whom she could not sexually satisfy did not stop her from loving him deeply. Her spirit sought out his spirit and was willing to love only his spirit until she understood that his body could also love but that it could never love *her* body. Her sense of guilt about her husband's suicide is compounded by her inability to save the older relatives for whom she had to be the primary caregiver back at Belle Reve. Whereas the threat of death in the fever epidemic halts John's descent in *Summer and Smoke,* it accelerates Blanche's; she seeks comfort in one-night stands with soldiers from the local army base and in affairs with teenage boys, giving to them what she could not give to her young husband. Again, for Williams in this play, it is Blanche's spirit, not her body, that lacks the emotional resources to cope with adversity. Her pose as the fine lady is the doppelgänger of her shame, and her obsession with her looks is the doppelgänger of her panic, that she can no longer turn the trick, that she will no longer find any lasting comfort.

Mitch, however, also encourages the pose, putting her on the pedestal of chastity, telling her that he's never met anyone like her, and imploring her to slap him whenever he steps out of bounds (*Streetcar* 91). Blanche rolls her eyes and propositions him in French, almost wanting to be found out. The playwright is not only revealing the good girl/nice girl sexual mores of his era but also commenting on spirit. Williams portrays the quality of spirit and sensitivity through Mitch as prissy, somewhat ineffectual—needing the consent of his mother to choose whom he loves—and prone to illusions. And Mitch abandons her precisely for shattering the illusion, not for what she has done. The lie is worse than the deed. Mitch feels "had" but does not see his own part in the pretense that he encouraged, nor does Blanche acknowledge her part or his anger, preferring instead to hide behind a euphemism, giving people "magic" instead of the truth, her version of "spin doctoring," which, sadly, she thoroughly believes. Spirit, cut off from the flesh, denying its needs, becomes insensitive and badly deluded. This denial makes spirit weak and easily vanquished. Corrigan characterizes Stanley's conquest as the "oft-told tale of the defeat of the weak by the strong" (the power duality) and quotes Joseph Riddel's analysis that Blanche's "schizoid personality is a drama of man's irreconcilable split between animal reality and moral appearance," the Puritan/sensualist duality (*Mod-*

ern Drama 392). For Corrigan and Riddel, all of this material has the certainty of a geometric theorem, but if we look at these schisms in terms of the mind-body conflict, it is wrong to conclude that spirit must necessarily reside in a mirage and that the split between it and body is irreconcilable.

It is the *lie* that Williams finds irreconcilable and condemns with even greater vehemence in *Suddenly Last Summer*. Since the play takes place after Sebastian's death, we know him only through his mother, Mrs. Venable, and his cousin, Catharine, who also represent the mind-body split. His mother presents his public persona as chaste, celibate at the age of forty. His life as a poet is also pure. He desires no literary reputation and will publish only after his death. His poems are equated with births. He writes one a year, and each one gestates for nine months until he travels for the summer and gives life to the work on the page. This is his surrogate for sex, but unlike Alma and Mitch, Sebastian is neither shy nor squeamish about the world. He sees God in the savage struggle of life and death in the Galapagos Islands and rejects the monastic life of the monk for the Ritz in Paris. He surrounds himself with an entourage of the beautiful, the talented, and the young. And unlike Blanche's youth, his own has not faded. When the doctor cannot tell the difference between a photo of him at twenty and at forty, his mother brags, "It takes character to refuse to grow old . . . , discipline . . . , one cocktail before dinner, not two . . . , a single lean lamb chop" (*Five Plays* 246). There is no languishing in the bathtub for Sebastian, unlike Blanche, no paper shades to hide the light of a lamp. His life seems a vital, spiritual work of art.

Still, we have misgivings about the authenticity of Mrs. Venable's depiction of Sebastian even before we hear Catharine's version. Sebastian's relationship with his mother has the suggestion of incest. Mrs. Venable boasts, "I was the only one in his life that satisfied the demands he made of people" (*Five Plays* 247). No one else was pure enough for him. They were a famous couple at the fashionable European resorts, and her voice takes on the sentiment of the lover as she reminisces: "We would carve out each day of our lives like a piece of sculpture" (*Five Plays* 248). And there is the jealousy of the lover, an upper-class echo of Miller's Eddie Carbone, when the mother refers to Catharine as a "vandal" (*Five Plays* 248) for taking Sebastian from her. Corruption also rears its head in the form of bribery. Mrs.

Venable wants Catharine lobotomized to silence her and makes clear to the doctor that her financial support for his work depends on his doing as she says.

The truth serum is a plot device to help us judge the veracity of Catharine's account, since it's her word against Mrs. Venable's. But the device seems superfluous because Catharine speaks with the simplicity and directness of the body. When asked about her feelings for Sebastian, she replies, "He liked me and so I loved him" (*Five Plays* 267). When asked how she loved him, she replies, "The only way he'd accept—a sort of motherly way" (*Five Plays* 267), implying that she would have given her body if he so desired. And when the doctor shows concern for her, the loneliness of being institutionalized is expressed directly and physically when Catharine fiercely presses her lips and body against him. Andrew Sofer's article in *Modern Drama,* using many of the same examples cited here, offers a view of Catharine's sexuality as manipulation of the doctor, and her drug-induced confession as a gambit, a performance (342–43). Sofer's interpretation is unconvincing because, first of all, anyone who has sat in a dentist's chair in a drug-induced stupor or reverie knows that such a conscious performance would be impossible. Moreover, anyone who has seen the play in a theater (and I have seen several productions) sees a frightened, troubled woman desperately trying to understand what has happened to her and her cousin. Although we may see the Prince feigning madness in some performances of *Hamlet,* we have no indication that this is happening here onstage. Those of us who write about drama ought to watch plays, not just deconstruct words.

Catharine's version of Sebastian exposes the lie about his spirit and has the ring of truth because she seeks not so much to undermine his reputation as to understand the shocking event that was his death. She tells the doctor that she tried to save him from the image of himself as a sacrifice to a cruel God (*Five Plays* 267). She feels that she failed him and that she was, and still is, somehow responsible.

Through her, we see that Sebastian's need for beauty is corrupt, that Catharine, like the mother, was used to procure men for him. Suddenly, that summer, Sebastian could not write a poem. The spiritual, creative absence is replaced by an insatiable appetite for passing out tips to the hungry, homeless kids who follow him into the bathhouses; he becomes a pied piper leading a growing, penniless entourage that wants more and more. The sex has the quality of imperialism, the rich Yankee flinging coins to the poor in exchange for favors. Steven Bruhm's essay in *Modern Drama* amplifies in much greater detail the hypocrisy of Sebastian's commodity mentality against his image of pure spirit (530–31). Bruhm views the cannibalism in several ways, including Williams's ambivalence about homosexuality. But Catharine's anguish indicates a broader concern: "I know it's a hideous story but it's a true story of our time and the world we live in" (*Five Plays* 259). Bruhm expands Catharine's vision and grapples with another duality: "The [cannibalism] scene collapses the barrier between the city and the jungle. . . . The city had tried to transform the primal need for consumption—including sexual consumption—into an orderly, regulated system of trade. But by collapsing back into its primal, repressed form, the jungle exposes the underside of consumption upon which the city is founded" (*Modern Drama* 533).

This dynamic, viewed from the mind-body split, broadens the analysis even further. Williams's play is a tale not of descent, as in *Summer and Smoke,* but rather of metamorphosis. Sebastian, as spirit, is a Dorian Gray whose mask is intact as long as he stays in polite society where exploitation can be cloaked in pretense; the same type of charade that almost allowed Catharine to be date-raped by the stranger feigning concern at the Mardi Gras ball. But let Sebastian loose in a grittier world, and not just as an observer as in the Galapagos but as a player in Mexico, and his hidden corruption surfaces. If Blanche represents deluded spirit and her punishment is madness, then Sebastian represents evil spirit, and the playwright's punishment for the devourer is to be devoured.

The mind-body battle does have its truces. *Cat on a Hot Tin Roof* offers a more compassionate body in Maggie and Big Daddy to a more self-aware spirit in Brick. Maggie is often contrasted with Blanche, Alma, and Laura (Cafagna, Bigsby, Prenshaw), using the gender or illusion and reality duality (*Confronting Tennessee* 120–21), but she also has the practicality of the body, like Stanley in some ways. She wants her husband to stop drinking and give her a child to please his dying father and not get cut out of the will. Like Stanley, she does not mince words: "Brick, y'know, I've been so God damn disgustingly poor all my life. . . . Always had to suck up to people I couldn't stand because they had money. . . . You can be young without money, but you can't be old without it" (*Cat* 41–42). She has the same kind of earthy perspective as Stanley, admiring Big Daddy because he didn't come from and is unaffected by money, for still being a redneck. She also has the longing of the body. Maggie may not scream out Brick's name, but she spares herself no pride in trying to get him to desire her again. When Brick tells her to take a lover, she replies that she can't see anyone but him, even with her eyes closed, and that she wishes he'd get ugly so she could stand the estrangement (*Cat* 31). Like Stanley to Stella, she speaks frankly to Brick about sex: "[You] did it naturally, easily, slowly, with absolute confidence and perfect calm, more like opening a door for a young lady or seating her at a table than giving expression to any longing for her. Your indifference made you wonderful" (*Cat* 25).

Maggie has none of Stanley's malice, however, and is no mercenary. David Savran, citing Lacan (*Communists, Cowboys, and Queers* 107), characterizes her as castrating. Yes, she is jealous of Brick's friendship with Skipper to the point of seducing Skipper, but the seduction is not the covert plotting of Stanley who "outs" Blanche. Maggie is guilt-ridden and takes responsibility for what happened: "In this way, I destroyed him, by telling him truth that he and his world which he was born and raised in, yours and his world, had told him could not be told! . . . I'm not tryin' to whitewash my behavior. Christ, no! Brick, I'm not good . . . , but I'm honest! Give me credit for that, will you please?" (*Cat* 45). And unlike Stanley, who humiliates Blanche in front of Stella, Maggie as body is much more circumspect about attacking Skipper and pleads with Brick (spirit) to see the truth from her vantage point: "I'm naming it so damn clean that it killed poor Skipper! You two had something that had to be kept on ice, yes, incorruptible, yes!—and death was the only icebox where you could keep it" (*Cat* 44). But Brick is having none of it and perhaps with good reason. As spirit, Brick is no brick. He's described by Maggie, even in anger, as a superior creature, a godlike being who asks too much from those who love him. He has none of Alma's anxiety or Blanche's desperation, although Dianne Cafagna, citing Riddel, likens him to Blanche, pointing out that he drinks "to induce illusion" (*Confronting Tennessee* 127). But Brick creates no false past or present when he drinks. The alcohol hardly allows him to feel more at home in the world or his marriage, and while liquor dulls his disgust, drinking cannot remove it.

Big Daddy, like Maggie, won't accept the vagueness of Brick's disillusionment. Body dwells in the concrete. Both characters push Brick to confront his friendship with Skipper and Skipper's death. Much has been made of Brick's sexual identity, using the hetero-homo duality, but if Brick's self-hatred is examined more closely, the schism is too narrow. The fact that Brick debates his sexual identity is proof, in itself, that he is in the closet according to David Savran (*Communists, Cowboys, and Queers* 105). But why dismiss his defense, which is straightforward and unapologetic? In response to Gooper and Mae's insinuation of homosexuality, he upholds his feelings in spiritual terms to Big Daddy: "Why can't exceptional friendship, real, real, deep, deep, friendship between two men be respected as something clean and decent without being thought of as—Fairies . . . Normal? No!—It was too rare to be normal, any true thing between two people is too rare to be normal" (*Cat* 89). For Brick this is Platonic love in the true sense of the word. Even Maggie describes the friendship in Hellenistic imagery: "It was one of those beautiful, ideal things they tell about in the Greek legends, it couldn't be anything else, you being you, and that's what made it so sad, that's what made it so awful because it was love that never could be carried through to anything satisfying or even talked about plainly" (*Cat* 43). But it *is* satisfying to Brick until Skipper plainly confesses his feelings. Brick's self-loathing comes not from any confusion about his sexual identity but from his abandonment of Skipper when his friend needed him the most. What he had described to Maggie as the "one great good true thing in his life" (*Cat* 44) is now tainted with reproach and guilt. From the standpoint of the mind-body duality, Brick represents a wounded spirit, alienated from the greedy squabbling over the family fortune, alienated from a father who loved him but never talked to him, and alienated from a world full of mendacity, which now includes his friendship with Skipper. This fall from grace, and not his fear of being homosexual, as asserted by Kataria (*Faces of Eve* 75), has landed Brick in the bottle.

In *Cat*, however, the thematic bottom line does not solely belong to body. Big Daddy forces Brick to face his guilt. Brick, in turn, forces Big Daddy to face the truth that he is dying from cancer. Maggie insists that Brick see the truth about his friend, but her husband's estrangement forces her to see the truth about seducing Skipper and his impotence. Her conduct led to his drunken phone confession to Brick and eventually to Skipper's alcoholic death. Key to all of these revelations is the desire for body and spirit to help each other. The need to vanquish that pervades *Streetcar* and *Suddenly Last Summer,* the competitive need to be right in *Summer and Smoke*—all of this is replaced by kinder motives in *Cat.* Big Daddy is abusive to his wife and Gooper's family, but he pushes Brick out of a genuine desire to understand his son, and Brick is genuinely sorry for exposing the lie about the spastic colon.

These more generous emotions emerge as both archetypes become more aware of their own shortcomings. Spirit as represented by Brick is not self-righteous like Blanche. Just listen to Brick turning his disgust on himself: "In some ways I'm no better than the others, in some ways worse because I'm less alive. Maybe it's being alive that makes them lie, and being almost not alive makes me sort of accidentally truthful" (*Cat* 94). And there is just as much disgust in Big Daddy at the compromises and lies in his life, from the Elks to the Rotary Club, to Sunday church, to having sex with a wife for whom he no longer cares. He calls it all crap. And body experiences as much pain as spirit in Big Daddy's cancer and Maggie's anguish at being cut off by her husband: "Oh, Brick! How long does it have t' go on? This punishment? Haven't I done time enough, haven't I served my term, can't I apply for a—pardon?" (*Cat* 31).

And in the end, body looks out for spirit as well as its own interests. Maggie tells the lie about being pregnant to soothe Big Mama and keep her inheritance secure. And she will make the lie true by locking up Brick's liquor on this night when it is her time of the month to conceive and make him satisfy her. But this is not just to satisfy her desire for money but also out of concern for her husband's interests and out of a real need for him. And Brick will join her. Mark Royden Winchell's article in the *Mississippi Quarterly,* using the hetero-homo duality, finds the resolution unconvincing and claims that Williams "may simply have lost his nerve," returning Brick to the heterosexual fold to placate the audience (712). But from the point of view of the mind-body duality, the ending, as stated earlier, is a truce, not a resolution, an open-ended recognition of mutual need between body and spirit that is evoked by the bittersweet accommodation in the last exchange of the play, the original version, when Maggie says: "Oh, you weak people, you weak, beautiful people!—who give up. What you want is someone to take hold of you—Gently, gently, with love! And I do love you, Brick, I do!" (*Cat* 123). And Brick acquiesces by replying, "Wouldn't it be funny if that was true?" (*Cat* 123).

It is self-awareness and mutual need that hold out this possibility of mending the tear between spirit and body in Williams's last great play (before alcohol and drugs controlled him), *The Night of the Iguana*. The play is also a more complex arrangement of the body-spirit archetypes. We are offered a trinity: Maxine as body, Hannah as spirit, and Shannon as the tormented embodiment of both.

Shannon, like Blanche, appears at the beginning of the play as a protagonist on the verge of a nervous breakdown. Like Miss DuBois, he has come down in the world. A defrocked minister who once conducted exclusive worldwide tours for the rich, he arrives at Maxine's hotel in a broken-down school bus with a group of schoolteachers from a Baptist female college who want his head on a platter. But unlike Blanche, Shannon knows he's in trouble and makes an immediate, full confession. He tells Maxine that he's been accused of statutory rape for sleeping with a minor, that losing this job is the end of the line, and that he is losing his grip; the "spook" has moved in with him.

One might argue that Shannon is as deluded as Blanche in thinking that he'll return to the church, but the declaration is uttered in panic and serves as a shield against the accusations hurled at him by one of the teachers, Miss Fellowes. His awareness is once again revealed a moment later when, at the crescendo of her attack, he shows just how frail the shield has become, screaming: "Don't do what you're doing. Don't! Break! Human! Pride!" (*Three by Tennessee* 31). And when he rails at Latta about being a gentleman, later in the play as he's being fired, we sense that this is a plea for his dignity and that there is little pretense in his claim. Also, Shannon's desire to return to his former vocation belies a deeper spiritual crisis to return to his God. More on that below, but first let's look at the other component of his crisis.

Shannon's life is the battlefield for the war between spirit and flesh. As spirit, he's perceptive in spotting Hannah's generosity. He notices that she rations her last two cigarettes to herself but then reflexively offers him one when asked. And he, too, is generous, interceding on Hannah's behalf with Maxine. Shannon is also compassionate, careful not to wound Hannah's pride about being broke. He also helps her grandfather, Nonno, through one of his "cerebral accidents," sets the trapped iguana free, and, in the end, frees Hannah by giving her his gold cross to pawn until her circumstances improve.

As Body, both as minister and tour guide, he has sex with the young women in his flock, but there is little pleasure in the act, as he slaps these women afterward and forces them to pray with him for forgiveness. Rita Colanzi's article in *Modern Drama* uses Sartre's duality of the rebel and the revolutionary to explain this behavior. Unlike the revolutionary who wants to change and transcend the world, the rebel, Shannon, wants to preserve the abuses, in Shannon's case traditional values, so that he can continue to rebel against them (456). Colanzi makes a valid point: why doesn't Shannon just leave the church rather than continuing to sin within it? While Sartre's bad faith describes Shannon's contradictory impulses, the model doesn't adequately explain why he is trapped in them. Maxine explains his proclivities as the result of his being spanked for masturbating as a child and then being told that he had offended God. But Williams, like Arthur Miller, is too good a dramatist to allow a character's dilemma to balance on the head of a Freudian pin. The mother's intrusion is not the singular, traumatic turning point. Shannon would have wound up at the brink even if he didn't get caught masturbating. His crisis is much more pervasive. He is angry at the smug complacency of his former suburban parishioners and the tourists he leads around the world and their God, whom he calls "a senile delinquent . . . , the sort of old man in a nursing home that's putting together a jigsaw puzzle and can't put it together and gets furious at it and kicks over the table" (*Three by Tennessee* 60). Shannon rejects the spirit of his former parishioners as feeble. He is looking for his God in wild thunderstorms that will declare: "*Here I am* on this dilapidated verandah of a cheap hotel, out of season, in a country caught and destroyed in its flesh and corrupted in its spirit by its gold-hungry Conquistadors that bore the flag of the Inquisition along with the cross of Christ" (*Three by Tennessee* 61). Colanzi identifies this God as nihilistic and, echoing Sartre, sees Shannon as refusing to face his existential anguish, evading the nihilistic

God, refusing to accept nothingness in favor of redeeming a mean-ingless world (456). If we look more closely at the description above, however, God seems not nihilistic but Rousseauean, closer to na-ture, of the body. Kevin Matthews also sees Shannon's God in this way: "Shannon reverts to a primitive, elemental God. . . . He does not choose a God that will somehow minimize the imperfections of the universe, but one that embodies those faults" ("Evolution" 80). Shannon runs not from but to this God, leading his flock "off the grand boulevards" (*Three by Tennessee* 93) to see, feel, and be touched by the underbelly of life, finding God in starving people scavenging a dung heap for bits of food, seeing the profane as holy. That this realization has brought him no peace, only more pain and isolation, that he cannot reconcile the Rousseauean God with the spiritual, is proof of his existential anguish. As Hannah notes, his fleeting se-ductions of young women are proof of "how lonely the intimate connection has been. . . . You have always traveled alone except for your spook" (*Three by Tennessee* 112).

Unlike Brick, who medicates his spook, Shannon is unwilling to escape into Maxine's soothing rum-cocos; nor is he willing to invent illusions, as Blanche does, to buffer the crisis. He knows that his spook is not easily placated and that he is in for a battle, one that could end in what he calls "the swim out to China" (*Three by Ten-nessee* 96). Although Shannon may be a drowning man, he at least grabs for a lifebuoy. Rather than self-destruct as do many of Wil-liams's earlier protagonists, Shannon seeks help, and here he turns to Hannah rather than Maxine, to spirit rather than body.

It's not that Maxine isn't willing. In their first encounter, she lit-erally offers her dead husband's shoes and his old bedroom. Maxine as body doesn't judge Shannon in the way that Stanley judges Blanche. When she discovers his predicament, she knowingly laughs and says, "So you took the young chick and the old hens are squawk-ing about it" (*Three by Tennessee* 15). Body recognizes body's need. Indeed, Maxine has young hired hands who swim and copulate with her nightly. Her only admonishment to Shannon is more of an ad-vertisement; she asks him why he doesn't lay off the young ones and cultivate an interest in grown-up women like herself. Maxine as body is also much more generous than Stanley when threatened. Rather than vanquish the indigent Hannah by throwing her per-ceived rival out in the street, Maxine is honest about her feelings

and straightforward about her needs. She tells Hannah that she's noticed Shannon's interest in her and that if Hannah doesn't respond
to him, she and her grandfather can stay as long as they like. As
body, Maxine is also a more mature Maggie, exhibiting not only
more awareness but also less desperation. She tells Shannon that the
trysts with her hired hands grew out of her late husband's indifference and that she knows the difference between just sleeping with
someone and loving someone: "We've both reached a point where
we've got to settle for something that works for us in our lives—even
if it isn't on the highest kind of level" (*Three by Tennessee* 86). Early
in the play she lays the proposition on the table, pointing out that
he could do worse than to stay with her, but he replies: "If I could
do worse, I'll do worse" (*Three by Tennessee* 32).

Does Shannon initially reject Maxine in favor of Hannah because
he doesn't want to *settle* for someone? Shannon's choice is a result
of his mind-body split, not taste. Shannon, as body, not just spirit,
has been with too many bodies. What Maxine has to offer is more
of the same thing that has brought him to the edge. He finds Maxine
repugnant in the same way that he now finds even the smell of alcohol revolting. Rather than offering relief, they've led him to his
spook. This is why he insults Maxine when she thrusts her hips at
him, and he articulates his sense of emptiness to Charlotte, the
young girl he has seduced, when she wants his love: "I don't have a
dime left in my nervous emotional bank account—I can't write a
check on it, now" (*Three by Tennessee* 53). Shannon is world weary,
in a spiritual crisis that calls for a spiritual healer.

At first glance, Hannah Jelkes seems to resemble Alma. She calls
herself a middle-aged spinster, and she's chaste. But Hannah has not
led an insulated life. As spirit, she's like Shannon in many ways.
She's traveled all over the world, and she, too, has seen life away
from the grand boulevards, watched the old die in the opium dens
of Shanghai, complimented tourists with flattering portraits to pay
the bills, and found herself with her back to the wall, flat broke on
Maxine's verandah with her dying grandfather. Shannon spots his
kindred spirit, affectionately calling her "a hustler, a fantastic cool
hustler" (*Three by Tennessee* 62). But Hannah is not a "user" of people.
And unlike Blanche, she never hustles herself. Hannah has trod
Shannon's perilous path, what Hannah calls "the subterranean travels, the journeys that the spooked and bedeviled people are forced

to take through the unlighted sides of their nature" (*Three by Tennessee* 108). And she, too, has doubted God and almost cracked up. But Hannah has something that Shannon has not yet found, something that Blanche could never find: the will and grace of the survivor. She has outlasted her spook, her "blue devil" (*Three by Tennessee* 107), by paying close attention to the world around her rather than focusing on herself.

Hannah's deep compassion for others makes her Williams's most realized envoy of spirit. Gulshan Rai Kataria, using the gender duality, calls her "a reconciliation of masculine and feminine polarities. . . . Hannah is a complete . . . human being whose love-life manifests itself through helping people" (*Faces of Eve* 126). Her mere appearance soothes Shannon's tension "like that of someone going under hypnosis" (*Three by Tennessee* 33). Hannah's empathy has none of the piety of the devout. She respects Shannon because he has had to "fight and howl for his decency" (*Three by Tennessee* 102) as, no doubt, she has. She'll lie to the teacher Miss Fellowes about Shannon's whereabouts because Hannah knows what it means to be harassed by petty tyrants, those hotel managers and maître d's who now look at her and her grandfather with suspicion. And when others hear the band playing down on the beach, Hannah hears the iguana trapped at the end of its rope, because she's come to the end of hers.

She also leads by example. She shows Shannon the meaning of grace under fire with her resourcefulness in looking after her grandfather, whether that entails slashing the prices on her paintings or pawning a valuable piece of jade. And her dignity is not for sale. Listen to her constancy as she tells Maxine that she's broke: "I'm not proud of it or ashamed of it either. It just happens to be what's happened to us, which has never happened before in all our travels" (*Three by Tennessee* 47). Nor will she be bullied by Maxine, even though she depends on her. She is prepared to brave a storm with Nonno in a wheelchair rather than stay where she is not wanted. In this way, she also proves Maggie wrong; one can be older without money and still have one's pride.

Hannah also helps Shannon by listening to and understanding him, yet hers is no pliable ear to bend or inert shoulder to cry upon. She confronts Shannon with her honesty, as spirit has to body and body has to spirit in many other plays by Williams. In this play,

however, and in Hannah as spirit, we encounter a unique development, the evolution of spirit: tenderness, unfailing tenderness, beneath the honesty. She gets Shannon to see how self-involved he's
been, so much so that he can't tell when others are trying to help
him. And she points out that while she doesn't care for his busload
of schoolteachers any more than he does, they still paid their hard-
earned money to be at "home away from home" (*Three by Tennessee*
100) and were entitled to the tour they wanted, not the one that he
wanted. She also calls his breakdown an "almost voluptuous kind of
crucifixion to suffer for the guilt of the world" (*Three by Tennessee*
99), not questioning the sincerity of his anguish but challenging
him to have some perspective about his pain. All her words to Shannon are served with poppyseed tea and a sympathetic voice.

Finally, Hannah opens up about her life, allowing Shannon to understand himself by recognizing a fellow traveler. Here spirit exposes what might be her Achilles heel to body. But when Shannon
confronts her chastity, there is none of Alma's defensiveness or
Blanche's illusions. Her two sexual experiences are somewhat pathetic. The first is a man pressing his leg against hers as a teenager
in a darkened movie house, and in the second, in a sampan on a
Singapore night, a lingerie salesman asks for an undergarment while
he turns his back and masturbates. Shannon labels the second encounter disgusting. But Hannah matter-of-factly calls it a love experience, and while it may have been profoundly lonely, she says,
"Nothing human disgusts me unless it's unkind, violent" (*Three by
Tennessee* 117). Spirit, in this play, is accepting of body and therefore
accepting of, and at peace with, herself. And this acceptance, the
mingling of the spiritual and the profane as part of life and death,
is certainly echoed at the climax of the play in Nonno's poem just
before he dies.

Still, Shannon winds up staying with Maxine, while Hannah will
move on. Hannah is right, of course, when she concludes that she
and Shannon traveling together would be impractical, the oddest of
all couples, one person preferring celibacy, the other likening it to
lunacy and death. On the other hand, Shannon's moving in with
Maxine has the feel of an arrangement, that he *is* settling, that body
and spirit can never be soulmates. But consider how these characters, like the iguana, are trapped, in their case by their own limitations, and still through the course of the play, they are capable of

facing their lives without lying to themselves. Moreover, they are able to reach out to one another, albeit in painful, difficult ways, and to help one another, however imperfectly, without descending into madness, alcoholism, or cannibalism; and in this way body and mind are able to move past the impasse, to begin again, to get on with the business of living, not destroying.

Even more remarkable is that the business of living is set against a tableau of destruction, the Nazi tourists who parade across Maxine's verandah and who are amused at the other characters' suffering and delight in it. For Williams, the greatest crimes are committed neither by body nor by spirit but by deliberate cruelty, and so these gilded Nazis, "pink and gold like baroque cupids" (*Three by Tennessee* 15), are given only a few lines throughout the whole play. They are made mute by the playwright and yet serve as a constant reminder of a world where there is no attempt at understanding. How remarkable, then, are Hannah's words, a life support system for both mind and body: "I think of a home as being a thing that two people have between them in which each can, well, nest—rest—live in, emotionally speaking. . . . I'm not a bird Mr. Shannon, I'm a human being and when a member of that fantastic species builds a nest in the heart of another, the question of permanence isn't the first or even the last thing that's considered" (*Three by Tennessee* 111).

Hannah's words just might answer those uttered years earlier by Blanche, offering at last a map out of the "dark march toward whatever it is we're approaching" (*Streetcar* 72).

Works Cited

Bentley, Eric. *Bentley on Brecht*. New York: Applause, 1998.

Bruhm, Steven. "Blackmailed by Sex: Tennessee Williams and the Economics of Desire." *Modern Drama* 34 (1991): 532–33.

Cafagna, Dianne. "Blanche DuBois and Maggie the Cat: Illusion and Reality in Tennessee Williams." In *Confronting Tennessee Williams's "A Streetcar Named Desire": Essays in Critical Pluralism*, edited by Philip C. Kolin. Westport, Conn.: Greenwood Press, 1993.

Colanzi, Rita. "Caged Birds: Bad Faith in Tennessee Williams's Drama." *Modern Drama* 35 (1992): 456–57.

Corrigan, Mary Ann. "Realism and Theatricalism in *A Streetcar Named Desire*." *Modern Drama* 19 (1976): 392.

Griffin, Alice. *Understanding Tennessee Williams*. Columbia: University of South Carolina Press, 1995.

Falk, Signi. *Tennessee Williams*. New York: Twayne, 1961.

Kataria, Gulshan Rai. *The Faces of Eve: A Study of Tennessee Williams's Heroines*. New Delhi: Sterling Publishers, 1992.

Kolin, Philip C., ed. *Confronting Tennessee Williams's "A Streetcar Named Desire": Essays in Critical Pluralism*. Westport, Conn.: Greenwood Press, 1993.

Kleb, William. "Marginalia: *Streetcar,* Williams, and Foucault." In *Confronting Tennessee Williams's "A Streetcar Named Desire": Essays in Critical Pluralism,* edited by Philip C. Kolin. Westport, Conn.: Greenwood Press, 1993.

Matthews, Kevin. "The Evolution of *Night of the Iguana:* Three Symbols in the Manuscript Record." *Library Chronicle of the University of Texas* 25.2 (1994): 70–85.

Riddel, Joseph N. "*A Streetcar Named Desire:* Nietzsche Descending." *Modern Drama* 5 (Spring 1963): 426.

Savran, David. *Communists, Cowboys, and Queers: The Politics of Masculinity in the Work of Arthur Miller and Tennessee Williams*. Minneapolis: University of Minnesota Press, 1992.

Sofer, Andrew. "Self Consuming Artifacts: Power, Performance, and the Body in Tennessee Williams's *Suddenly Last Summer*." *Modern Drama* 38 (1995): 342–45.

Williams, Tennessee. *Cat on a Hot Tin Roof*. New York: New American Library, 1955.

———. *Five Plays by Tennessee Williams*. London: Secker and Warburg, 1962.

———. *Four Plays by Tennessee Williams*. London: Secker and Warburg, 1957.

———. *The Glass Menagerie*. New York: Dramatists Play Service, 1975.

———. *A Streetcar Named Desire*. New York: New American Library, 1947.

———. *Three by Tennessee*. New York: Signet, 1979.

Winchell, Mark Royden. "Come Back to the Locker Room Ag'n, Brick Honey!" *Mississippi Quarterly* 48.4 (1995): 702–12.

Zeineddine, Nada. *Because It Is My Name*. Great Britain: Merlin, 1991.

7

The Family of Mitch

(Un)suitable Suitors in Tennessee Williams

Philip C. Kolin

Perhaps more frequently than any other American playwright, Tennessee Williams knew the promise and the pain of (un)suitable suitors. His *Memoirs,* letters, essays, and even paintings record his mismatched liaisons; the roll call of suitors rejected by Williams or rejecting him is long and includes Pablo Rodriguez-Gonzales, Kip Kiernan, and all the boys of desire whose anatomies he temporarily cruised to dispel loneliness. Frank Merlo stands out as the bright exception. Turning his courting performances into text, Williams energized many of his dramatic works—and his fiction, too—around the quest for suitors and the disappointment their discovery effected.

Unsuitable suitors—failed gentleman callers, if you will—are obsessively persistent in Williams's imagination. Some of these suitors are spectral—Miss Lucretia Collins's lover in *Portrait of a Madonna;* Shep Huntleigh in *A Streetcar Named Desire;* and Merriwether in Williams's one-act play, *Will Mr. Merriwether Return from Memphis?* Their invisibility is a sign of phantom, unattainable desire. Sailors, the quintessentially unanchored lovers, also appear often as ill-fated suitors—Blanche's analogue from whom she asks directions in the acting script of *Streetcar;* the drunken paramours whom Violet entertains in *Small Craft Warnings;* and the predatory sailor of vicious and vulgar carriage in *Something Cloudy, Something Clear.* Serafina in the *Rose Tattoo* knows the type all too well when she asks her daughter's boyfriend, the sailor Jack Hunter: "What are you hunting, Jack?" Ironically, Sailor Jack in *Not About Nightingales* is the first casualty of cruel Warden Whalen's attack on desire in Williams's early play

(1938). Few suitors, if any, in Williams offer honest love, commitment. Jake Torrence is the most mean-spirited suitor Lady ever had. Bill is rapacious and cruel in *The Long Good-bye,* trying to get sex from Joe's sister and denouncing her when she refuses. Another Bill, the aging stud in *Small Craft Warnings,* delivers a selfish paean to "Junior" (his penis), which seems more wish fulfillment than accomplishment.

The most famous group of unsuitable suitors belongs to what might be termed the "Family of Mitch," after Harold Mitchell in *Streetcar.* They share a repertoire of similarities, chief among which is that their narratives of self compete with and become emasculated in the plays in which they appear. These unsuitable suitors suffer from interrupted/incomplete sexuality, branding them as representatives of a desire that is fathomable, disappointing. Characteristically, Williams portrays their attempts within sacramental symbolism. Unsuitable suitors are caught in anticipated but ultimately annihilated epiphanies, made emblematic through Williams's numerous connections between the sacred and the profane. I would like to explore in some detail here the ways in which Williams develops and then radicalizes unsuitable suitors by focusing on Jim O'Connor in *Glass Menagerie,* Mitch, Alvaro Mangiacavallo in *The Rose Tattoo,* and Chicken Ravenstock in *Kingdom of Earth.*

I

Incomplete/interrupted sexuality is at the very center of Williams's most famous gentleman caller, Jim O'Connor in *The Glass Menagerie,* Williams's memory play. But *Menagerie* is Jim's memory play, too, for he tries to recall and to recuperate his image as a lover/powerfully sexual man that the script undermines. Jim's performances of hyperbolic virility are driven by his narratives of boundless masculinity. He brags to Laura that, when he was in school, "I was beleaguered by females in those days" (218) and reminisces that with his manly voice he "sang the lead baritone in that operetta" *The Pirates of Penzance,* not sensing the incongruity between the diminutive ("operetta") and his sexual self-importance. Believing that his manly ambition was effectively realized through public speaking, Jim thought he would go to the White House, the male seat of power, but he ended up at the shoe factory. His masculine hubris

governs his ersatz courtship of Laura. Jim injects several illocution-
ary anatomical references to his manly physique. Although the remark is made in a "gently humorous" way, when he tries to get
Laura to drink some wine—a frequently used male ploy to seduce a
woman—Jim brags, "Sure I am superman" (210). Earlier, narrator
Tom mocks Jim's superhuman ego: "He always seemed at the point
of defeating the law of gravity" (190). Performing his manhood before Laura in the candle-lit room, Jim boasts: "Look how big my
shadow is when I stretch" (225). His fatuous shadowed self conflicts
with the reality of pettiness in which he is enclosed. Even Jim's ex-
pletives attempt to reinforce his masculinity—"Why man alive"
(221). "My interest happens to lie in electro-dynamics," he informs
the gullibly adoring Laura as if to substantiate in language a sexual
dynamism he can only fabricate.

Yet *Menagerie* includes another version of Jim's reality, not the
shadow script he offers to Laura, but one that interrogates his sexual
inadequacies, revealing him as a fabulist of desire. Williams deflates
Jim's own representations of manhood, unpacking into the script
of *The Glass Menagerie* the problematics of the gentleman caller's
virility. No icon of male sexual beauty, Jim is "medium homely." His
masculinity is underwritten by bovine femininity when he claims
that he is as "comfortable as a cow!" (212). In that he is an advocate
of chewing gum, Jim's mastication, not Tom's, further confirms the
bovine in his repertoire. Appropriately, Jim is a shipping clerk, not
one of the workers who make or manufacture, twice removing him
from manly labor. Deflecting Jim's tauted masculinity again, Williams often situates Jim within a context of failed light and power.
His self-announced manly expertise in "electro-dynamics" is futile
when it comes to restoring the lights in the Wingfield apartment—
"All the fuses look o.k. to me." Although he may have been cast as
a hero in *The Torch*, Jim never lived up to the manly dreams of lead-
ership that this publication augured. In signing Laura's copy of this
contract of undelivered promises, Jim shows how ineffectual his
manhood is. *The Torch* and the pen he uses to sign it—faint phallic
tropes—mock his failed accomplishments. Like the old *Torch*, Jim is
burned out, only pretending a passionate future. A perfect fetish of
his inadequate manhood is the candelabra that he carries into the
living room; as Amanda recalls, it "was melted a little out of shape,"
just like Jim, whose manly bravado dissolves into comic reality. Car-

rying such a melted symbol of light and fire, Jim, as Roger Boxill points out, "does not fulfill the role of redeemer" (75), still another indictment of his manliness.

Jim's self-proclaimed sexuality is further devalued in his (un)intentionally parodying courting rituals, all of which point to a disabling interruption of love. He is out of place in a romantic setting of shadows, candlelight, music, and dancing—tropes indicting his, and not just Laura's, diminished performance. Though claiming expertise about the technical world, Jim knows little about wooing. As a courtier, he is clumsy, awkward, gauche; he is a poseur in love. The gestures of his faux courtship are interruptive. No elegant, smooth dancer, "he moves about the room in a clumsy waltz." As he dances with Laura, "they suddenly bang into the table, and the glass piece on it falls to the floor. Jim stops the dance." One of the most blatant attacks on Jim's virility comes from his own lips; he twice refers to himself as a "stumblejohn" after inappropriately kissing Laura. Jim is indeed the inept, stumbling john, or man in search of sex. After kissing her, "he coughs decorously and moves a little farther aside" —again interrupting the space and spirit of romance. Further breaking any love spell, he "fishes in his pocket for a cigarette" and then for a piece of gum, for, as he says, "my pocket's a regular drugstore" (229). Props of amorous engagement, gum (freshened desire) and the cigarette (seduction) become signs of evasion, disruption. Jim's fatuous discourse on these objects in his pockets interrupts the performative amorous script that he initiates and the desire-starved Amanda directs. As he fumbles in his pockets, Jim physicalizes both the banality and the concealment of his romantic overtures.

Structurally, the entire episode with Laura is an interruption in Jim's involvement with Betty, to whom he is engaged; he leaves Betty out of the picture and meets Laura and then returns to her after he breaks Laura's heart—"I hope it don't seem like I'm rushing off. But I promised Betty that I'd pick her up at the Wabash depot. . . . Some women are pretty upset if you keep 'em waiting" (234). The script hints that Jim's future relationship with the impatient Betty will be uxorious—"I've got strings on me" (229). He will learn much more about what Amanda labels "the tyranny of women" (234). Jim's temporary tryst with Laura, then, says as much about his future love relationship as hers; both face alienation.

Williams invests the script heavily in religious symbolism to deflate Jim's sexual heroics, to underscore a failed epiphany for him as well as for Amanda and Laura. In setting and trope, Williams relates sacred to secular. The lighting is both romantic and sacramental, the one fusing with the other. The melted candelabra comes ironically from the "Church of Heaven's Rest" (210). The "Blue Roses" and "a floor lamp of rose colored silk" contribute to the aura of sacramentality Williams creates around Jim's courtship of Laura. Music drifts in from the Paradise Dance Hall across the street. Amanda, too, contributes to the sacramentality of the moment in action and allusion. Hiding behind the kitchenette curtains, she behaves like a giddy angel at the Annunciation or, even more ironic, one of the foolish virgins (she is presented as "Amanda as a girl" on one screen) waiting for the bridegroom of the biblical parable. But Jim does not cooperate with the biblical subject, despite her bringing in macaroons and fruit punch (secular, romantic communion) after his unholy kiss. Drinking the punch, Amanda exclaims: "Oooo! I'm baptizing myself!" (232). In fact, Jim undercuts any expected sacramental revelation or epiphany. "The holy candles on the altar of Laura's face have been snuffed out" (230) by his antiepiphanic revelation of his approaching marriage to Betty. The long-waited redeemer leaves for uxoriousness, and in his wake, two foolish virgins—Laura and Amanda—inherit a bleak, loveless future, a triangulation of the lost.

II

In *Streetcar,* Mitch also repeatedly projects an incomplete/interrupted sexuality in word and act, the hallmarks of the unsuitable suitor. Significantly, when he asks Blanche whether he may have a kiss, she responds: "Why should you be so doubtful?" Mitch's doubt, though, is a consequence of his insufficient sexuality. As Elia Kazan rightly pegged him in his *Streetcar* "Notebook," Mitch's "spine" is that of a "mama's boy," neither man nor boy, caught somewhere in between, incomplete. William Kleb wisely refers to Mitch's "arrested adolescence, even sexual confusion." Like a child, Mitch even looks sensitive, unmanly. No wonder Blanche calls him "angel puss," her most salacious epithet. Among his male friends, Mitch—the boy/man —is comically harangued for his unmanly ways; he needs a "sugar tit." He is accused of saving his poker winnings in a piggy bank for his mother. Occupationally, his sexual incompleteness is suggested by his work in the "spare parts department" at Stanley's plant. During the poker game, Mitch twice says, "Deal me out" (51,52), separating himself from male sport. Domestically he is still caught in his mother's apron strings, metonymically represented in the Kazan film of 1951 by his leaving the washroom (Blanche's domain) still holding a towel, something literally left out that should have been left in. The incompetent wooer, Mitch is suspended between the worlds of desire and dependence, trapped in diminishment.

Mitch's language also demonstrates his sexual incompleteness—his lack of originality, psychic wholeness, integrity. He often leaves his sentences unfinished and even speaks without the benefit of connective syntax—"You . . . you . . . you . . . brag . . . brag . . . bull . . . bull" (131). Another indication of Mitch's insecurity and lack of confidence is his awkward reliance on the language of trite, conventional romance in wooing Blanche. He is so invested in the antiquated symbology of romance that it is easy for Blanche to trap, and then undercut, him. Among three of Mitch's many examples of stilted romancespeak are (1) "in all my experience I have never known any one like you" (87), a pickup line that serves as wonderful bait for Blanche's hook; (2) "you may teach school but you certainly are not an old maid" (56); and (3) perhaps his most disjunctively melodramatic line—"You need somebody. And I need somebody, too. Could it be—you and me, Blanche?" (96), cycling Mitch's banal sensitivity through the doubtful interrogative, the tentative.

Mitch's passing status in Blanche's life as well as his liabilities as a suitor are epitomized at the end of scene 5—Blanche "blows a kiss at [the newspaper boy] as he goes down the steps with a dazed look. She stands there dreamily after he has disappeared. Then Mitch appears around the corner with a bunch of roses" (84). A young, dashing rosenkavalier leaves Blanche's life as Mitch, the retreaded rosenkavalier, enters late, almost as an ominous second thought. Quite literally, Mitch is a runner-up who will run out of time in Blanche's world. His roses will be replaced by the Mexican woman's *flores*, the florilegia of grief.

Mitch's props of love are equally incomplete, cues to his amorous incompetence and failure. Blanche too easily snares him by asking for a cigarette (Murphy), thus giving Mitch an opportunity to recount his narrative about the deceased girl who loved him and then to produce the silver cigarette case with the poetic inscription "I shall love thee better after death." Mitch's past love affairs, like this one with Blanche, ended in defeat. He will never know recrudescence. He smokes Luckies, a choice that ironically and bluntly indicts him as "never getting lucky in love" and suggests that all sorts of sexual rituals/overtones go unfulfilled. The cigarette case he carries is equivalent to Blanche's trunk, the remnants of his former life—dead, unresurrectable. Mitch's narrative of self contains too many ghostly lacunae.

Scene 6, which might be entitled "The Date's Over," contains two pejorative symbols of Mitch's sexual folly, his inability to be a whole man. Coming home from his date with Blanche on Lake Pontchartrain, Mitch "is bearing, upside down, a plaster statue of Mae West, the sort of prize won at shooting galleries and carnival games of chance" (85). Williams could not have found a more salient reminder of Mitch's sexual ineptitude than the shabby relic of the queen of burlesque, the boastful, domineering woman of hyperbolic assignations fueling male fantasies in the 1930s and 1940s. Like the statue, all of Mitch's sexual ardor and sexual plans are upside down, an icon of his failures. He has not won a prize of merit at the shooting gallery (phallic implications noted). Instead, his upside-down Mae West suggests that Mitch does not know how to shoot or that his shot is limp, sexually. For his foolish efforts he has won the most appropriate prize symbolizing the Blanche he courts—a woman who pretends to eschew Mae West's vulgarity but who has engaged in the type of sexual escapades for which the burlesque diva was infamous. Romantic possibility and the fulfillment of desire are upside down, topsy-turvy in Mitch's world. In the acting version of *Streetcar,* Kazan substituted a Raggedy Ann doll for the Mae West statue, a change that also marginalized Mitch as a complete adult man. The message: men don't carry dolls.

In the second set of symbols in scene 6, Blanche's purse and keys are involved. "See if you can locate my door-key in this purse," instructs Blanche, using sexual shorthand as old as Chaucer—keys = phallic; purse = vagina. "Rooting in her purse," Mitch comes up with the wrong key ("No, honey, that's the key to my trunk which I must soon be packing"). Searching some more, he utters another line of characteristic interrogative tentativeness, "This it?" As if she were reaching a sexual climax, Blanche shouts, "Eureka. Honey you open the door" (86). Through this calculatingly realistic stage business, Williams broadcasts to an attentive audience that Blanche is out with a man who cannot find a key and cannot carry a woman (Mae West) the right way because he is forever trapped by/in spare parts, held captive to a castrating matriarchy.

When Mitch does attempt physical intimacy, he is a fumbling clown whose actions are repeatedly interrupted, at first comically but then tragically for him and for Blanche. Mitch's desire is severed from sexual competence. When he is parked at the lake with Blanche, she allows him to kiss her but to go no farther—"It was the other little-familiarity—that I—felt obliged to—discourage" (87). Mitch's sexual advances are not only discouraged but disrupted. When he lifts her up a few minutes later, still with his "hands on her waist" (90), Blanche again, though politely, says first "release me" and then "I said unhand me, sir." "He fumblingly embraces her. Her voice sounds gently reproving" (91), halting Mitch's awkward journey toward intimacy. In between these two failed attempts to become sexual with Blanche, Mitch is thwarted, mocked in his overtures. Blanche coquettishly says in French, "Voulez-vous coucher avec moi ce soir?"—a line omitted from the Kazan film by the censors—knowing that he does not understand French. (Ironically, the audience may know that he could not do what she asks even if he did understand.) Mitch is no student of the language of love. When he begs to lift her, she taunts him using an allusion to one of the greatest victims of foolhardy love. "Samson. Go on and lift me!" Like his biblical antecedent, Mitch is shorn of strength, satiety; he will lose whatever sexual promise of success he anticipates, thanks to Blanche and his own blindness. Claiming adherence to "old-fashioned ideals," Blanche "rolls her eyes, knowing he cannot see her face." At the end of this playlet in the middle of scene 6, Blanche histrionically sighs like a lovelorn maiden, while the disconnected Mitch can only "cough," two gendered gestures of amorous interruption. Mitch's cough represents male capitulation and isolation after a failed attempt; Blanche's sigh is an expression of feigned female longing, forced desire. Like Jim in *Glass Menagerie,* Mitch's cough marginalizes/derhapsodizes his wooing.

In scene 9, Mitch's interrupted sexuality turns tragic, violent. Revisiting his date after the date—he is always a victim of poor self-timing—Mitch replays tragically the comic interlude of scene 6.

Once more he "places his hands on her waist and tries to turn her about" (120). In this repetitive behavior Mitch again misses closure; he is caught in disruption, denounced desire. When Blanche asks him, "What do you want?" and he replies, "What I been missing all summer," Mitch admits his lack of connection, his miserable luck in love, the numerous times he started but failed—"Fumbling to embrace her" (120). Mitch's gestures are the signatory of interruption; a fumble is a failed attempt. When Blanche offers him the only way he can complete his amorous quest—"Then marry me, Mitch!"—he refuses not with an explanation based on his feeling, a sign of wholeness, but with an appeal to maternal jurisprudence—"You're not clean enough to bring in the house with my mother." Blanche screams, stopping Mitch in his tracks and conclusively interrupting his final attempt to get lucky. "With a startled gasp, Mitch runs and goes out the door, clatters awkwardly down the steps and around the corner of the building" (121). This event is scripted in interrupted motion—*gasping, clattering, hiding around a corner*—graphically reducing Mitch from a beau to a petty thief or arsonist, foiled in his botched quest for manhood and easily frightened out of purpose by Blanche's three monosyllables—"Fire! Fire! Fire!"

Time and sex are destructively intertwined for an unsuitable suitor like Mitch. His sexual clock is not in keeping with Blanche's, nor is hers with his. Blanche's love clock is kept by the Pleiades, undulating according to celestial harmony. The ill-suited suitor Mitch, however, takes the "owl car" home (85). He is not on the same track as Blanche; neither of them connects. She won't go out with him on Sunday afternoons, and his mother is alarmed about Blanche's biological clock. Mitch tells Blanche that "my mother worries because I am not settled" (94), yet paradoxically, when he is ready to settle down, Blanche is not, and vice versa. His first words in scene 6—"I guess it must be pretty late—and you're tired"—are the most (unconsciously) prophetic pronouncements that Mitch makes about Blanche. When he bursts into Stanley's apartment in scene 9, Mitch, drunk and disheveled, is greeted by Blanche's temporal unreadiness —"Just a minute." A few lines later Blanche tries to redeem time and love again: "She offers him her lips. He ignores it and pushes past her into the flat" (113). Pushing past her, Mitch will not wait for a kiss. Their schedules, like their lips, are not synchronous. When she was playing hard to get, she reproved Mitch for too much intimacy in scene 6. What Mitch wanted then, Blanche, desperate, offers in scene 9, but at this point the stakes for Mitch have both gone high and disappeared.

Throughout his encounters with Blanche, Mitch is plagued by expected but failed epiphanies. Like Jim O'Connor, he experiences an annihilated epiphany, sensing the arousal of passion but not experiencing its consummation. As in *The Glass Menagerie,* the unsuitable suitor's lack of sexual connectedness is tied to imagery both secular and sacred in *Streetcar,* diffusing body and soul. Nowhere is this link clearer for Mitch than at the end of scene 6 when, suggesting the inevitability of commitment, Blanche utters one of the most famous lines in the play—"Sometimes—there's God—so quickly" (96). The eternal (God) for Mitch is short-circuited by the ephemeral (quickly) as he moves away from Blanche, signaled beautifully by Williams's use of dashes. The ultimate failed epiphany is recorded in Blanche's reference to the cathedral bells, "the only clean thing in the Quarter." As she leaves with her new beau/gentleman caller—the courtly doctor dressed in black—Blanche proceeds off the stage as if she were a triumphant bride going on her honeymoon, leaving the inconsolable Mitch, the failed suitor, to contemplate his loss, spiritually and physically, with his head down on the bastion of male gamesmanship, the poker table. Interestingly, Jessica Tandy's Blanche in 1947 suggested a bride—she wore a white veil and a white dress as she exited with the doctor—while in the John Erman *Streetcar* of 1984, Ann-Margret's Blanche was driven away with her new gentleman caller in a stately black car headed right for the St. Louis Cathedral in the distance, its spire welcoming her as it might some heavenly bride preparing for a heavenly climax.

III

Alvaro Mangiacavallo in the *Rose Tattoo* is the quintessential comic unsuitable suitor, the generic embodiment of the type. Serafina sees him as a ridiculous version of her handsome and romantic husband Rosario—"My husband's body with the face of a clown." A creature of mental and physical deformities for Serafina, Alvaro is the grandson of the village idiot, a "buffone," "cretino" (394), a "paintetela." His ears stick out, he is short, he hitches his shoulders in nervous agitation, traits that call attention to his status as the buffoon.

When Serafina first sees Alvaro, he is "sweating and stammering," and he later makes ridiculous sounds like a bird. He physicalizes awkwardness, a fumbling sexuality.

Alvaro's sexual potency is weakened, interrupted, as was Jim's and Mitch's. If Rosario was the priapic benefactor of fruitfulness, Alvaro is frequently portrayed as unregenerative. Though at one point Alvaro is called "one of the glossy bulls," and he vows to give Serafina endless nights of pleasure, his behavior suggests otherwise. When he first appears onstage, Alvaro receives a comically painful priapic injury. The salesman who runs Alvaro off the road, and whom this "Macaroni" dares to challenge, "brings his knee up violently into Alvaro's groin. Bending double and retching with pain, Alvaro staggers over" to Serafina's porch. After this altercation, Alvaro weeps profusely, admitting that "crying is not like a man" (355). Later, attempting to persuade Serafina to make love, Alvaro professes that his fingers are so cold from a lack of love that "I live with my hands in my pocket," a masturbatory allusion and gesture. But then he "stuffs his hands violently into his pants' pockets, then jerks them out again. A small cellophane wrapped disk falls on the floor, escaping his notice, but not Serafina's." She indignantly asks whether that was "the piece of poetry" Alvaro claimed to offer her. For Serafina, Mangiacavallo's rubber symbolizes interrupted love, sex without passion's juices, an insult to both her lustiness (she does "glance below the man's belt freely" [Robinson 31]) and her protective prudery. The condom is also a sign of Alvaro's less than manly amor, which puts him in stark contrast to the diurnally fruitful and sanctified Rosario.

The most salient instance of interrupted love occurs in the last scene of *Rose Tattoo,* where Alvaro, drunk and disoriented, is accused of trying to rape Rosa, a hilarious analogue to the tragic encounter that Mitch had with Blanche in scene 9 of *Streetcar.* The parallels are many and once again marginalize Alvaro's lovemaking. Like Mitch, Alvaro is chased for his life by Serafina, who screams "Fire"—as Blanche did—and who beats him. The scene is both grotesque and comic, all at Alvaro's expense. It should be "played with the pantomimic lightness . . . of an early Chaplin comedy," according to Williams's stage direction (405). Being denied Mitch's flurry of forcefulness, Alvaro is even further deromanticized. He is a comically weakened Mitch.

Alvaro's position as the ungentlemanly caller is part of the larger psychic narrative of replication in the *Rose Tattoo* that contributes to the cycle of interrupted/incomplete sexuality. Imitation, copying, is the dynamic of this Williams play. Estelle gets a rose tattoo copied on her chest to brand herself as Rosario's inamorata; Serafina copies dress patterns and also reifies, imaginatively, her husband's rose on her chest; Alvaro, too, apes Rosario by having the patronymic emblem of Serafina's first husband emblazoned on his chest and, further, by wearing Rosario's shirt, given to him by Serafina. In the process, Alvaro invests in a feminine version of a man. He becomes a copy of a copy by imitating the women who are imitating Rosario, an act that amounts to a feminization of Alvaro's masculine agency, the deromanticizing of the Don Juan (masculine) amor he proffers to Serafina. Like Jim and Mitch, too, Alvaro arrives with prior experience in love, further casting him as a casualty in imitation. He gave his previous girlfriend "a zircon instead of a diamond. She had it examined. The door slammed in my face" (377). Alvaro is presented as the zircon lover, cheap, laughable, gender voluble. Not surprisingly, the emblematic bird of the play is the polly, the parrot, the totem of squawking mimesis.

My reading of Alvaro is squarely in keeping with the standard received opinion of the gentleman caller in *The Rose Tattoo*. Yet this Williams comedy is more subversive than festive. He alters and radicalizes this character type, establishing Alvaro as among the first strain of the valorized ungentlemanly callers. Forever the champion of the underdog, Williams is the apostle of transformation. Alvaro is the loser who becomes a winner, a character in Williams's performative rhetoric of investing the other with power, just as he does Chicken Ravenstock as suitor in *Kingdom of Earth,* as we shall see. Through Alvaro, Williams both fictionalizes and celebrates the instability of Otherness, the character who does most textual violence to the conventional image of male sexual prowess. In *Rose Tattoo,* Williams marshals his resistance to conventional romantic nostalgia by disrupting the romantic hegemonies that Rosario represents and, even in death, insists upon. Through Alvaro, Williams attacks a complacent audience's romantic assumptionality and consumption.

By disrupting and resisting the vestigia of romanticism in the Rosario script, Alvaro is significantly redeemed through an act of unremembering, ejecting the expectations the script encourages Serafina to harbor. As Rosa implores her gentleman caller, Jack Hunter: "I want you not to remember" (399), that is, to disregard Serafina's command to abstain from sex. Unremembering is precisely what Serafina (and we as audience) must do with Alvaro's literary/theatrical heritage as the unsuitable suitor. We must erase the clown image as we simultaneously reject the dashing allure of a romantic Rosario implanting roses—fictional or tattooed—in his lovemaking. As he does politically in *Camino Real,* Williams dislodges nostalgia from representation. Thwarting any audience's proclivity to valorize Rosario and depreciate Alvaro, Williams reconfigures our notion of the romantic. Love for Serafina, like love for Williams, comes from unexpected quarters. E. E. Cummings's poem "The Balloon Man"— rather than "Cara Mia"—could serve as Alvaro and Serafina's love song. As in the other unsuitable suitor plays, Williams invokes the religious in *Tattoo* perhaps most overtly. Serafina's prayers to the Virgin are efficacious. Through the power of Her son, Mary brings Serafina's heart back to life again. Once Serafina exorcizes the Rosario lie/nostalgia from her memory and comes back into real time by accepting Alvaro, she can escape the past and recoup love, an act of unremembering analogous to our unremembering that her new honeymoon lover was the grandson of the village idiot. Serafina's Alvaro is Tennessee Williams's Frank Merlo.

IV

Even more than Alvaro, Chicken Ravenstock in *Kingdom of Earth* may be the most ungentlemanly suitor in the canon. A mixed breed, or "wood's colt," Chicken is "someone with colored blood." He and his half brother, the landowning pale white Lot, had the same white father, but Chicken's mother was "very different," marginalized racially. The quintessential black man, Chicken cannot buy liquor, is forbidden to have relations with white women, and is dismissed as "untutored"—hardly romantic assets in Williams's bigoted Two River County. Branded a "misfit," an "outsider," a sexual deviate, Chicken has one of the strongest libidos in the canon. Don Rubincam observed that Chicken "had the sexual appetite of a satyr." He is unashamedly priapic with his hip-hugging boots and overt sexual gestures. At one point, Chicken "consciously or not drops one of his large, dusky hands over his crotch, which is emphasized, pushed out by his hip boots" (144). He carves lewd words into the kitchen table and bluntly probes his and others' sexual backgrounds. But what most infuriates critics is that Chicken receives fellatio from a white woman between acts 2 and 3.

Chicken's role as unholy suitor plays out within one of Williams's perpetual triangles—in this instance two men (Lot and Chicken) and one woman (Myrtle, the white "bride" whom Lot brings home). Triangulation in Williams always leads to disruption of the conventional. Myrtle is the female linchpin around whom the brothers' rivalry oscillates. Lot lures Chicken back to the family estate with the promise that if he comes back to work, Lot will include him in the inheritance, and Lot gives him a paper to that effect. But Lot changes his mind, arguing that he would turn over the family estate to a white woman he has known barely a few days—and whom he denigrates as a "whore"—rather than see his "colored" half brother get the land. To defraud Chicken, Lot instructs Myrtle: "Get Chicken drunk but get drunk yourself, and when he passes out, get this legal paper out of his wallet, tear it to bits and pieces, and burn 'em up." If Myrtle does this, "Then as my wife, when I die, the place will be yours, go to you" (168). She is to do this in Chicken's domain, the black servant's kitchen, a place that links him with cooking, subservience, and shadows.

Like Alvaro, Chicken's liminal status sets him apart as a special Williams suitor who succeeds, the critics' disgust notwithstanding. In Williams's theater of unsuitable suitors, Chicken powerfully thwarts, even threatens, an audience's expectations about courtship, marriage, union. Yet Williams boldly shows Lot's inferiority as a suitor by contrasting him with Chicken's actions. Lot, the spoiled aristocrat, diseased, is a tubercular transvestite whose own sexuality (and hence suitability as a lover) is intentionally linked to the satanic: "Lot remains in the wicker chair, still smoking with his mother's ivory holder and wearing now her white silk wrapper. His 'Mona Lisa' smile is more sardonic and the violent shadows about his eyes are deeper" (177). Secluded in his whites-only parlor, Lot can offer Myrtle only "the sexless passion of the transvestite" (212), the perverse pleasure of a lifeless Narcissus.

As he did to discredit Jim and Mitch but to valorize Alvaro, Williams contextualizes Chicken's actions within the sacramental promise of a fulfilled, not annihilated, epiphany. Unlike Jim or Mitch,

Chicken's raw sexuality and blunt courtship are, in Williams's radicalization of the (un)suitable suitor, imprinted with a procreative and proleptic biblical seal. In fact, Williams invokes several biblical narratives—epiphanic validations—to valorize Chicken. One of these clearly relates to Noah and the Flood, in which Chicken is cast as the survivor/savior. At play's end, when Lot is dead, Chicken saves Myrtle from the flood and participates Noah-like in the rechristening of the farm, affirming, "Floods make the land richer" (183). Closely associated with the flood, of course, is the fall of Sodom and Gomorrah—Lot's empire. But unlike Lot's wife, Myrtle does not look back and is redeemed/recuperated through her new husband Chicken. The second biblical narrative on which Williams draws to situate Chicken in an epiphanic light is that of Adam and Eve. Chicken is the new man, the rechristened Adam. And paradoxically, the "whore" for Chicken will become the new Eve, the mother of succeeding generations of Ravenstocks who will own the kingdom of earth as men and women of color. "Always wanted a child from an all-white woman," announces Chicken.

In this religious context, sex becomes a means of salvation for Chicken and Myrtle. The so-called perverse act between Myrtle and Chicken takes on almost a religious quality rather than something unnatural, revolting, or suspicious. Sex is not interruption, as for Jim or Mitch, but continuation. Their lovemaking is the summum bonum for a postlapsarian world. As Chicken says, "There's nothing in the world, in the whole kingdom of earth, that can compare with one thing, and that one thing is what's able to happen between a man and a woman, just that thing, nothing more, is perfect. The rest is . . . almost nothing" (211). The way Myrtle's response is described in one stage direction speaks volumes about a comedic conclusion: "Myrtle is still on a chair so close to the table that she's between his boots, and she looks as if she had undergone an experience of exceptional nature and manipulation" (203). Thanks to Chicken, she has had an epiphany of her own. Foster Hirsch eloquently comments on the secularization of Williams's sacramental vision: "The approach of the orgasmic flood coincides with Chicken's inheritance of the land. The flood symbolized the full release of the 'lust' body" (10).

As Williams's plays progressed, he took the unsuitable suitor farther and farther away from the conventional—Jim or Mitch—and into new, bold, revolutionary directions, Alvaro and Chicken being the two leading examples. In the course of this evolution, though, Williams retained or radicalized the symbolism of disrupted sex and annihilated epiphanies that helped him to create the characters who sought but rarely captured love.

Works Cited

Boxill, Roger. *Tennessee Williams.* New York: St. Martin's Press, 1987.

Hirsch, Foster. "Sexual Imagery in Tennessee Williams's *Kingdom of Earth.*" *Notes on Contemporary Literature* 1.2 (1971): 10–13.

Kazan, Elia. "Notebook for *A Streetcar Named Desire.*" In *Directors on Directing: A Source Book of the Modern Theatre,* edited by Toby Cole and Helen Krich Chinoy. 2d (rev.) ed. Indianapolis: Bobbs-Merrill, 1976.

Murphy, Brenda. *Tennessee Williams and Elia Kazan: A Collaboration in the Theatre.* Cambridge: Cambridge University Press, 1994.

Robinson, Marc. *The Other American Drama.* New York: Cambridge University Press, 1994.

Williams, Tennessee. *Glass Menagerie.* In *The Theatre of Tennessee Williams.* Vol. 1. New York: New Directions, 1971.

———. *Kingdom of Earth.* In *The Theatre of Tennessee Williams.* Vol. 5. New York: New Directions, 1971.

———. *Rose Tattoo.* In *The Theatre of Tennessee Williams.* Vol. 2. New York: New Directions, 1971.

———. *Streetcar Named Desire.* In *The Theatre of Tennessee Williams.* Vol. 1. New York: New Directions, 1971.

8

In the Bar of a Tokyo Hotel

Breaking the Code

Allean Hale

Even before *The Night of the Iguana*, in 1961 Tennessee Williams had said: "Nobody writes my kind of play any more." He was then America's most celebrated playwright, having won two Pulitzer Prizes and four awards from the New York Critics' Circle; he had had seventeen New York openings in sixteen years and had written blockbuster plays that changed the American theater. Now at age fifty he was casting around for a new medium. He recognized that serious theater had changed drastically with the rise of the European dramatists. He had helped to introduce Beckett to the United States by putting money into the first performance of *Waiting for Godot*. He was overcome by Pinter's *The Caretaker*, in particular by the way in which Pinter used silence to create tension. His own writing was tied to a profusion of words. He admired the sheer theatricality of Jarry, Ionesco, and Genet, whose surreal and ritualistic drama attempted to restore theater to its magical origins. This had been his own credo as a novice playwright, first expressed in his foreword to *The Glass Menagerie* when he called for a "plastic theatre": antirepresentational, using music, dance, and lighting to express the characters' inner motivations. At the end of the 1950s, he saw that the experimental and daring drama that was his natural milieu was to be found in small theaters Off Broadway, while he was expected to stay in his "slot." As the richest and most produced playwright in America, he had been trapped by success. The pressure was always to deliver another *Streetcar*. Success also made him a target for a younger and irreverent generation of American playwrights who both imitated him and parodied him. In the same season that *Iguana* appeared, so did Arthur Kopit's *Oh Dad, Poor Dad, Mamma's Hung You in the Closet and I'm Feelin' So Sad*—a direct spoof of Tennessee Williams. The next season, Edward Albee had a brilliant success with *Who's Afraid of Virginia Woolf?*, which parodied a scene from *A Streetcar Named Desire.*

The Night of the Iguana was later recognized as Williams's last "big" play. While it won the New York Drama Critics' award, these same critics found in it a puzzling new strain that was metaphysical, even religious. Williams was enshrined on the March 9, 1962, cover of *Time* magazine and was proclaimed, "barring the aged Sean O'Casey, the greatest living playwright." This triumph ironically marked the beginning of what he later called "his stoned age," almost a decade of deep clinical depression brought on by the death of his longtime partner, Frank Merlo. In his desperation, he fell under the influence of Dr. Max Jacobson, a sort of alchemist to the rich and famous, whose revitalizing miracle treatments of "vitamin" mixtures and medication turned out to be mostly amphetamines and addictive drugs. (Jacobson eventually lost his medical license.) During this decade of the 1960s Williams became, as he said, "the ghost of a writer," seldom heard from or seen. What was not realized is that he kept on writing but in a very different vein.

These new plays were so uncharacteristic in style that critics dismissed them as examples of the playwright's "decline and fall." They tended to be dark in mood, antirealistic, even fantastic. Now, after some thirty years, these late plays are being reassessed and are being found of unique interest. But one, *In the Bar of a Tokyo Hotel*, written in 1969, remains almost unexamined, still condemned as Williams's greatest failure. It is a challenge as perhaps his most difficult and devious play. On the surface it appears to be one of his simplest. One of his shorter works, in only two parts, *Tokyo Hotel* seems almost the abstract of a play. It has none of the characterization or poetic language for which Williams was famous; even the players are abstractions, and much of their dialogue is in fragmented lines. To critics these were obvious signs of the playwright's failing literary powers.

One voice disagreed drastically with the general verdict that *In the Bar of a Tokyo Hotel* was weak and ineffectual Williams when

Donald Newlove hailed it as "Williams' great crucifixion play" (176). I felt prompted to reconsider it in depth. The fact that the dissident was a writer, not a critic, seemed to warrant an examination on his terms. A careful reading of the text is needed, for here, more than in any other Tennessee Williams play, "the medium is the message." I believe we should consider this as a play written in code.

To decipher the code we need to consider factors that are not apparent on the surface: we need to know that, in response to the changes in theater that Williams saw around him, he was trying experiments in his writing that involved an extreme move away from the literary, poetic, psychological, and expressionistic quality of his usual drama toward the spareness and silence of a Pinter or Beckett. In the paranoia induced by the drugs taken for his depression, he may have been deliberately concealing these experiments under difficult titles like *The Gnädiges Fräulein* and *In the Bar of a Tokyo Hotel* to confound the critics. He did provide one clue that is essential for an understanding of this particular play. In the 1960s after a trip to Japan, he casually mentioned to a reporter that he was writing a Japanese Noh play, but the reporter did not follow up on the hint. Later, Williams would remark with almost saintly mildness that the critics hadn't taken the trouble to understand *In the Bar of a Tokyo Hotel*.

"In the bar" was the phrase they pounced on, making quick allusions to the author as an alcoholic. He might have said that before condemning the play they should at least have been seated in the right theater—a Japanese Noh playhouse, as his title suggests. Here Williams was using a simple form of free association or wordplay that works as in the game of charades. "Bar" can be a "gate," "Tokyo" implies "Japanese," and "hotel" is "house"—in this instance a playhouse or theater. He had used "hotel" as "house of life" or "house of death" in previous plays and originally planned to call his memoirs *Flee, Flee, This Sad Hotel*. A distinctive feature of the open-stage Noh playhouse is that it resembles the gateway to a shrine, the *Torii* of Japanese prints. Thus, "in the bar of a Tokyo hotel" can translate simply as "inside a Japanese playhouse." If "shrine" hints at religion, "Bar" evokes "crossing the bar," a euphemism for death. Combined with hotel-as-house-of-death, "in the bar of a Tokyo hotel" might translate *At the Gate of the House of Death,* a play in a very different mood from the alcoholic confessional its critics assumed.

Reviewers were unaware that Williams's latest drama was actually a variant of an unpublished manuscript, "The Day on Which a Man Dies," which he had written in 1960. In 1959, Williams had gone to Japan, where he met Yukio Mishima, Japan's leading playwright, who introduced him to the idea of Japanese Noh drama (Hale). He saw a number of Kabuki plays and became fascinated with Japanese theater in general. On his return home, as a compliment to Mishima, he wrote his own version of a Japanese drama, more Kabuki than Noh, although he subtitled it "An Occidental Noh Play." It was never performed but still rests in a library collection, an unintended literary secret (Williams, *Day*). It is not necessary to read this script to understand *Tokyo Hotel,* but the fact that he wrote a Noh play is our key to unlocking the mysteries of *Tokyo Hotel.* We need to understand that Noh is the opposite of Western drama, so an "occidental Noh play" is a contradiction in terms. Influenced by Zen, Noh plays are philosophical lessons on the folly of human passions. The principal character may be the abstract embodiment of some passion; in *Tokyo Hotel,* Miriam may personify "Jealousy." There is little plot development of the sort we see in Western drama. Both action and speech are highly stylized.

The basic story is the same in both Williams's Noh play and *Tokyo Hotel:* Mark, an established painter, is struggling to create a new style. His vision is that through pure paint, he can capture the essence of color and light on canvas. The interplay of color will replace the subject in painting, will itself become the subject. Obsessed, he literally fights the canvas to control his medium; if he succeeds, he will achieve a revolutionary new advance in art. If he fails, he will feel that his creative ability is dead. Paralyzed by self-doubt, he frantically seeks the support of the woman who has been his other half—Miriam. Jealous of his work, embittered by his neglect and convinced that his enterprise is insane, she is threatening to leave him. His creative self urges him toward the visionary; his earthbound partner tells him to settle for the familiar. The play follows Noh conventions: the opening action tells us "this is a Noh drama" when the barman raises a metal shaker to signal the start of the scene, imitating the shoulder drum raised by the Japanese drummer who sets the Noh play's rhythm. The barman is a clever condensation of orchestra, stage assistant, and chorus as he pointedly repeats and comments on the two characters' lines. If "bar" is the gate to the house of Death, he is the gatekeeper.

Miriam is seated at a small round table in a circle of intense light. She wears a fantastic hat of blue-black cock feathers. Her preening neck, croaking voice, and incessant pecking at her husband Mark emphasize "cock" as her image. "Cock" also suggests sex, and Miriam makes clear her sexual frustration. "Crock" is what she calls her alcoholic husband, so the play is set up on the surface as a marital battle. But "crock" metaphysically is "clay"—man as a spiritual vessel in the hands of the divine potter. Cock versus Crock, carnal versus spiritual; Williams has restaged his flesh-spirit duel in the Orient. (For another discussion of the duel, see Robert Siegel's essay elsewhere in this volume.) In Eastern mythology, "cock" would have another meaning: the cock's crow signifies creation. Miriam's opening lines are about vitality and suicide, indicating a play about creativity and death.

Here Williams seems to be venturing into Taoist philosophy. Miriam's lines; "convex demanding concave," refer to the yin-yang symbol, a circle divided into two equal sections by a sigmoid line, the white section (yang) having a black spot within it, and the black (yin) a white spot. These two spots signify that there is something of the feminine in the masculine and something of the masculine in the feminine—a favorite contention of Williams's (see figure). The two halves forming a circular whole stand for the Taoist principle of balance intrinsic to order in the universe. The stage directions enforce the yin-yang idea. They specify that "the cyclorama should be a perfect half circle" (Dramatist's Play Service edition 1969). Projected on this are two large Mandala-type circles. The semicircular shape of the playing space, the three small round tables, and the spot lighting enforce Miriam's theme that to stay inside the "circle of light" is the norm. In Taoist philosophy the alternation of light and dark relates to the alternating sexual principles of yin and yang. The yin represents terrestrial matter, the yang, creative power. If Miriam represents the yin—the earthly, negative, passive, dark, and female elements, Mark stands for the yang—the heavenly, positive, active, light, and male components. Both must be in balance to create the whole or normal person.

Early in the play Miriam confronts Mark with the possibility that they are two sides of the same person—that the artist is tied to the animal. Williams had been fascinated by the Noh "ghost" plays' concept of the person inhabited by his opposite spirit. This seemed to him much like the doppelgänger, or double, that he had used in *Summer and Smoke*. In Noh, the dark side of the protagonist's nature is personified onstage by a character who may be deceptively attractive at first but during the course of the play is revealed as a destructive force. In fact, the action of *Tokyo Hotel* suggests as its model the well-known Japanese classic drama *Dojoji (Dojo Temple)*. In 1960 Williams had seen the Grand Kabuki's production of *Dojoji* on their first American tour and had written a glowing endorsement of the troupe. In *Dojoji* the woman is in love with a priest, who flees from her to the temple compound, where a great new bell is being dedicated, and takes shelter inside the bell. As the woman pursues him, in her fury she is revealed as a dragon. She twists herself about the bell, lashes the bronze with her tail, and spits flame from her mouth. The heat melts the bell and the priest dies in the molten mass. The artist consumed by his work is a classic mythical theme. It is also one of the themes of *Tokyo Hotel*.

If *Tokyo Hotel* were being performed as Noh, Miriam's solicitation of the barman would represent the maiden in *Dojoji* trying to persuade the gatekeeper to let her into the temple; their contrapuntal conversation is a sort of verbal pas de deux that might stand for the opening dance of a Noh play. Williams's signature comedy appears in this encounter, as Miriam tries to seduce the young Japanese bartender. He uses the formal rituals of his society and impeccable conformity with manners to keep her at a distance and protect his virtue. With words as mismatched as their motives, they dance through a dialogue of misinterpretation but absolute understanding. The two

languages, each foreign to the other, produce nonsequiturs and ironies as both duel with double-entendres. Wordplay is a characteristic of Japanese drama, and in interpreting *Tokyo Hotel* no word
is too insignificant to study.

The playwright's insistence on Miriam's hat—a hat crowned with
blue-black cock feathers, underscores the play's resemblance to *Dojoji.* "Cock" may allude to the mythical cockatrice—a serpent. In
Dojoji the snake woman wears a traditional costume patterned with
shining scales. Miriam's serpent image is established in the stage directions early in *Tokyo Hotel:* "Miriam touches the feathers on her
hat and makes a humming sound, then rearranges the bracelets on
her arm and moves her head from side to side more noticeably" (act
1, scene 7). In his review of *Tokyo Hotel,* Clive Barnes observed,
"Anne Meacham, as the wife, maintained constantly the expression
of a startled rattlesnake" (Barnes 44 M). Miriam, who wears the mask
of "beautiful lady," is surely a demon. She calls herself "a woman
who burns" and carries a snuff box containing a poison pill. Even
the drink she mixes—a stinger—"equal parts brandy and crème de
menthe," suggests Hell versus Heaven. In the second act, which begins with a miniature vision of Hell—steam rising as the barman
sterilizes glasses—Miriam both paralyzes and sterilizes Mark, as she
attacks his artistic and sexual potency. When the barman confuses
the two words "paralyze" and "sterilize," the playwright is not making "feeble jokes," as Clive Barnes wrote, but giving clues to the
play's action.

The fragmented dialogue between Miriam and Mark most annoyed the reviewers. Mark enters, covered with paint, and sinks into
a chair opposite Miriam. He is so tense that he cannot hold his glass.
He tries to tell Miriam what is happening in his work that causes his
tension.

MARK: For the first time, nothing that sep, sep!
MIRIAM: Are you trying to say separates?
MARK: Yes, separates, holds at some dis!
MIRIAM: To translate your incoherence, holds at some distance,
is that it? . . .
MARK: There was always a sense of division till! Gone! Now, ab-
solute one-ness with!
MIRIAM: You're shaking the table so that I have to grip the other
side of it to keep it from.

MARK: If I said that I'm—
MIRIAM: What?
MARK: Actually *terrified* of. Would you believe me?
MIRIAM: I have no reason to doubt it.
MARK: . . . The images flash in my brain, and I have to get them on nailed-down canvas at once or they.
MIRIAM: Flash back out of your brain . . .
MARK: . . . What I'm saying is—color isn't passive, it. It—has a fierce life in it!
MIRIAM: That's right. Color. On your suit, your hands, even in your hair. (Part 1, 17–24)

Hearing such exchanges, the more compassionate reviewers speculated on some psychic fragmentation in the author himself: "a terribly naked work that reveals more about its author than he could have possibly intended," wrote one. "I don't think anyone should be allowed to see it" (Hirsch 81n.). Others, like C. W. E. Bigsby, called the writing hysterical (114). The verdict was that Tennessee Williams could no longer complete a sentence. Only a few saw the lines as a new literary device with which the playwright was experimenting or noted that in this play he was working in an adventurous vein. Nancy Tischler pointed out that Williams, always concerned about human failure to reach out and touch another, is commenting on the failure of his chosen tool—words (Letter). David Savran has voiced a gay interpretation, suggesting that after Williams "came out of the closet" and was no longer forced to conceal homosexual allusions with dramatic artifice, he lost his power of words and was reduced to stuttering! (137). No one recognized in the exchanges between Miriam and Mark an attempt to reproduce the duet style of dialogue in Noh plays in which two characters share the lines phrase by phrase to build to a climax. This technique of chanted response corresponds somewhat to a feature of Western oratorio. The omitted words or silences in the characters' dialogue may correspond to the empty spaces in a Japanese painting, which are considered as meaningful as what is pictured. Actually, most of the unfinished sentences here leave no meaning in doubt but are like simple puzzles that the listener easily completes. Also, if Miriam and Mark are halves of one person, there is no need to complete the sentences.

As part 1 of *Tokyo Hotel* depends on a Noh interpretation and Eastern philosophy, part 2 moves westward. (Remember that Tennessee Williams called his secret version "an Occidental Noh play.") If we keep in mind that Noh is defined as religious drama and accept the code of hotel-as-playhouse-as-shrine, part 2 immediately alerts us to the religious aspects of the play. With the entrance of the character Leonard, the metaphors change from Taoist to Christian. Again, Williams resorts to a simple code, using puns and wordplay as in Japanese drama. Leonard is the representative of "Aunt Grace," the artist's agent. Miriam has summoned him, hoping that he will convince Mark that his present style of painting is worthless. Coming from "the Gallery," symbolically Leonard is the angel or messenger of grace from on high. (In today's less subtle theater, he might have flown down from the wings like the angel in Kushner's *Perestroika*— a play that in fact owes something to Williams.) His every speech is conciliatory; he is the placator, the mediator who pleads with Miriam for understanding and mercy. But Miriam is adamant. She insists that Mark is insane and should be hospitalized. Leonard shows Miriam his "star sapphire," a gift from "Raymond"—"Raymond," literally, "the light of the world"—reemphasizing his heavenly mission. Then follows a brief battle between Heaven and Hell, as Miriam counters with her Regency snuffbox. Hers is a different Regent and her lines, "Snuff, snuff, enough" pronounce the judgment, death.

Meanwhile, Mark has capitulated to Miriam's threat of leaving him. Accepting her judgment on his painting, he has thrown down his brushes and is anxious for a reconciliation. Mark enters to the tinkling of wind chimes—a liturgical symbol of the Holy Spirit. He is dressed in a clean white suit. (White in Japanese drama is worn in preparation for death.) Mark has shaved and cut himself; there are bloodied bits of tissue paper scattered over his face. Like a man carrying a heavy weight he stumbles and nearly falls. Then come the strange speeches of Leonard when Mark explains his bleeding— speeches that make no sense without the biblical interpretation.

MARK: . . . you see, I forgot my . . .
LEONARD: What did you forget, Mark.
MARK: My electric razor . . .
LEONARD: I think that unconsciously we resent shaving. I've often made trips and forgotten my razor. But this time Ray-

mond packed for me, so I have my electric razor. Of course you're welcome to use it . . .

"The Japanese make such lovely, compact electric appliances . . . " [adds Leonard, in what I take to be Williams' reminder of the Japanese origin of his play.] "Very relevant . . . " [says Miriam sarcastically.] (II 44)

This conversation *is* irrelevant on a realistic level, but if we dissect the coded words in a simple translation, the whole crucifixion story emerges. Williams writes as a poet; words are seldom casual in his work; names, almost never. "Mark" was the first of the gospel writers, the disciple who was on the scene. A "mark" is a target, pierced by shots or arrows, so Mark is a victim. One's mark is a cross; the cross refers to crucifixion. Mark's bleeding face is a reference to the flagellation of Christ. "Leonard" means "Lion," which is the liturgical emblem of St. Mark. Leonard, the messenger from on high, brings from *Raymond* the electric *razor.* The sounds "ray" and "razor" reverberate in this passage, like "rays." Leonard, the heavenly messenger, is offering Mark—the Christ figure—his halo. This suggests a painterly image: the circle of golden rays around the head of a Renaissance painting of Christ. Or is it the crown of thorns, as the sharpness of a razor suggests? With either interpretation, in the crucifixion story Leonard's offer represents the revelation, "Behold the son of God." From the time Mark staggers on stage—as Christ stumbled under his cross—the play becomes a minimalist enactment of the journey to Golgotha. Miriam even says, "let's go into the garden." Now Miriam's cock-feathers suggest another allusion: to the cock crowing three times as His dearest disciple denies his Lord.

There is the emphasis on the time—noon. Mark has been offered the wine, which he refuses. We learn that as he showered before donning his white garment, the shower curtain was torn down. "And the curtain of the temple was torn in two, from top to bottom," reads the Gospel of Mark, 15:38. The suffering on the cross, the fighting for breath, is enacted as the others talk. There is even the hint of an ascension in Mark's key speech: "A serious painter has two requirements. . . . A long white beard and a stepladder and a commission to paint, on the ceiling of the Sistine Chapel" (II 48). Then come the lines to which critics so objected as voicing Williams's self-pity: "Nobody ever gave me a magnum or a quart or a baby's bottle of confidence, and I didn't have a long, white beard and a stepladder to the vault of the Sistine Chapel to paint the creation of creation" (II, 50).

This outburst may, however, be Williams's version of the biblical accusation: "My God, my God, why hast thou forsaken me?" Then the entombment: "Put the words back in a box and nail down the lid," Mark says. "Fini." (John 19:28, "It is finished.") Even the removal from the tomb and the resurrection are predicted, as Mark tells them: "I'll remove the tissue and talcum my face and be back." Then he slumps to the floor and dies. Leonard and the Barman carry him offstage while Miriam appears to see and feel nothing. If there seems to be some doubt about the Ascension—"no stepladder to Heaven"—Mark's promise, "I'll be back," is prophetic of Williams. In the end, Miriam's evil is revealed. In destroying Mark's belief in his vision she has caused his death. Just as Noh plays end in a revelation, here the final recognition is Miriam's. Without Mark, she has made herself incomplete. The circle is broken. "I have nowhere to go," she says as she casts off her bracelets (circles that symbolize the whole). Her circle of stage lighting is extinguished and she is left in darkness as the play ends.

If we accept this as Williams's crucifixion story, it does indeed "blow the mind." For here the playwright has taken the enormous risk that this work will be seen *only* as his personal complaint. The cry for understanding here, however, is not simply his own; the crucified martyr is the Artist as such, and this is the playwright's declaration that to create Art is a divine commission. Williams's subject is no longer the sensitive individual as an outsider in an insensitive world—the Blanche of *A Streetcar Named Desire* or the Alma of *Summer and Smoke*—but the Artist as Outsider in an alien society. In *Tokyo Hotel* he is investigating what it takes to be an artist: grappling with the creative problem that in being obsessed with capturing the essence of life, one may fail to live it; warning that for the artist not to be able to change his art can mean artistic death.

Evidence that this play is not simply Williams having his "nightmares in public" (Hirsch 79) is supplied also by the script's reference to a specific artist. Jackson Pollock, who went from supreme success and notoriety to disillusionment and suicide, was Williams's obvious inspiration for the artist figure in his play. This premise is the final component in our understanding *Tokyo Hotel*. Williams had met Pollock in Provincetown in 1940 and through the years had followed the rise and fall of Pollock's career, which in so many ways resembled his own. In 1949 Jackson Pollock had been pictured in *Life* magazine as America's greatest living painter, just as Williams had been celebrated in 1962 as its greatest playwright. Ironically, for each the acclaim was followed by decline. Biographies of Pollock stress his experiments in a new technique, his "drip painting"— work with no preconceived image but with pure paint, which he poured onto the canvas with no intermediary brush. Like Mark, Pollock was seeking the essence of color and light. (He had in fact one painting called "White Light.") Just as Mark struggles to control his canvas, Pollock referred to his as "the arena." Derided for painting on the floor, he pointed out that this was a standard Japanese method. This way, he could attack the canvas from all angles, could in fact become a part of his painting. Pollock once said, "When I am *in* my painting, I'm not aware of what I'm doing. . . . the painting has a life of its own" (Friedman 100). Like Mark he was painting from the unconscious—a Surrealist method—lines and whirls that had no representational function but created a purely optical phenomenon: "Energy Made Visible," his biographer called it, noting a correlation between splitting the atom, which in 1945 set off the atomic age, and Pollock's atomized paintings of the same era. To Pollock and serious artists of his time, conventional modes of representation could no longer express the terrors of the modern world, and so they were obliged to deal in abstraction. *In the Bar of a Tokyo Hotel* as a text reflects some of the abstraction, the surrealism and— in its broken sentences—the atomization of Pollock's painting. It also reflects Williams's belief that he himself was forging a new style of expression and his consequent self-doubt when this was described as disintegration.

In *Tokyo Hotel* Williams reproduces the period when Pollock suffered a block in his painting and could not face the empty canvas— the end of his life when he took refuge in drugs and drink, had a psychiatric breakdown, and, in a deliberate reckless act, brought on his own death. Williams was quite aware of his own paranoia. In a 1973 interview, looking back on this play, he said: "Writers are paranoid, because they're living two lives—their creative life, of which they're most protective, and their life as a human being. . . . I put a premium on the creative life. One risks one's personal life in order to work, and when one cannot work or when one expects total failure, there is a crisis" (Jennings 245). *In the Bar of a Tokyo Hotel* centers on such a crisis.

More than one reviewer noted that the terror in this schizophrenic play was real. When Williams thought he was dying, he became a Catholic. However, for more than a decade he had been studying Eastern religion. In these Noh-inspired plays, when he feared he was going mad, he seems to have been searching for absolutes in Buddha or Tao. Williams at his most withdrawn was writing about the artist's fear of not being able to separate himself from his material. For Mark to destroy the bafflers between his painting and himself is to break with reality, as Miriam points out. But what in Freudian terms is a psychotic break may be in eastern mysticism a merging with the cosmic unconscious: Zen's *satori*—total enlightenment. So the artist is the supreme gambler, prisoner to the judgments of time.

Whether read as Williams's exercise in Noh drama, his "great crucifixion play," another in his portraits of the artist, or an experiment in linguistic and dramatic form, *In the Bar of a Tokyo Hotel* has the problem that its meaning cannot easily come through in production. There is much more here than can be enacted onstage. Like Noh drama itself, which was written for the elite, it will be most appreciated by those who are acquainted with the text. So again Williams has written an intrinsically private play and condemned himself to being misunderstood. If he wrote *Tokyo Hotel* while on drugs, as his brother claims, this might help to explain its hallucinatory quality and the schizophrenic effect of multiple obsessive ideas shooting off in every direction like fireworks. Still—to maintain two consistent allegories, one Eastern, one Christian, under the surface of a third realistic plot is a tour de force that would seem to require authorly control. Williams was well aware that audiences found it hard to empathize with the turn in his work of the 1960s toward a new style of creative expression. Interviewed about his "stoned age" by Richard Christianson he declared: "Actually. I wrote two or three of my best plays then, even if they were a little weird: 'In the bar of a Tokyo Hotel' . . . and the two-character play sometimes called 'Out Cry.' In these, I began experimenting with writing in incomplete sentences" (81). It should be mentioned that in the two decades of his "decline" Tennessee Williams wrote thirty-five new plays!

In the years since his death, *The Two-Character Play* has been revived several times and is being recognized as an important, if challenging, work. A revival of *Tokyo Hotel* is still waiting in the wings. *In the Bar of a Tokyo Hotel* opened at the Eastside Playhouse Off Broadway on May 11, 1969, with Herbert Machiz as director; after twenty-two previews and twenty-five performances it closed. Donald Madden and Anne Meacham had done their best, but even the cast had trouble understanding the play. Williams, in a desperate effort to forestall its failure, published a letter in the *New York Times* before the play opened, asking that it be read to the company to clarify the play's meaning (146). The letter is a strangely simplistic restatement of his artist's dilemma. Unfortunately, the only interpretive comments he added were so personal as to be embarrassing: his confessions that he wondered whether his work had any essential value opened the play to charges of self-pity and hysteria. In this self-destructive act it would seem that a frightened playwright was out to sabotage his own play before the critics could get to it.

By now nothing could assuage the critics' exasperation. *Time* magazine, which had always targeted Williams, moved in for the kill. "Tennessee Williams is lying on the sickbed of his formidable talent," it announced. "*In the Bar of a Tokyo Hotel* is more deserving of a coroner's report than a review "(75). On June 10, *Life,* its companion magazine, seizing an opportunity to bolster its dwindling circulation, took a full-page ad in the *New York Times* which may have been one of the most unprincipled acts in the history of journalism. It was printed in four-inch black letters surrounding a face shot of Tennessee Williams. "Played out?" it said. "Tennessee Williams has suffered an infantile regression from which there seems no exit. Almost free of incident or drama . . . nothing about *In the Bar of a Tokyo Hotel* deserves its production. . . . That's the kind of play it is, and that's the kind of play it gets in . . . *Life* ("Come to Life" 96). On June 16 *Life* printed a review by Stefan Kanfer entitled "White Dwarf's Tragic Fade-out," using a metaphor from astronomy. It was clear, Kanfer wrote, that the bright light Williams had once cast on the American stage could now be seen as coming from a cinder" (10). He used the word "senile." Three days later the playwright fled to Tokyo with his star, Anne Meacham, and in mid-September he entered the psychiatric division of Barnes Hospital, where the treatment for drug overdose brought on heart attacks that almost caused his death.

There is little doubt that the severe criticism of *Time-Life* killed *In the Bar of a Tokyo Hotel*. It was revived once, ten years later at Eve Adamson's Jean Cocteau Repertory Theatre and was ignored by reviewers. It is still almost unknown even to theater people. Must it in fact remain a chamber drama only to be read and studied? Under the surface, all of its references are allusive, symbols that cannot easily be expressed in production, but fascinating in the printed text. No doubt some day, somewhere, some producer will meet its challenge.

I can visualize it being done on the pattern of David Henry Hwang's *M. Butterfly*—or by someone like Michael Kahn, who has produced several Williams plays in Kabuki style. It could be stunning staged like a Noh drama, with the harsh attacks of Miriam against Mark danced out as a choreographed battle. One can imagine Leonard performing the traditional Noh-Kabuki "lion-dance" meant to ward off evil spirits—and Miriam's final symbolic throwing off of her serpent costume as she casts off her bracelets. In the text of *Tokyo Hotel* where the painter simply drops dead and is carried offstage, the symbolic finale that Williams wrote into his Noh play would be spectacular—the painter bursting through a series of rice-paper screens until he disappears.

Meanwhile, until the day when it will be reevaluated and better understood, *In the Bar of a Tokyo Hotel* must stand as the courageous experiment of a writer who was not afraid to take risks—an artist who dared to try to create his own light—then shrank from the critical light of those who misunderstood it.

Works Cited

Barnes, Clive. "Williams Play Explores Decay of an Artist." *New York Times,* 13 May 1969, p. 44M.

Bigsby, C. W. E. "Tennessee Williams." In *A Critical Introduction to Twentieth Century American Drama*. Cambridge: Cambridge University Press, 1984.

Christiansen, Richard. "Sharp, Selfish, Sentimental—and Seventy." *Chicago Tribune,* 17 April 1981, p. 81.

"Come to Life." Advertisement, *New York Times* 10 June 1969: 96.

Dojoji: Twenty Plays of the New York Theatre. Edited by Donald Keene. New York: Columbia University Press, 1970.

Friedman, B. H. *Jackson Pollock, Energy Made Visible.* New York: McGraw-Hill, 1972.

Hale, Allean. "The Secret Play of Tennessee Williams." *Southern Review* 27 (Spring 1991): 363–75. (Source for an account of Williams's friendship with Yukio Mishima and subsequent interest in Japanese theater)

Hirsch, Foster. "Portraits of the Playwright as Failure." In *A Portrait of the Artist: The Plays of Tennessee Williams.* New York: Kennikat, 1979.

Jennings, C. Robert. "Playboy Interview: Tennessee Williams." In *Conversations with Tennessee Williams,* edited by Albert J. Devlin. Jackson: University Press of Mississippi, 1986.

Kanfer, Stefan. "White Dwarf's Tragic Fade-out." *Life,* 13 June 1969, p. 10.

Newlove, Donald. "A Dream of Tennessee Williams." *Esquire,* November 1969, pp. 172–79.

Savran, David. "The Incomplete Sentence." *Communists, Cowboys, and Queers.* Minneapolis: University of Minnesota Press, 1992.

Tischler, Nancy, to Allean Hale. October 10, 1995. (Letter re: *Tokyo Hotel*). In the author's collection.

"Torpid Tennessee." Review of *In the Bar of a Tokyo Hotel. Time,* 23 May 1969, p. 75.

Williams, Tennessee. "The Day on Which a Man Dies. An Occidental Noh Play." Unpublished manuscript. Special collections, University of California, Los Angeles.

———. *In the Bar of a Tokyo Hotel.* In *The Theatre of Tennessee Williams.* Vol. 7. New York: New Directions, 1994.

———. "Tennessee Williams Talks About His Play *In the Bar of a Tokyo Hotel.*" *New York Times,* 14 May 1969, p. 146.

9

"Entitled to Write About Her Life"

Tennessee Williams and F. Scott and Zelda Fitzgerald

Jackson R. Bryer

STANLEY:. . . . now the cat's out of the bag! I found out some things!
STELLA: What—things!
STANLEY: Things I already suspected. But now I got proof from the most reliable sources—which I have checked on!
—*A Streetcar Named Desire*

"Who are you anyhow?" broke out Tom. "You're one of that bunch that hangs around with Meyer Wolfsheim—that much I happen to know. I've made a little investigation into your affairs—and I'll carry it further to-morrow."
—*The Great Gatsby*

Clothes for a Summer Hotel (1980) was Tennessee Williams's last Broadway production during his lifetime. This "dream play" about F. Scott and Zelda Fitzgerald was a critical and commercial failure that devastated Williams. In many ways he never recovered from this failure. Its effect is perhaps best captured in the oft-quoted recollection of José Quintero, the play's director, who remembers that, on the morning after its out-of-town opening in Chicago, where, aside from a positive review from Claudia Cassidy, the notices had not been very good, he found the playwright "in front of the Art Institute": "He was sitting on the steps, in the snow, like some half-demented creature. I said, 'What are you doing, Tom?' He said, 'I'm waiting for them to open because this is a place for artists where I can catch my breath to go on living'" (Galligan 46). The play fared no better in New York, where Robert Brustein, cruelly but not atypically, began his assessment: "You couldn't possibly be interested in my opinions of a work you'll never get a chance to see; and I suspect the playwright would just as soon let the moment pass in silence while he licks his wounds and ponders his next move (perhaps a flight to Three Mile Island on a one-way ticket)" (Brustein 27).

Brustein's prediction was correct. The play, which had opened on March 26 (Williams's sixty-ninth birthday), closed on April 16, almost a month before Brustein's review appeared. And in the years since its inauspicious debut, it has received little attention from Williams scholars and critics. In an admittedly cursory survey, I have found, aside from passing mentions, just three full-length essays on the play (by Thomas P. Adler, Hilton Anderson, and Peter L. Hays) and a brief but incisive two pages in Bigsby's *Volume 2* on Williams, Miller, and Albee in *A Critical Introduction to Twentieth-Century American Drama* (125–27).

Most of those who have written about *Clothes* have taken their cue from Elliot Martin, the producer of the original production, who observed, "It's not about the Fitzgeralds, it's about a brother and sister, about Tennessee and his sister. . . . it's a play with a certain transferred paranoia—from the situation of Rose to that of Williams himself who . . . was blaming the critics and the media for his own failures" (Spoto 345). Williams himself lent additional credence to Martin's assertions when, in many of the interviews he gave prior to and during the run of the play, he acknowledged his sympathy for and understanding of the Fitzgeralds. Like Scott, Williams observed, "At one point I went through a deep depression and heavy drinking. . . . And I, too, have gone through a period of eclipse in public favor" (Weatherby); he added that the Fitzgeralds "embody concerns of my own, the tortures of the creative artist in a materialist society. . . . They were so close to the edge. I understood the schizophrenia and the thwarted ambitions" (Sandomir 5). At least one reviewer of the New York production agreed: Jack Kroll suggested that the play "may be really about the tension, both creative and lacerating, between the male and female elements in Williams's own psyche."

Adler's essay, along with most of the briefer comments on the play, also read it pretty much entirely in terms of Williams's life and career. "The autobiographical impulse remains uppermost in *Hotel*," according to Adler (6), who then proceeds to place it artistically, thematically, and chronologically with respect to *The Glass Menagerie, Out Cry, Sweet Bird of Youth, Summer and Smoke,* and *Vieux Carré.* Partly because this territory has already been covered and also because I am not a Williams scholar and have some credentials as a Fitzgerald critic, my interest here is less with the Williams portion of the equation and more with the Fitzgerald portion.

Having said so, however, I will begin by acknowledging that, thematically, the story of the Fitzgeralds and of Zelda in particular is clearly one that resonated with Williams. As evidence of this point, I would refer readers to the essay by Michael Paller in this volume and also cite some of Roger Boxill's generic remarks about typical Williams themes, techniques, and characters in order to make the connections between them and *Clothes for a Summer Hotel.* The "essential Williams condition," according to Boxill, "is that of a sensitive creature who has no home in an alien world" (26); "Nearly all of Williams's plays are . . . 'memory plays.' They look back with longing to a time that has been sweetened in the remembering" (27). Williams's interest in the story of Zelda Fitzgerald is implicit in Boxill's description of what he sees as one of the playwright's "two main character types," "the faded belle":

> In the story of the faded belle, an attractive young woman of sensitive nature, born in the South of good or even of aristocratic family, and having a refinement of taste and sensibility and a puritanical fastidiousness about sex, is disappointed in love at an early age, and as a result either ends her life as a recluse or abandons herself to promiscuity, especially with younger men, but in either case probably becomes deranged and, after losing her youth, her looks, and sometimes even a home of her own, is taken away to an institution. (35)

Of course, one instantly recognizes Blanche DuBois as a "faded belle," but it is also not necessary to belabor the connections between this figure and Zelda Fitzgerald—both in her real life and as Williams depicts her in his play. It is worth mentioning, however, that in selecting aspects of Zelda's story to dramatize, Williams emphasizes her affair with French aviator Edouard Jobin (that is, Zelda's "promiscuity" with another man), which occupies a disproportionately large portion of the play, as well as her dissatisfaction with Scott's sexual performance. This last element Williams probably based on the famous chapter "A Matter of Measurements," in Ernest Hemingway's *A Moveable Feast*, in which Hemingway graphically recounted Fitzgerald's sexual insecurities. This possibility in turn brings us to the larger question of Williams's sources and emphases in his retelling of the Fitzgeralds' lives. As Adler has shown, the acknowledged biographical "genesis" (Adler 13) of *Clothes* is Nancy Milford's 1970 feminist biography *Zelda*, which takes as one of its principal premises the contention that Fitzgerald stifled his wife's quite abundant creative talents and appropriated Zelda's life "as his raw material" (Milford 115): because he "was the professional writer and . . . supporting Zelda, . . . the entire fabric of their life was his material" (Milford 273). In a 1979 interview with John Hicks, Williams virtually echoed Milford's thesis: "Well, his material was Zelda's life! Naturally she felt she was entitled to write about her life."

But in that same interview, Williams goes beyond Milford in claiming that "Zelda has as much talent as her husband did." He calls her novel *Save Me the Waltz* "a beautiful book," adding "There are passages in it that have a brilliancy that Fitzgerald was unequal to" (Devlin 322). This assertion could well be implicit in Milford's book, although she never states it explicitly; but Sara Mayfield, another Zelda biographer whom Williams probably read, does state it. According to Mayfield, both Fitzgerald and Hemingway "were jealous of the fact that Zelda was the born 'natural' and the 'original' that neither of them, for all their skill in construction and craftsmanship, would ever be" (187). *Save Me the Waltz*, Mayfield contends, is as good as *This Side of Paradise* or *The Sun Also Rises* (186) and better than *Tender Is the Night* (187).

There is abundant evidence in the text of *Clothes* of how heavily Williams was influenced by this at least debatable view of Zelda's talents. In fact, Williams's continual unsubtle reiteration of this theme is one of the play's principal weaknesses. It is introduced barely five pages into the published text—I am using the text included in *Volume 8* (1992) of *The Theatre of Tennessee Williams*—in a conversation between Fitzgerald and his friend Gerald Murphy:

scott: I had to discourage her attempt to compete with my success as a writer. . . . Have you seen Zelda's writing?

MURPHY:—Yes. That was her talent. I hear you made her promise not to publish *Save Me the Waltz* till your *Tender Is the Night* had come out.

SCOTT: Without apology, yes, I did. . . . So much of Zelda's material was mine and she put it into her novel—a beautiful but cloudy, indistinct mirror of—(209)

Thereafter, this point is hammered into us time and again—by Zelda's remark to her husband, "What was important to you was to absorb and devour!" (215; italicized in the original), by her complaint, "Never in all these years of coexistence in time did you make the discovery that I have the eyes of a hawk which is a bird of nature as predatory as a husband who appropriates your life as material for his writing" (216), and her statement, "I respect your priority in the career of writing although it preceded and eclipsed my own" (218); and by Scott's response to Zelda's plaintive question, "What about . . . my *work*?": "Your work is the work that all young Southern ladies dream of performing some day. Living well with a devoted husband and a beautiful child" (240). This demonization of Scott at the hands of his highly talented and legitimately embittered wife reaches its logical climax when Dr. Zeller, Zelda's psychiatrist, tells Scott, "I like to read important writing, and I feel that your wife's novel *Save Me the Waltz*—I'm sure you won't mind me saying that there are passages in it that have a lyrical imagery that moves me, sometimes more than your own" (259).

Oddly enough, in his review of the original Broadway production, John Simon noted that in only one scene had Williams introduced "the not entirely novel notion that Fitzgerald jealously sabotaged what might have turned out to be his wife's superior talent for writing," adding that if "that had been the main thrust of the play, the result might have been, however unfounded as literary criticism, something of greater dramatic and human interest" (84). One wonders whether either Simon wasn't paying very close attention or Williams substantially altered the script between the original production and the final published version. If the latter is the case, he severely weakened the play.

My theory is that, already sympathetic to both Fitzgeralds' story and especially to Zelda's—in that it so closely paralleled that of so many of Williams's own dramatic heroines—the playwright read

Milford, Mayfield, Hemingway, and others on the subject of the Fitzgeralds. Finding ammunition therein for his own predisposition toward their story (a story that, undeniably, also paralleled in a number of significant ways his own relationship with his sister, Rose), he felt empowered to tell a version to which he was extremely sympathetic, namely one in which Scott is the villain and Zelda is the victim. It is also worth noting here that in March 1937 when Rose Williams's mental illness worsened, her family unsuccessfully "attempted to place her in Highland Hospital in Asheville, North Carolina" (Devlin and Tischler 99). Highland Hospital, of course, is where Zelda Fitzgerald spent much of the last decade of her life and where she died in a fire in 1948. It is also the setting for *Clothes for a Summer Hotel*. That Williams wants to side with Zelda against Scott is suggested in the play's opening scene when Scott replies to one of the two nuns guarding the gates of Highland Hospital, who tells him that the suggestion has been made that the gates be painted red "to look cheerful": "If the objective is to create a cheerful impression, I would begin by removing the two of you from beside the gates" (206). Because our sympathies throughout *Clothes* are manipulated to be entirely with Zelda, Williams sacrifices ambiguity, one of the major positive attributes of his best plays.

Williams's recognition that ambiguity was a desirable strength is amply demonstrated in his essay "Critic Says 'Evasion,' Writer Says 'Mystery,'" originally published in 1955 in response to Walter Kerr's criticism of the character of Brick in *Cat on a Hot Tin Roof* as ambiguous and evasive. "The truth about human character in a play, as in life, varies with the variance of experience and viewpoint of those that view it," says Williams. "No two members of an audience ever leave a theater, after viewing a play that deals with any degree of complexity in character, with identical interpretations of the characters dealt with. This is as it should be" (Williams, *Where I Live* 70–71). And of course, it is the principal strength of Williams's greatest creations—Blanche, Amanda, Brick, Maggie, Stanley, and many others—that we can legitimately have such divergent responses to them. We are not permitted to do so in *Clothes for a Summer Hotel*. Williams himself may well have been aware of this weakness in his script; he commented to an interviewer during the play's pre-Broadway run in Washington, when he was still revising: "I hope to make Zelda and Scott more balanced, as the play progresses" (Kriebel 76). This aim, I would submit, he never achieved.

One of the other weaknesses of *Clothes* that I would like to mention briefly also relates to the method of its composition suggested earlier, a hasty reading of secondary sources. The play is filled with passing references to extremely arcane biographical details that no reasonable playwright could expect even a few members of his audience to understand. Many, but not all, would know, as mentioned above, that Zelda Fitzgerald died in a fire at Highland Hospital in 1948, hence her fear of fire throughout the play and the playwright's pervasive use of fire imagery. But how many would realize that, when Zelda mentions "how careless I am with Caesar's things" (251), it is an allusion to her second, unpublished, novel, "Caesar's Things"? Do many readers or viewers of the play understand that Scott's seemingly disproportionate distress at hearing of Conrad's death (254–56) relates to the critically popular notion that Fitzgerald based the narrative technique of *The Great Gatsby* on Conrad's *Lord Jim* and *Heart of Darkness* (Long 85–118)? Similarly, an exchange between Ernest and Hadley Hemingway—in which the latter asks, "Will I still be your girl?" and Ernest answers, "Be good"—to which she replies, "You mean entirely devoted to you, even when discarded for the next?" refers to the fact that Hemingway left Hadley for her best friend, Pauline Pfeiffer, who became his second wife.

When one adds to the above examples references to Scott's having helped Hemingway revise *The Sun Also Rises* (269), to a motor trip that Hemingway and Fitzgerald took to Lyon (described in *A Moveable Feast*), during which, Scott says, "You cared for me with the tenderness of—" and Hemingway interrupts, "The night?" (270; get it?), or to the Garden of Allah, one of Fitzgerald's final residences during his final stay in Hollywood (276)—to name just a few—it is clear that the script is full of obscure references that depend on specialized knowledge. Perhaps the most extreme of these occurs toward the end of the play when Zelda says, "Poor Scott," and he responds "Meaning 'poor son of a bitch'" (277). The quotation marks around "poor son of a bitch" (which are obviously apparent only to someone using the published script) are the key here; because this is an echo of the exact words that "the owl-eyed man" utters about Gatsby at the latter's funeral (176). A few readers and carefully attentive viewers might catch that reference; but how many would know that they are also the words that Dorothy Parker is reputed to have muttered when she visited a funeral parlor in Hollywood to pay her last respects to Fitzgerald (Mizener 298)? No, the play has too much of the aroma of the library and not enough of that of the playhouse. Again, Williams himself probably recognized this flaw when he admitted to an interviewer, "I wrote this very quickly, and I wasn't as careful as I usually am" (Kriebel 76).

II

I will now turn to a perhaps more felicitous pairing of Fitzgerald and Williams and one that, to my knowledge, has never previously been noted. It is what my more savvy colleagues might call, I think, an intertextual connection—the similarities between *The Great Gatsby* and *A Streetcar Named Desire,* most especially in the two romantic triangles central to the works. In each case, there is a romantic dreamer (Gatsby's counterpart is Blanche) opposed by a pragmatic realist out to destroy them (Tom in the one case, and Stanley in the other), with a figure in the middle who is, to some extent at least, torn between the two, although married to one—with whom she eventually chooses to remain (Daisy and Stella). In both cases, realism triumphs over romance, although it is clear in each instance that the author probably sides with the romantic dreamer while at the same time realizing that their attempt to achieve happiness will ultimately prove fruitless. Williams's famous remark, in his foreword to *Sweet Bird of Youth,* surely applies to *Gatsby* as accurately as much as to *Streetcar:* "All my life I have been haunted by the obsession that to desire a thing or love a thing intensely is to place yourself in a vulnerable position, to be a possible, if not a probable, loser of what you most want" (*Where I Live* 106).

Starting from this premise, there are some quite remarkable additional parallels that devolve from the similarities in the basic triangular situation. Of necessity, in the brief space of this essay, I can do no more than suggest them—in the hope that they will provoke further exploration.

1. In both works, the romantic dreamer figure is depicted as totally incapable of understanding or existing in the world represented by the figure of brutal reality; and the gulf between the two worlds is thus emphasized.

The best example in *Gatsby* occurs when Tom Buchanan and two of his East Egg friends show up, unexpectedly, on horseback at Gatsby's house. When Gatsby invites them to stay for dinner, the unnamed woman in the party "enthusiastically" says, "You come to supper with *me*." Gatsby leaves for a moment and the following conversation ensues between Nick and Tom:

> "My God, I believe the man's coming," said Tom. "Doesn't he know she doesn't want him?"
> "She says she does want him."
> "She has a big dinner party and he won't know a soul there."
> (104)

They leave without waiting for Gatsby to return, "disappearing under the August foliage just as Gatsby, with hat and light overcoat in hand, came out the front door" (105).

We see the same sort of collision of two worlds in *Streetcar* on numerous occasions—when Blanche enters the poker night party saying, "Please don't get up," and Stanley replies, "Nobody's going to get up, so don't be worried" (48); or when Blanche, having just arrived, tells Stella, "I brought some nice clothes to meet all your lovely friends in," and Stella says, "I'm afraid you won't think they are lovely" (23); or when Stanley correctly observes, "The Kowalskis and the DuBois have different notions" (37).

2. In both works, in several instances, the world of reality cruelly crushes the world of romance.

In *Streetcar*, of course, the ultimate example is Stanley's rape of Blanche; but that act is foreshadowed earlier in the play when he snatches Blanche's husband's love letters from her trunk, causing her to exclaim, "Now that you've touched them I'll burn them!" (42), explaining, "Everyone has something he won't let others touch because of their—intimate nature" (42); or when Stanley tells Blanche that Stella is going to have a baby (43), despite Stella's admonition to him not to do so until Blanche "gets in a quieter condition" (33). At the very end of the play, when Stanley "seizes the paper lantern, tearing it off the light bulb, and extends it toward" Blanche, her exposure is complete and total.

Similarly, in *Gatsby*, Tom's eventual triumph over Gatsby is foreshadowed very early in the novel, when Fitzgerald's light, airy description of Daisy and Jordan sitting on "an enormous couch . . . buoyed up as though upon an anchored balloon," with "their dresses . . . rippling and fluttering as if they had just been blown back in after a short flight around the house," is brought to an abrupt end with "a boom as Tom Buchanan shut the rear windows and the caught wind died around the room, and the curtains and the rugs and the two young women ballooned slowly to the floor" (8). And if we grant that Myrtle Wilson is another, "junior," version of the romantic figure in this novel—she is described as having "an immediately perceptible vitality about her as if the nerves of her body were continually smouldering" (25)—then Tom's action of brutally breaking her nose "with his open hand" (37) is still another example of this pattern.

In both works also, the triumph of the realist over the romantic is accomplished partially through the exposure of the true past of the romantic by the realist. This is suggested by the two passages I used as epigraphs for this essay, the first in which Stanley tells Stella that he's found out "some things" about Blanche from "the most reliable sources" (98) and the second in which Tom tells Gatsby that "I've made a little investigation into your affairs" (134). In both cases, the exposure of the "truth" of the romantic's existence is the coup de grace that seals their defeat. As Nick says in *Gatsby*, " 'Jay Gatsby' had broken up like glass against Tom's hard malice" (148) and as Stanley says to Blanche, "We've had this date with each other from the beginning!" (130).

3. In *Streetcar*, Stella and Blanche share a past from which Stanley gradually realizes he is excluded; in *Gatsby*, Daisy and Gatsby also share a past from which Tom eventually sees he is excluded. But in both works, there is an added complexity that relates to this one: Stella and Stanley also share something Blanche can't touch, just as Tom and Daisy also share an intimacy that Gatsby cannot destroy.

We see evidence of the past that Stella and Blanche share, their *Belle Reve* past, when Stella says she likes to wait on Blanche because "it makes it seem more like home" (79), or when she tells Stanley, "You didn't know Blanche as a girl. Nobody, nobody, was tender and trusting as she was" (111); or Stella's response to Stanley when he rebukes her for getting Cokes for Blanche: "Blanche is sensitive and you've got to realize that Blanche and I grew up under very different circumstances than you did" (98). That Stanley is threatened by this shared past is apparent in his tirade at the end of scene 8, when he says, "You showed me the snapshot of the place with the columns. I pulled you down off them columns and how you loved it, having them colored lights going! And wasn't we happy together, wasn't it all okay till she showed here? . . . Hoity-toity, describing me as an ape" (112). And Stanley's rape of Blanche, of course, is the most vivid evidence of her perceived threat to his life with Stella; he must bring her down to his level in order to defeat her.

Gatsby's past with Daisy is first described to Nick by Jordan. It is a highly romantic picture of a couple "so engrossed in each other that [Daisy] didn't see me until I was five feet away," of Gatsby looking at Daisy "in a way that every young girl wants to be looked at some time" (76). And there is the view of Daisy on her wedding day, drunkenly clutching a letter, presumably from Gatsby, and instructing all who were listening to "Tell 'em all Daisy's change her mine" (77). Then, when they are reunited, clearly the romance has endured: "I'd like to just get one of those pink clouds and put you in it and push you around," says Daisy as she looks out the window of Gatsby's mansion (95).

It is much later in the novel that Tom recognizes the shared past: he sees Gatsby and Daisy's eyes meet, "and they stared together at each other, alone in space. . . . "

> "You always look so cool," she repeated.
> She had told him that she loved him, and Tom Buchanan saw. He was astonished. (119)

Then, in the Plaza Hotel room scene, he hears the full story for the first time and responds aggressively, clearly disturbed by what he learns—his voice "groped unsuccessfully for the paternal note" (131).

But ultimately, in both works the world shared by the two realists triumphs over the world shared by the dreamers. And it is another similarity that, in both *Streetcar* and *Gatsby*, the dreamer/romantic figure cannot believe, accept, or understand this resolution. In *Streetcar*, Blanche cannot fathom why Stella returns to Stanley after the disaster of the poker night; "You're married to a madman!" (64), she says, to which Stella replies, "I'm not in anything I want to get out of" (65), and then later, "There are things that happen between a man and a woman in the dark—that sort of make everything seem—unimportant" (70). Blanche's line, "I don't understand you" (65), sums up her feeling about Stella's relationship with Stanley.

Similarly, in *Gatsby*, when Tom says to Gatsby in the Plaza Hotel room, "Why—there're things between Daisy and me that you'll never know, things that neither of us can ever forget," he speaks the truth, a truth that foreshadows Nick's view of Tom and Daisy sitting at their kitchen table after discussing the fatal automobile accident: "They weren't happy, and neither of them had touched the chicken or the ale—and yet they weren't unhappy either. There was an unmistakable air of natural intimacy about the picture, and anybody would have said that they were conspiring together" (146). Just as Blanche is incapable of accepting the validity of Stanley and Stella's world together, so too is Gatsby unable to grasp the "natural intimacy" between Tom and Daisy. In the Plaza Hotel room, unaware that he's lost Daisy to Tom, he tells Tom that "Daisy's leaving you" and "you're not going to take care of her any more" (134); and then, after the accident, he stands guard outside the Buchanans' house, explaining to Nick, "I'm just going to wait here and see if he tries to bother her about that unpleasantness this afternoon. She's locked herself into her room, and if he tries any brutality she's going to turn the light out and on again" (145). As Nick explains, "He couldn't possibly leave Daisy until he knew what she was going to do. He was clutching at some last hope and I couldn't bear to shake him free" (148). And the last time Nick sees Gatsby, the latter refuses to believe that Daisy "ever loved" Tom, adding, "Of course she might have loved him just for a minute, when they were first married—and loved me more even then" (152). Then he walks back into his mansion to await a call from Daisy that we know will never come.

4. In both works, there is a character (Stella and Daisy) who is caught in the middle between the realist and the romantic; and this character, although she eventually chooses to remain with her realist husband, evidences considerable ambivalence before making that decision. She is clearly attracted to the romantic figure and, to some extent at least, repelled by her husband.

Stella throughout chides Stanley for his treatment of Blanche, trying to protect her sister from her husband. She tells him, "This is my house and I'll talk as much as I want to!" (51), when he tells her to shut up; and she admonishes him at Blanche's birthday "party," "Your face and your fingers are disgustingly greasy. Go and wash up and then help me clear the table" (107). At the same time, while she is, as was mentioned earlier, drawn back to some extent into the world of her girlhood by her sister's reappearance, she also recognizes, as she tells Blanche, that "Stanley's the only one of his crowd that's likely to get anywhere," because it's "a drive he has" (50).

In a similar way, Daisy is caught in the middle. She is painfully aware of Tom's continual infidelities and is sporting a bruised finger when Nick first sees her ("You did it, Tom. . . . I know you didn't mean to, but you *did* do it. That's what I get for marrying a brute of a man, a great big hulking physical specimen" [12]). Then, in the Plaza Hotel room scene, when Tom tries to declare his love for her, she calls him "revolting" (132) and announces, albeit "with perceptible reluctance," that she "never loved" Tom. Clearly, she sees Tom for who he is and chooses to remain with him, just as Stella sees Stanley clearly and chooses to stay with him.

5. Finally, in each work, a marriage survives because of a lie that both husband and wife agree to perpetuate.

In *Streetcar*, Stella and Stanley stay together despite Blanche's having told her sister that Stanley raped her. "I couldn't believe her story and go on living with Stanley" (133), Stella tells Eunice. In *Gatsby*, we assume that Daisy allowed Tom to tell Wilson that she was not driving the car that killed Myrtle. Perhaps he knows the truth, perhaps he doesn't; but she does and Nick does—"There was nothing I could say, except the one unutterable fact that it wasn't true" (180)—and the lie is allowed to stand.

Those are a few of the parallels between the two works. There are others—the similarities between the physical descriptions of Stanley ("Animal joy in his being is implicit in all his movements and attitudes" [29]; Stella calls him "a little bit on the primitive side" [39–40]) and Tom (first seen "standing with his legs apart" [7] and possessing a body of "enormous power . . . a body capable of enormous leverage—a cruel body" [7]), for example. Or we could consider Blanche's famous line, "I don't want realism . . . I want magic! . . . I tell what *ought* to be truth" (117) next to Gatsby's "extraordinary gift for hope" and "romantic readiness" (2) and his equally well-known line, "Can't repeat the past? . . . Why of course you can!" (111).

I have offered these brief remarks on intertextual affinities between Williams and Fitzgerald to suggest that, long before the former sat down to write *Clothes for a Summer Hotel,* the two shared thematic interests. *Clothes,* then, becomes the culmination and most overt example of these affinities rather than the sole focus of them. Williams was attracted to the Fitzgeralds' story by more than autobiographical parallels. As he admitted to an interviewer in 1980, Scott and Zelda had "haunted me for a very long time" (Silverman 26). Perhaps one of the ways their story—which many critics see as the basis for much of Fitzgerald's fiction—haunted Williams was through the resonances between his work and Fitzgerald's, especially *Gatsby* and *Streetcar.*

Works Cited

Adler, Thomas P. "When Ghosts Supplant Memories: Tennessee Williams' *Clothes for a Summer Hotel.*" *Southern Literary Journal* 19 (Spring 1987): 5–19.

Anderson, Hilton. "Tennessee Williams' *Clothes for a Summer Hotel:* Feminine Sensibilities and the Artist." *Publications of the Mississippi Philological Association* (1988): 1–8.

Bigsby, C. W. E. *A Critical Introduction to Twentieth-Century American Drama.* Vol. 2. *Williams/Miller/Albee.* Cambridge: Cambridge University Press, 1984.

Boxill, Roger. *Tennessee Williams.* London: Macmillan, 1987.

Brustein, Robert. "Robert Brustein on Theater: Advice for Broadway." *New Republic,* 3 May 1980, pp. 27–29.

Devlin, Albert J., ed. *Conversations with Tennessee Williams.* Jackson: University Press of Mississippi, 1986.

Devlin, Albert J., and Nancy Tischler, eds. *The Selected Letters of Tennessee Williams. Vol. 1, 1920–1945.* New York: New Directions, 2000.

Fitzgerald, F. Scott. *The Great Gatsby.* New York: Scribners, 1953.

Galligan, David. "Director José Quintero: Recollections of a Friendship." *Advocate,* 15 September 1983, pp. 42–43, 45–46.

Hays, Peter L. "Tennessee Williams 'Outs' Scott and Ernest." In *The Author as Character: Representing Historical Writers in Western Literature,* edited by Paul Franssen and Tom Hoenselaars. Madison, N.J.: Fairleigh Dickinson University Press, 1999.

Hemingway, Ernest. *A Moveable Feast.* New York: Scribners, 1964.

Kriebel, Charles. "An Afternoon in Gray with Tennessee Williams." *Dance Magazine* 12 (April 1980): 39, 76.

Kroll, Jack. "Slender Is the Night." *Newsweek,* April 7, 1980, p. 95.

Long, Robert Emmet. *The Achievement of "The Great Gatsby": F. Scott Fitzgerald, 1920–1925.* Lewisburg, Pa.: Bucknell University Press, 1979.

Mayfield, Sara. *Exiles from Paradise: Zelda and Scott Fitzgerald*. New York: Delacorte Press, 1971.

Milford, Nancy. *Zelda*. New York: Harper & Row, 1970.

Mizener, Arthur. *The Far Side of Paradise: A Biography of F. Scott Fitzgerald*. Boston: Houghton Mifflin, 1951.

Sandomir, Richard. "Tennessee Williams: On Age and Annoyance." *New York Sunday News*, March 23, 1980, Leisure Section, pp. 5, 12.

Silverman, Stephen M. "Tennessee Takes Aim at Zelda's Life." *New York Post*, January 12, 1980, pp. 26, 27.

Simon, John. "Damsels Inducing Distress." *New York*, April 7, 1980, pp. 82, 84.

Spoto, Donald. *The Kindness of Strangers: The Life of Tennessee Williams*. Boston: Little, Brown, 1985.

Weatherby, W. J. "Scott and Zelda Relive the Jazz Age." *London Sunday Times*, March 30, 1980, p. 38.

Williams, Tennessee. *Clothes for a Summer Hotel. The Theatre of Tennessee Williams*. Vol. 8. New York: New Directions, 1992.

———. *A Streetcar Named Desire*. New York: Signet, 1974.

———. *Where I Live: Selected Essays*. Edited by Christine R. Day and Bob Woods. New York: New Directions, 1978.

10

"It's Another Elvis Sighting, and . . . My God . . . He's with Tennessee Williams!"

Barbara M. Harris

"Fortunately, there are also a great many people who don't think of me as a bum; a lot of them think of me as Tennessee Ernie Ford!"
—Tennessee Williams, *Playboy*, 1973

Toward the end of his life, Tennessee Williams sensed that, despite the enormous extent of his published and produced dramatic work and his numerous professional prizes, he remained outside the general American culture, his very name confused with that of a country and western singer.[1] To some writers familiar with his work, even his acceptability within the academic literary world appeared questionable. The following, from *Evolving Texts: The Writing of Tennessee Williams,* the catalogue of a collection of Williams papers and artifacts published at the University of Delaware Library in 1988, illustrates this academic attitude:

> This approach reflects the uneasy niche Williams and his writing occupied in the scholarly world throughout his career. He was a playwright of emotions rather than ideas; his work, especially the films which were adapted from his plays, brought him a great deal of commercial success; finally, and perhaps most crucially, Tennessee Williams, the public figure, eventually overshadowed his own work. . . . the scholarly world came to regard him as a popular author. All of these factors have helped to diminish Williams's critical reputation as a writer. (5–6)

By the 1990s, however, things had begun to change drastically. Using elements of cultural theory to facilitate interpretation, I will argue here that at the millennium both Tennessee Williams and his works have risen phoenixlike to the status of popular American icons. Before I present evidence of Williams's rise, however, I will offer a brief review of reactions to Williams and his oeuvre during and after the 1960s. This review will be helpful, especially as it contrasts with the treatment of Williams today in both popular and specialized media.

"Deliberate cruelty is not forgivable," Blanche tells Stanley in *A Streetcar Named Desire*.[2] Tennessee Williams endured a lot of cruelty from writers who evaluated his works from the late 1960s until the time of Williams's death in 1983. Deliberate or not, many "critics" incorporated ad hominem attacks on Williams in reviews of his works or quarreled with a style he attempted to make organic to his purpose by incorporating words in their reviews like "silly" and "trivial," words too amorphous to be enlightening. Anthony West, later in the same review from which I quoted above, says, "There is a sad moment in the career of an artist of the second rank, a point of no return, beyond which his work ceases to develop."[3] Such comments, arguably, have no place in a productive discourse of "literature and theater," in which West says he is participating;[4] and therefore are conscious in their cruelty. Even before these words, written in 1963, Williams found himself censured by satire.

Probably because of the popularity of 1950s films made from his work, the second annual edition of the comic book *The Worst from Mad* satirized Tennessee Williams in 1959. In "Sin-Doll Ella," the comic book juxtaposed the Cinderella story with the world of Williams. Featured in addition to the notorious "Baby Doll" were caricatures of Burl Ives as "Big Daddy," Marlon Brando as "Stanley Kowalski," and Anna Magnani as "Serafina delle Rose." Nonetheless, though academia was slow to publish literary criticism of Williams, 1961 saw three excellent books of serious Williams criticism and scholarship: Nancy M. Tischler's *Tennessee Williams: Rebellious Puritan;* Signi Falk's *Tennessee Williams;* and Benjamin Nelson's *Tennessee Williams: The Man and His Work*. The tide of critical acceptance, at first so promising, however, was about to recede. On December 28, 1961, Williams's *The Night of the Iguana* opened on Broadway, later winning Williams his fourth and last New York Drama Critics'

Circle Award. The equally successful film version appeared in 1964. Though other Williams plays would open on Broadway, *The Night of the Iguana* represented Williams's last successful Broadway play, and the film version was the last Williams film to be well received by the critics.

Though Williams, after 1961 and until his death in 1983, appeared to have a certain amount of celebrity, especially on the East Coast, he seems to have dropped from the general cultural scene. Furthermore, with a few outstanding academic exceptions during the 1970s, such as Ruby Cohn's fine work in *Dialogue in American Drama* and Esther Merle Jackson's *The Broken World of Tennessee Williams,* "scholarly investigations of Williams and his work dwindled to almost nothing in the early 1980s. . . . Critical literary attention having dwindled, [he] was at the mercy of theater critics and reviewers in the popular press who attacked him regularly during the 1970s and 1980s."[5] In the academy's classrooms, Williams seems to have fared even less well. From 1964 to 1974, in the English department at the University of Missouri in Columbia, Missouri—chosen not because it is necessarily representative but because it was the university Williams attended from 1929 to 1933—an upperclass/graduate seminar in modern drama used as the textbook *The Dramatic Moment,* edited by Eugene M. Waith of Yale University. The undergraduate courses in the introduction to world drama used, first, *Drama,* edited by Otto Reinert of the University of Washington, and then *Types of Drama: Plays and Essays,* edited by Sylvan Barnet of Tufts, Morton Berman of Boston University, and William Burto of Lowell State College, who also edited *a Dictionary of Literary, Dramatic, and Cinematic Terms.* None of these texts includes a selection from Tennessee Williams, though each has work by Edward Albee. The absence of Williams's work from the curriculum at the University of Missouri at any time is amazing, especially when one considers that originals of his earliest known plays, *Beauty Is the Word,* and *Hot Milk at Three in the Morning* (later revised and renamed *Moony's Kid Don't Cry*) were written while Williams attended the University of Missouri and are archived at the university's Ellis Library. Such a situation in the classroom appears to serve as further evidence during the time after the mid-1960s of the "uneasy niche Williams and his writing occupied in the scholarly world." The mid-1990s, however, brought tremendous changes; and suddenly Tennessee Williams and his works appeared everywhere in the media's reflections of public consciousness.

Since the death of Tennessee Williams on February 24 or 25, 1983, and especially after the death of his somewhat difficult literary coexecutor, the Lady Maria St. Just, on February 15, 1994, academic writing activity has burgeoned; new film treatments of the plays have appeared, and new productions have been mounted. The first volume of Williams's authorized biography by Lyle Leverich, *Tom: The Unknown Tennessee Williams*, appeared in 1995. The first volume of the collected Tennessee Williams letters appeared in 2000, and his journals are also being prepared for publication. The flood of new Williams literary criticism has finally included sensitive and adulatory work with the many plays completed after the mid-1960s.[6] New Directions, Williams's lifelong publishing house, has begun publishing early manuscripts found among Williams's papers, such as *The Notebook of Trigorin: A Free Adaptation of Anton Chekhov's "The Sea Gull"* in 1997, *Not About Nightingales* in 1998, and *Spring Storm* in 1999. Williams's unproduced play *Not About Nightingales* had languished among his other papers at the Harry Ransom Humanities Research Center of the University of Texas at Austin, until 1998–1999, when productions were mounted first in London and then in New York. The New York production garnered six Tony Award nominations, including one for best new play, more than sixty years after the play had been written. (Only the Tony for Best Scenic Design went to *Nightingales*, unfortunately.) Though an attempt had been made to publish a Tennessee Williams literary journal beginning in 1979, no journal at all was in operation between 1983 and 1989. The premier issue of the *Tennessee Williams Literary Journal*, edited by W. Kenneth Holditch, appeared in spring 1989; and *The Tennessee Williams Annual Review*, edited by Robert Bray, began in 1998.

In *Time* magazine for February 3, 1997, Richard Zoglin, in an article entitled "The Kindness of Foreigners" (72), writes that in the early 1980s, Howard Davies, associate director of the Royal Shakespeare Company, had unsuccessfully tried to promote Williams revivals. In 1997, in contrast, London producers were suddenly presenting several plays by Williams as well as plays by Arthur Miller and Edward Albee. Lauren Bacall played the "Princess" of *Sweet Bird of Youth*, and Sir Peter Hall, director of England's National Theatre, imported Jessica Lange to duplicate her 1992 Broadway performance as "Blanche" in *A Streetcar Named Desire* with an all-English cast that included Toby Stephens, the son of English actress Maggie Smith, as "Stanley." Zoglin quotes David Thacker, the director in residence of the Royal Shakespeare Company, who justified the wave of American theater, especially Williams, by saying, "We'd have to look back to Shakespeare to see drama at that level" (72). Thacker's mention of Shakespeare may have been more apt than he realized. Williams, his famous characters and their equally famous words, like no other author or dramas in English with the exception of Shakespeare, are everywhere in America: in the academy, in positive critical discourse, on television, in the popular press, on Broadway, on Off and Off Off Broadway, in advertising, and just below the conscious level of the cultural public, which constitutes the prime requirement in the definition of cultural icon. And like Shakespeare, Williams now has a ballet—specifically, with a film score by Alex North; a short opera of "Lord Byron's Love Letter," adapted and performed by Raffaello de Banfield; an opera of *Summer and Smoke,* composed by Lee Hoiby; and the new three-act opera of *Streetcar* composed by André Previn, which premiered in San Francisco in December 1998.

Anyone who doubts such iconology did not pay attention to televised news in the fall of 1998, when then First Lady Hillary Rodham Clinton coyly dropped her eyes upon returning from a trip to India with her daughter and answered a reporter's inquiry about the success of her trip by saying, "I have always depended upon the kindness of strangers." Surely Mrs. Clinton would have no desire to incorporate, by poetic device, Blanche's personality into her own. In the 1990s, Blanche's famous exit line has simply fastened itself to the tip of the public tongue. In 1991, Bette Bourne, Paul Shaw, Peggy Shaw, and Lois Weaver wrote their Obie Award–winning play *Belle Reprieve,* whose title, of course, intentionally echoes Blanche's plantation, "Belle Reve," in *Streetcar. Belle Reprieve* does not simply satirize Williams as, for example, the *Mad* comic book did; the play takes a serious look at the relationship between gender and power in Western life and theater. The authors use a farcical mixture of cross-dressing and cross-gendering, often in layers, in a treatment that also explores the gender and sexual tensions that many critics have found in the major characters in *A Streetcar Named Desire,* both in film and stage versions. The references to the original lines include, in act 1:

BLANCHE: (*From inside box*) I've always depended on the strange-ness of strangers.

. . . .

STELLA: Look, I'm supposed to wander around in a state of nar-cotized sensuality. That's my part. (*Blanche and Stanley speak simultaneously from inside the two largest boxes*)

BLANCHE: You didn't see, Miss Stella, see what I saw, the long parade to the graveyard. The mortgage on the house, death is expensive, Miss Stella, death is expensive.

STANLEY: Is that so? You don't say, hey Stella wasn't we happy before she showed up. Didn't we see those colored lights.

STELLA: And anyway, it's too late. It's already started.

STANLEY: Hey Stella! (*Coming out of stage right box*)

STELLA: Don't holler at me like that, Stanley.

STANLEY: Hey Stella, Stella baby! Catch!

STELLA: What!

STANLEY: Meat. (992)

This playscript is no simple postmodern pastiche of Williams; the authors treat *Streetcar* with respect. The play functions as a canoni-cal backdrop against which MITCH ("a fairy disguised as a man"); STELLA ("a woman disguised as a woman"); STANLEY (a butch lesbian); and BLANCHE ("a man in a dress") suggest enigmatic questions con-cerning the visible signifiers of sexual orientation and whether or not gender is simply a costume ball wherein each attendee masks important aspects of identity.

In our culture, however, television measures the pervasiveness of an icon as no other medium can. Susan Harris, creator, writer, and producer of the popular early 1990s network television sitcom *The Golden Girls,* felt a popular acceptance of the Williams canon so in-tensely that the television show frequently constitutes a crossword puzzle of Williams signifiers. The sitcom involves three main char-acters, all widows or divorcees, now living together in Miami, Florida:

1. DOROTHY: A wise-cracking, well-read teacher of English and lit-erature. ("Dorothea" is a teacher/character from Williams's play, *A Lovely Sunday for Crève Coeur.*)

2. ROSE: A naive, simple-minded but kind, good-hearted midwest-ern woman who "suppresses" the sexual talk of the others but yearns for a relationship with a significant other. (Rose, of course, is the

name of several Williams characters but is, more important, the name of his beloved sister. Rose Isabel Williams, eventually the victim of a prefrontal lobotomy in 1943, as Williams himself said, had torn "herself apart mentally and physically by those repressions imposed upon her by Miss Edwina's monolithic Puritanism") (*Memoirs* 151). In the television series, Rose's mother is named, "Alma," Williams's heroine from *Summer and Smoke,* and his favorite female character as well as, in his opinion, "the best female portrait I have drawn in a play."[7]

3. BLANCHE: A woman who grew up on a southern plantation, covets trinkets and clothes, and continues in middle age a nymphomaniac romp that, she tells us in one of the episodes, began in high school because "women just mature faster in the south. I think it's the heat." This Blanche's younger brother, interestingly, is gay.

Supporting characters of note include:

1. SOPHIA: Dorothy's mother, an Italian immigrant who tells at least two Italian stories or folktales, mostly her own fabrications, in each episode. Of course, Williams set several of his works either in Italy (*The Roman Spring of Mrs. Stone*) or among Italian immigrants (*The Rose Tattoo*). Williams loved the Italian people; he found them warm and refreshingly honest. Like Williams, Sophia is a purveyor of conscious illusion within a real world.

2. Blanche's father: She refers to him as "Big Daddy." ("Big Momma" has died before the series begins.) In one episode, "Big Daddy," who ironically is short and slight, arrives at Blanche's door with the announcement that he has decided to leave the plantation to become a folk singer. These references, of course, are to *Cat on a Hot Tin Roof* and to the folksinger, Burl Ives, who played "Big Daddy" both in the Broadway production and in the film. In other episodes of the sitcom, we see "Big Daddy" achieving the company of a different lady each night of his visits with Blanche, reminiscent of his namesake's promise to strike out and find a good woman with whom to party after he thinks he has gotten a reprieve from death.

3. STANLEY: This Stanley (Dorothy's ex-husband), no longer sexy or macho in his golden years, wears an ill-fitting toupee; and the only feather boas or rhinestone tiaras he will throw around are what remains of the inventory of his bankrupt novelties business.

In one episode, Blanche's adult daughter, who approaches middle age with neither boyfriend nor husband, decides that she wants to start a family with the help of an artificial insemination clinic. Blanche is horrified. Eventually Blanche's roommates persuade her to visit the clinic at least. While the four women stand huddled in apprehension, a doctor joins them to explain the procedure that Blanche's daughter will experience. At one point, Blanche runs from the room, crying out "impregnated by a stranger!" When the doctor asks what Blanche's problem is, Dorothy responds that she has no idea; Blanche, after all, "has always depended on the kindness of strangers."

A later episode finds the three women attempting to win money on a television quiz show named, "Grab That Dough!" The penultimate question, "What famous Tennessee Williams play was filmed and directed by Paul Newman?" is appropriately answered by Rose, who announces proudly the name of the play that constituted, in part, a love letter to her namesake from her famous brother: *The Glass Menagerie*. In another episode worth noting, Blanche, about to go on a date with "Dirk," a much younger man, says, "I'm going to live forever." Dorothy comments, "Not outside an institution."

Dorothy, the teacher, brings home an "intellectual author friend" in another episode. The author friend simply cannot remember Blanche's name and continually calls her "Madge." This reference recalls "Madge" from William Inge's play *Picnic*, and the "Blanche-Madge" confusion alludes to the Williams-Inge rivalry that occurred during the 1950s. Williams befriended William Inge in December 1944, when Williams had briefly returned home to St. Louis. At that time, Inge was writing for the (now defunct) *Star-Times* as drama and music critic and had arranged to interview Williams. The two men found they had much in common. Both were homosexuals; both had lived in Columbia, Missouri, though at different times; and Inge, as he finally admitted, was an aspiring playwright. Williams became Inge's early mentor and introduced him to Williams's own agent, Audrey Wood. Shortly after Williams's successes with *The Glass Menagerie* (1945) and *A Streetcar Named Desire* (1947), Inge's own star rose harmoniously with *Come Back Little Sheba* (1950). Then came 1953. "Blanche" had been a hit in *Streetcar*, and Williams was elected to the National Institute of Arts and Letters. Inge's "Madge" in *Picnic*, produced by the Theatre Guild, opened on

Broadway on February 19, 1953, to rave notices. Twenty days later, Williams's *Camino Real* opened to mixed notices. Williams had previously endured an abysmal failure with the Theatre Guild involving his play *Battle of Angels;* and now he had another "failure" with *Camino,* while Inge had an award-winning hit. Licking that wound, Williams was also aware that his failed *Angels,* which he was still revising, shared the same mythological structure as the successful *Picnic,* that is, the Orpheus myth. Little doubt exists that Williams was jealous of Inge at the time. But little doubt also exists that, a half century after their first appearances, anyone would seriously confuse Blanche with Madge.

The name of Tennessee Williams was heard ever more frequently through the 1990s from the little box of mass entertainment. At the 1997 Tony Awards ceremony, for example, actor Rip Torn, who has appeared in several Williams plays and movies, included Williams in a short tribute. No other playwright, except those directly involved in the nominated plays, was mentioned that evening. In 1998, the movie of *Streetcar Named Desire* was among the movies named on television as The Hundred Best Movies In History as selected by the American Film Institute. Shortly thereafter, that most "mass" of mass publications, *TV Guide,* included *Streetcar* among its picks of the "Fifty Greatest Movies on TV and Video." Ranking the movie at number twenty-five, this description went into millions of homes:

> The performances in Elia Kazan's landmark adaption of Tennessee Williams's play remain among the most electric in American film. The brutish Stanley Kowalski reminds us how Marlon Brando became Marlon Brando. And Vivien Leigh's Blanche DuBois is a heartbreak, and not just because she evokes an aging Scarlett O'Hara; of all the screen actresses who played one of Williams's doomed heroines, Leigh best personified the fate that befalls fragile souls in a world of Stanleys. Censors forced Williams to alter the play's ending, but "Streetcar" is still a steamy hothouse of a movie (22).

In the 1997–1998 television season, allusions to Tennessee Williams occurred in the extremely popular, Emmy Award–winning sitcom *Frasier.* The writers on *Frasier* use a device borrowed from silent films; they flash sayings on the screen between scenes, a device also reminiscent of the noteboard signs Williams first intended for *The Glass Menagerie*. In one episode about Frasier's tendency to hypochondria, a tendency shared by Williams, the scene-dividing phrases included: "Cat Fight on a Hot Tin Roof," "Suddenly This Summer," "The Night of the I Wanna," and "The Bath Menagerie." Niles, Frasier's brother, complains at one point about the heat, saying he feels "like a tortured character in a Tennessee Williams play." Niles also mentions that his wife has a slight webbing between her toes that "makes her feel self-conscious," suggesting, of course, Laura's slight limp in *The Glass Menagerie*. Over fifty years after its Broadway opening, *Glass Menagerie* surfaces in the minds of television sitcom writers; and they seem assured that their audience will connect with their references. In another episode, Niles addresses Roz, a lead female character, "Like in that great play, *A Streetcar Named Desire*, when the brutish Stanley says to the ultra-refined Blanche, 'We've had this date with each other from the beginning.'"

Williams allusions have also embellished television scripts in such shows as *Northern Exposure, Magnum, P.I.*, and an entire episode of *The Simpsons*. In *Beverly Hills 90210*, a nighttime soap opera for twenty-somethings, a character conspicuously displays a scholarly book with Williams's picture on the cover in an attempt to appear interested in serious theater. (The book is Al Devlin's *Conversations with Tennessee Williams;* Devlin gave the sitcom producers permission to use it.) In an episode of *Wings*, Lowell, one of the two male leads, meets a man who supposedly cannot be beaten at "Simon Says." Lowell challenges him. The man says, "Simon says do the Stanley scene from *Streetcar*"; Lowell grabs the flaps of his coveralls, closes his eyes and with his head up, cries, "Stella!"[8] Premiering in the 1998–1999 season, the sitcom *Maggie Winters* includes in its first episode a reference to Maggie as a "cat on a hot tin roof." In *Will and Grace,* premiering the same season, Will says to Grace during an argument, "Hello Blanche; they'll tell you all about it at the nervous hospital." This last script, interestingly, neither identified *A Streetcar Named Desire* nor Williams anywhere in the television show; apparently these writers felt confident that the name "Blanche" alone was sufficient allusion for television viewers. In an episode of *Murder, She Wrote*, Mrs. Venable (the actual name of the mother in Williams's *Suddenly Last Summer)* arrives at a steamy and decaying island estate with her author son. In another episode, a female playwright, who only allows her current plays to be produced Off Broadway, arrives at a plantation near Savannah. She has "let her personal feelings toward family take over" in her work and now has "a lot to pay for from the critics"; the script writers accurately summarized the problems Williams had with the drama critics during the late 1960s and 1970s. Even television psychiatrists apparently use Williams as a way of omitting technical terminology from their instant diagnosis. On *The Montel Williams Show,* March 5, 1999, a Dr. Halpern, in discussing multiple personality disorder, said, "In other words, when you're feeling sexy, you're Blanche. Later, when you're having trouble with your partner, as in Tennessee Williams' great masterpiece, you leave your home and rely on the kindness of strangers."

Popular television and screen stars of the 1990s may still aspire to do Shakespeare some day, but it seems that more and more of them also aspire to do Williams. Nathan Lane, Broadway comedian, popular star of Mike Nichols's hit movie *The Birdcage* and television pitchman, told an *Esquire* interviewer in May 1996, that his "dream" is "to play Tom in *The Glass Menagerie*" (Blum 90). In June of 2000, Lindsay Wagner of *The Bionic Woman* fame, on the television program *Intimate Portrait,* attributed a change in the direction of her life to her reading of Williams's *This Property Is Condemned.* The same month, Katie Brown, of *Next Door with Katie Brown,* told her viewers that she first fell in love with southern gardens when she fell in love with Tennessee Williams's *Suddenly Last Summer.* Actual recent appearances in Williams's plays include those by movie and television stars Alec Baldwin and Ann-Margret, somewhat of an American icon in her own right. Even the now burlesque actor Leslie Nielsen talks about his dream of doing Williams in his 1993 book spoof *The Naked Truth.*

Though public broadcasting programs about Williams the man and author had been seen by limited audiences in the past,[9] Williams took his place beside the other literary giants when, in 1998, he was included in the venerated Arts and Entertainment Biography series. Furthermore, Williams's place as America's greatest playwright appears secure; in 1996–1997, at least five of his plays were presented on New York stages: *The Glass Menagerie, The Night of the Iguana, The Rose Tattoo, Suddenly Last Summer, Summer and Smoke, Kingdom of Earth,* and *Red Devil Battery Sign.* Off Broadway and Off

Off Broadway continue to produce Williams plays as well as plays about Williams, for example, the Red Light District's production of *Adjoining Trances,* by Randy Buck, which covers the friendship and careers of Williams and Carson McCullers through a series of imaginary conversations.

Tennessee Williams has indisputably become an American cultural icon, and like it or not, the unassailable test of iconology remains American mass advertising. Williams's iconic status is nowhere more apparent than in a 1999 television commercial for Pella Windows. It closes with a macho male model, complete with torn undershirt, yelling, "Pella! Pella!" Let us not overlook the print media. In *U.S. News & World Report* (December 28/January 4, 1999), a full-page Morgan Stanley Dean Witter ad begins with a headline in fifty-point type, "'You can be young without money, but you can't be old without it.'—*Tennessee Williams."* The quotation, of course, is Maggie's statement from *Cat on a Hot Tin Roof* (*The Theatre of Tennessee Williams* 3: 54).

International evidence of Williams's cultural influence can be found in the 1999 Australian film *Babe: Pig in the City.* In this film, Blanche is a pink poodle; Stanley is a pit bull; and Stanley is left with the puppies after their misalliance—each one a miniature pit bull with one tuft of pink hair atop his head. In 2000, America's Academy Award for best foreign picture went to Spain's *All About My Mother,* directed by Pedro Almodovar. The gender-bending movie's central metaphor revolves around Williams's *A Streetcar Named Desire:* the parents of a son who is killed early in the movie, met while appearing in Williams's play, and the now grief-stricken mother becomes a friend of a lesbian currently playing Blanche. By what process does a writer such as Tennessee Williams become such a pervasive cultural icon?

Cultural theory uses labeled categories to classify personages, ideas, and writings that invade the general public consciousness; these labels, with time, sometimes overlap. The labels "celebrity" and "legend" both usually involve personages as well as an admixture of truth and pretenses about the people involved. Celebrity, unlike legend, however, tends to be short-lived, usually generation-specific. Legend can continue for several generations—often beyond the death of the person so labeled—and even enter the culture's folklore. In the cultural medium of film, for example, 1920s film star

Ruth Chatterton had celebrity; James Dean has legend. Sometimes, a personage who had celebrity becomes legend, as did England's Princess Diana. Icons, unlike either a celebrity or a legend, usually entail ideas, words, and/or personifications. Like a celebrity, however, a pop icon is usually short-lived and, also like a celebrity, has usually been driven into the public consciousness through the efforts of third parties, for example, publicity agents or advertising copywriters. A cultural icon, contrarily, often enters the public consciousness slowly and has a long incubation period before it suddenly seems to engage vast numbers of the population. One explanation of this long incubation for a cultural icon is that, unlike a popular icon, it is progressive rather than instant (like a pop icon) or regressive (like a legend) in that it often quietly signals the beginnings of a change in the cultural direction. Examples of pop icons are legion: "the flapper" from the 1920s, the ubiquitous "Kilroy" from the 1940s (whom Williams used as his "everyman" in *Camino Real*), Elvis Presley (who has probably now achieved the status of pop icon legend) at the end of the sexually repressive 1950s and "Dirty Harry" getting tough on crime in the 1980s. The Ernest Hemingway "code hero" exemplifies the progressive growth of a cultural icon. Though Hemingway was a literary name from the late 1920s and even subsequently achieved celebrity, it was the machismo element in his personage and writings that began to incubate as idea in the collectivist 1930s, signaling the changes American culture would make in the postwar years when men were men, kings of their castles and involved with other men in the manly and individual pursuits of hunting and fishing. Hemingway's code hero had become a cultural icon; and his creator's name was recognized by undergraduate students prior to any literature classes. Cultural icons, unlike pop icons, usually remain in the public consciousness beyond the century in which their creators first published their words and ideas, beyond even the period in which they became cultural icons.

Tennessee Williams may not finally reach Presleyan proportions, but I hope that I have shown that "sightings" have been plentiful. As with Shakespeare and Hemingway, the familiarity of Williams's name to students entering American literature classes around the country eases the jobs of teacher/researcher/critics. The more culturally iconic his stature, the more publishing houses and magazines will show interest in Tennessee Williams criticism and biography. What this mass recognition of Williams signals about our changing culture will take time to identify, but at the very least, now more than ever, Tennessee Williams belongs to all of us. And few of us would currently confuse Williams with Tennessee Ernie Ford.

Notes

1. I witnessed the same phenomenon when, in 1969, a high school principal responded to an English teacher's request to take her students to hear Tennessee Williams. "Why," the principal asked, "would you want to take your students to hear a country and western singer?" My epigraph is taken from Devlin, *Conversations with Tennessee Williams,* 240.

2. Williams, *Theatre of Tennessee Williams,* 1: 397.

3. Crandell, ed., *The Critical Response to Tennessee Williams,* 211–12.

4. Ibid., 212.

5. Martin, *Critical Essays on Tennessee Williams,* 8.

6. See, for example, Ruby Cohn, "Late Tennessee Williams," 286–93.

7. Williams, *Memoirs,* 138.

8. I have now seen the episode, courtesy of the producers; but the occurrence was originally brought to my attention by a student who became so intrigued by Williams from this allusion that she read all the published volumes of *The Theatre of Tennessee Williams.*

9. See, for example, PBS's *Lion of the American Stage* in 1995.

Works Cited

Barnet, Sylvan, Morton Berman, and William Burto, eds. *Types of Drama: Plays and Essays.* Boston: Little, Brown, 1972.

Blum, David. "Enter Laughing." *Esquire,* May 1996, pp. 87–91.

Bourne, Bette, Paul Shaw, Peggy Shaw, and Lois Weaver. *Belle Reprieve.* In *Modern Drama,* edited by W. B. Worthen. New York: Harcourt Brace, 1995.

Bray, Robert, ed. *The Tennessee Williams Annual Review* 1 (1998).

Cohn, Ruby. "Late Tennessee Williams." In *Critical Essays on Tennessee Williams,* edited by Robert A. Martin. New York: G. K. Hall, 1997.

Crandell, George W., ed. *The Critical Response to Tennessee Williams.* Westport, Conn.: Greenwood Press, 1996.

Devlin, Albert J., ed. *Conversations with Tennessee Williams.* Jackson: University Press of Mississippi, 1998.

Falk, Signi. *Tennessee Williams.* Boston: Twayne, 1961.

"Fifty Greatest Movies on TV and Video." *TV Guide,* 8 August 1998, pp. 14–40.

Holditch, W. Kenneth, ed. *Tennessee Williams Literary Journal* 1 (Spring 1989).

Jackson, Esther Merle. *The Broken World of Tennessee Williams.* Madison: University Press of Wisconsin, 1965.

Leverich, Lyle. *Tom: The Unknown Tennessee Williams.* New York: Crown, 1995.

Martin, Robert A. "Introduction." In *Critical Essays on Tennessee Williams,* edited by Robert A. Martin. New York: G. K. Hall, 1997.

Murray, Timothy D. *Evolving Texts: The Writing of Tennessee Williams.* Newark: University of Delaware Library, 1998. (Catalog of an exhibition at the Hugh M. Morris Library)

Nelson, Benjamin. *Tennessee Williams: The Man and His Work.* New York: Obolensky, 1961.

Reinert, Otto, ed. *Drama: An Introductory Anthology.* Boston: Little, Brown, 1964.

"Sin-Doll Ella." In *The Worst from Mad.* 2d annual ed. New York: E. C. Publications, 1959.

Tischler, Nancy M. *Tennessee Williams: Rebellious Puritan.* New York: Citadel, 1961.

Waith, Eugene M., ed. *The Dramatic Moment.* Englewood Cliffs, N.J.: Prentice-Hall, 1967.

Williams, Tennessee. *Cat on a Hot Tin Roof.* In *The Theatre of Tennessee Williams, vol. 3.* New York: New Directions, 1971.

——. *Memoirs.* Garden City, N.Y.: Doubleday, 1975.

——. *Not About Nightingales.* New York: New Directions, 1998.

——. *The Notebook of Trigorin: A Free Adaptation of Anton Chekhov's "The Sea Gull."* New York: New Directions, 1997.

——. *Spring Storm.* New York: New Directions, 1999.

——. *The Theatre of Tennessee Williams.* vol 1. New York: New Directions, 1971.

Zoglin, Richard. "The Kindness of Foreigners." *Time,* 3 February 1997, pp. 72–73.

11

Tennessee Williams in New Orleans

W. Kenneth Holditch

In January 1979 Tennessee Williams was in New Orleans for his only public appearance in the city he had often called his "spiritual home." He was staying at 1014 Dumaine St., an elegant nineteenth-century Creole townhouse, which had several years before been divided into six apartments. Tennessee had bought the residence in 1962 but he did not move into the main apartment until 1972. After that, during his infrequent visits, it was his residence, the only one he had ever owned in the city. The day before his performance in 1979, I went with Don Lee Keith, a longtime friend of the playwright, to meet Tennessee and Robert Carroll, his secretary-companion at the time, at Marti's restaurant. It was a favorite dining spot of Tennessee's for several reasons: it was diagonally across the street from his house, and the chefs would prepare for him his favorite dishes, including a variety of seafood as well as vegetables cooked in the southern style, bacon fat and all. He also enjoyed sitting on the second-floor balcony some afternoons playing poker, which he had learned during rehearsals of *The Glass Menagerie*.

After lunch, the four of us strolled across Rampart Street to the Theater for the Performing Arts, where the next night's program would take place. Along the way, Tennessee asked me about the status of real estate in the French Quarter, and when I told him that prices were currently on the rise, he chuckled and, in that deep southern drawl he had clung to all his life, said, "You know, I'm just like a sly old fox. I've bought property wherever I went." He commented on what he saw as the unpleasant changes to the Quarter that had been occurring for the past decade or more, including the increasing sleaziness of Bourbon Street, the loss of permanent residents to businesses, and the influx of tourists that made walking through the streets of some areas increasingly difficult. He seemed almost to echo Eloi Duvenet, a character from his early one-act play *Auto-Da-Fé,* who ranted to his mother about the corruption of the area. Indeed, Tennessee's own mother, Miss Edwina, had written in her memoirs that in his early days in the Big Easy, he became "acquainted with a new kind of life in the French Quarter, one of wild drinking, sexual promiscuity and abnormality" (103). It was a region, as he writes in his short story "The Yellow Bird," where it was "not necessary to go into a good time house to have a good time" (207). Without Miss Edwina's knowledge, Tom Williams had adapted rather quickly to that easygoing life style, and now, ironically, forty years later almost to the day of his first arrival in the city, he seemed to be echoing her puritanical opinions.

The next evening, I introduced Tennessee Williams to a large assemblage that had gathered in the theater despite one of those sudden New Orleans deluges that can fill the streets with six to twelve inches of water in a matter of minutes. He read his own poetry, his short story entitled "Man Bring This Up Road," and some verses of Oliver Evans, an old friend and former Tulane professor who had been diagnosed with a brain tumor. Following the reading he was interviewed by Don Lee Keith, whose initial question was "Mr. Williams, what first brought you to New Orleans?" Tennessee's unhesitating response was "St. Louis, a city I loathe!" What the playwright probably disliked in the city in which he had been reared was not only the place itself, very much at odds with his early years in a southern small-town environment, but also the unhappy family situation in which he had lived since childhood. New Orleans came to represent for him, if not the paradise of his youth, an essential liberating element for the developing artist.

After the readings and the interview, a small group of us accompanied Tennessee across Rampart Street to the very popular Restaurant Jonathan, whose owners hosted a dinner in his honor. In the course of that leisurely meal—Tennessee was much more relaxed than he had been before his performance—I inquired of the playwright how long he would be in town, and he responded, "Not long. Carnival season is upon us. Too many people and too much noise." Later the conversation turned to literature, with his old friend Artis

Blackburn stating that she did not like Flannery O'Connor. Tennessee and I agreed that we did, and then he turned to me and inquired, "Do you read any of the northern writers?" When I responded that I liked John Updike and Philip Roth, he said that although he liked Roth, he was not familiar with Updike's work, then drew back, shaking his head, and announced, "But I can't read Saul Bellow." I told him that I had problems with Bellow myself, and Tennessee, an amused glint in his eye, said, "Well, there you have it!"

In a matter of days, he had departed for Key West, and I was only to see him once more, in 1983, when I stood in front of the house talking to Lyle Leverich, who would become the author's major biographer, and Tennessee waved to us from a second-floor window. A few weeks later, Tennessee died in a hotel room in New York, not, as he had wished in his *Memoirs*, "in my big brass bed in my apartment on Dumaine Street in New Orleans, which has so many wonderful memories" (248). The final visit had occurred forty-four years after he first got off a bus in the city that was to become the source of his creative freedom.

A combination of serendipitous circumstances led Thomas Lanier Williams to flee St. Louis in 1938 and head south to New Orleans, a decision that was to prove momentous in shaping his life and his career. The situation in the Williams home was intolerable for him, living as he had to in close proximity to a father whose attitude toward his sensitive and artistic older son was little short of contempt, hearing the almost constant bickering of his parents, and watching in pained helplessness as his beloved sister Rose slipped further and further away from him and disappeared into the "dragon-country" of her growing hysteria.

When his attempt to acquire a position with the WPA Writers' Project in Chicago failed, the direction Thomas Lanier Williams chose to move, not surprisingly, was south, to the area of the country where, he told Don Lee Keith in a January 1978 interview, he found life more congenial. It was December 1938, when, hoping to join Lyle Saxon's WPA team, he arrived in New Orleans, "like a migratory bird," as he said in a 1982 interview with Eric Paulsen, in full flight from St. Louis and hoping to find a better climate for his life and work. The shabby but genteel old French Quarter, at that time virtually unaffected by progress and modernization, was still more or less a self-contained village heavily populated by Italian,

Sicilian, and black families. By the 1920s it had become a gathering place for writers and artists, where cheap rents, good food, free-flowing liquor, and a Latin lifestyle at odds with that in most of the rest of the country were powerfully appealing. How very different Williams's career might have been had he remained in Chicago instead of moving to the city that proved to be a major liberating factor in his life and his work. Edwina Williams wrote of her son that when he set out on that journey, "I had the feeling this time, in one sense, he was never coming back to me" (98). Those words proved to be prophetic, in both a real sense and a metaphorical one, for never again would Tom live at home for long periods of time, and when next he visited his mother, the young man was hardly the son who had left the shelter of her nest. For the rest of Tennessee's life, New Orleans was to remain a place in which he felt free, an easygoing environment where he would write and enjoy the leisurely life of this most foreign North American city. Of the places he was to live from that point on, it was New Orleans that elicited such praise as this remark: "If I can be said to have a home, it is in New Orleans where I've lived off and on since 1938 and which has provided me with more material than any other part of the country" (qtd. in Tischler, 62).

When Thomas Lanier Williams arrived in the French Quarter in December 1938, he presented himself to Odette and Knute Heldner, artists who knew friends of his in St. Louis and who graciously gave him shelter. They showed him around the Quarter, introduced him to writers and artists, and helped him find a dwelling place: on 1 January 1939 he moved into a roominghouse at 722 Toulouse Street. A 1940 photograph of the three-story Creole townhouse shows it in a romantic state of decay, a stuccoed building with vines growing over one corner and a cast iron second-floor balcony. Williams's third-floor room, for which he paid ten dollars a month, opened onto a dormer window, while the other room with a matching dormer was occupied by Eloi Bordelon, an artist who became a close friend of the author. His mother notes in her memoirs that Tom wrote to his grandparents, Rev. and Mrs. Walter Dakin, that the house was owned and operated by a "lovely Mississippi lady" (101), but apparently there were three landladies, operating two adjoining houses, who had, the writer told his mother on another occasion, seen better days and now lived amid their antiques on the second floor at 722 Toulouse. They were such excellent cooks, his mother writes, that the young writer persuaded them to open a restaurant for which he provided the motto ("Meals for a Quarter in the Quarter"), which he hand printed on cards that he distributed in the area, later returning to work as waiter and cashier (101).

In *Remember Me to Tom,* Miss Edwina also records her son's account of a melodramatic episode that occurred in the boardinghouse. One of the landladies, a Mrs. Anderson, who, according to Tom Williams, "had a hard time adjusting herself to the Bohemian spirit of the Vieux Carré," created havoc when, after the first-floor tenant had ignored her complaints about the noise from a party he was giving, poured boiling water through holes in the floor, an act that the young author witnessed. She was charged, Tom wrote to his mother, with "malicious mischief and disturbing the peace" and her case was tried the next night at the Third Precinct police station on Chartres Street. Tom Williams was called as a witness, and when asked by the judge whether Mrs. Anderson had indeed perpetrated the act with which she was charged, cleverly evaded the question by responding that he thought "it . . . highly improbable that any lady would do such a thing!" (qtd. in *Remember* 102). His evasion probably spared his being asked to vacate his room at 722 Toulouse, but embedded within it is certainly a gentle rebuke for Mrs. Anderson.

The incident produced several significant results: a similar episode is described in *A Streetcar Named Desire,* and the pouring of the water and the subsequent trial became climactic scenes in *Vieux Carré,* the 1976 "memory play" in which he recreated the dramatic incidents of those important months in his life. (In the play, the photographer's party is transformed into an orgy, and when the guests flee into the street after the pouring of the water, they are nude.) In addition, as a result of the episode, Tennessee made the acquaintance of Mary Rose Bradford, a guest at the photographer's party, whose dress was ruined by the water; she lived with her husband, Roark Bradford, in a Creole cottage across the street from the roominghouse. Roark Bradford, the night city editor for the *Times-Picayune,* had made a name for himself writing books in black dialect, including his most popular work, *Ol' Man Adam an' His Chillun* (1928), adapted by Bradford and Marc Connolly into the long-running Broadway hit *Green Pastures.* The couple, whose home was a gathering place for writers—William Faulkner, Sinclair Lewis, and

John Steinbeck were among those who enjoyed their hospitality—
introduced Williams to Sam Byrd, a visiting producer, who, upon
hearing that Williams was an aspiring dramatist, volunteered to
read some of his work. Characteristically, Tom, his mother writes in
Remember Me to Tom, "had nothing to show him," since he had sent
all his plays to New York and had retained no copies (102).

If Mrs. Anderson found it difficult to adjust to the "Bohemian"
nature of the Quarter, young Tom Williams reveled in it once he had
adjusted himself to the free-wheeling Latin lifestyle there. He professed to have been shocked at a New Year's Eve party to which the
Heldners took him, the day before he moved into the room on Toulouse Street, but he was soon to immerse himself in the milieu that
had originally surprised him. The freedom the city offered transformed him, for there was a tension between it and what he termed
the "Puritanism" of his nature. This Calvinistic view of life, instilled
by early years living in his grandfather's rectory and the strong
influence of Edwina Williams—a straitlaced lady of the old school,
who probably viewed sexuality as a flaw in human nature—was to
provide him with dramatic material for work he produced for the
rest of his life.

Eloi Bordelon's brother, Charles Ayala, said that the Quarter
in those days was "like a little community where everybody knew
everybody else," and his memories of the roominghouse indicate
something of how it must have affected impressionable young Tom
Williams. Ayala, who was the son of his mother's second marriage,
was five at the time, considerably younger than his brother. He lived
with his mother in the Algiers community across the river from New
Orleans, and the two of them rode the ferry across the river every
Sunday to bring Eloi a basket of food and clean clothes. At the time,
Eloi was working as an artist for the WPA and later became a successful interior decorator in New York, quite a contrast to the portrait of the tubercular artist Nightingale, based on Bordelon and portrayed in *Vieux Carré.* It was Eloi who introduced Williams to the
New Orleans Athletic Club, where for the next forty-four years the
dramatist was to swim daily whenever he was in the city. One indelible impression on Ayala's memory involves Mrs. Wire, a landlady in
the house next door to 722 Toulouse, who had apparently operated
a bordello at one time—Williams uses her name in *Vieux Carré.*
Charles Ayala told me that Mrs. Wire's parrot would perch on the

balcony of the second floor and call out to men passing in the street below, "Come on up, boys, and have a good time." Tennessee, who was always fascinated by birds, particularly parrots, surely would have been impressed by this phenomenon.

Ironically, a man named Jim Parrott provided the dramatist an exit from the roominghouse and an entrance to the next phase of his life. Described by Tennessee in *Vieux Carré* as an itinerant saxophonist named Sky, Parrott stayed briefly at the house before the two of them left for Texas. Parrott, now a retired pilot who lives in Florida, recalls those times in his unpublished memoirs, "Travels with Tennessee," parts of which have appeared in the *Tennessee Williams Journal.* In later years, Tennessee, in what may or may not have been an apocryphal story, insisted that because he was behind in his rent, he had to slide down knotted sheets to leave the roominghouse.

Those few months on Toulouse Street constitute one of the most crucial periods in the life of Tennessee Williams. He was storing up material for later use. It is here that he set the story "Angel in the Alcove," as well as the one-act *The Lady of Larkspur Lotion* and the late play *Vieux Carré,* and he used the first name of Eloi Bordelon for the protagonist of the one-act *Auto-Da-Fé.* In 1939, the Musée Méchanique at 523 Royal Street, around the corner from the roominghouse, was operated by John Henry Hewlett and his wife, the former Lorraine Werlein. The museum, a collection of charming mechanical figures and clockwork pictures, must have made a strong impression upon the young playwright, for he retained the memory of this magical place until he needed it in 1964 for *Eccentricities of a Nightingale.* Mrs. Winemiller relates the story of Albertine, her sister, who, with her husband, Mr. Schwarzkopf, owned such a museum and met a tragic end, unlike the real-life models. (In reality, the Hewletts moved the museum to San Francisco for the World's Fair in 1939, and it ultimately went bankrupt. The pieces were dispersed, although some of them have turned up recently in San Francisco.)

If the twenty-seven-year-old Thomas Lanier Williams could return to the Vieux Carré today and see the Toulouse Street house, he would hardly recognize it. In the 1970s when it was renovated, some ill-advised alterations were instituted: the third floor, where the young playwright launched his career, was removed, the cast iron balcony railing was replaced with wood, and a plate glass window was installed in front of what was once the photographer's studio. The architects insisted that the third floor was an addition made in the 1930s, but an 1870s photograph of the building shows that it already existed. There is no plaque on the building to indicate its significance in the career of America's great playwright, but those who know the story of his life may pause to contemplate the building and realize the extent to which his residence here changed the history of American drama. (Volume 4, number 1, of *The Tennessee Williams Journal* contains a wonderful photograph by Christopher Harris of Williams standing in the ruins of what had been his attic room.)

Those critical months of his new existence, away from St. Louis, which he found stultifying, and from the tensions of his family life, months spent in a new and liberating environment in which he could be himself and begin for the first time seriously to explore his sexual nature, served to convert the proper young man, wearing a coat and tie and polished shoes, into the Bohemian author and, ultimately, the greatest American playwright. Of that first 1939 in the French Quarter, he remarked to Eric Paulsen in the 1982 interview in New Orleans, "Oh, it was my first contact with a free society, I mean a bohemian world, . . . which I really encountered with a bang there." Terming it one of the "last frontiers of Bohemia," he professed to Pen Wilson, a New Orleans newspaper reporter, that he himself was a Bohemian—a fact which Miss Edwina, his mother, disputed when she read the article; she insisted that her son ask the reporter to print a retraction.

To Don Lee Keith he remarked in the 1970s after they had observed a well-known local character, Ruthie the Duck Girl, in Jackson Square, "I shall always think of New Orleans—affectionately of course—as a vagabond's paradise. In New York, eccentrics, authentic ones, are ignored. In Los Angeles, they're arrested. Only in New Orleans are they permitted to develop their eccentricities into art." He always insisted that the city liberated him, made him feel completely free and secure in a way he had never felt before. It was here, he later insisted, that he developed into a mature writer. In a very real sense, it can be said that while Thomas Lanier Williams was born in Columbus, Mississippi, in 1911, Tennessee Williams was born in a roach-infested, cramped, and romantic garret in a roominghouse at 722 Toulouse Street in the French Quarter, the area he came to love and call his spiritual home.

On subsequent sojourns in New Orleans that ranged in length from weeks to months, he lived in a variety of places. In the early years it was other rented rooms, including one in the six hundred block of Toulouse and another in the four hundred block of Royal. Later, after the success of *The Glass Menagerie* had brought him a considerable amount of money, he could afford apartments for extended stays or hotel rooms if he was in town for only a few days or weeks.

In 1946, he rented a second-floor apartment on Orleans Avenue, whose most appealing feature for him was a balcony overlooking Père Antoine's Garden behind St. Louis Cathedral. It was to be his favorite balcony in the Quarter, affording him, as he recalled later in his *Memoirs,* his favorite view in the city, that of the statue of Christ in the garden, hands lifted, "as if to invite the suffering world to come to him" (99). According to a letter Williams wrote to Donald Windham, he was convinced that the apartment was haunted, since the wind chimes that Windham had given him would suddenly begin to vibrate during the night, even when all the windows were closed (180). While living here with Pancho Rodriguez, Tennessee was at work on "Ten Blocks on the Camino Real," which ultimately became the full-length *Camino Real.* It was in also this apartment that, unlikely as it seems, he gave a party in February 1946, during Carnival season, for a group of uptown debutantes. In *Memoirs* he recalled that when the young women discovered that he shared a bed with Pancho, the debutantes and their dates gathered their wraps and fled as though a storm was threatening. He added that it was, however, just as well, since he belonged in Bohemia and not in the society world the debutantes represented (100).

Later in the same year, he moved into a house on St. Peter Street owned by his friend Dick Orme, where the most charming feature in his apartment on the second and third floor was a skylight over his desk. At the time, he was working on the script that would become *Summer and Smoke,* but he put that aside after a while to return to the play that had undergone numerous changes in setting and content and had been given a variety of titles, including "Blanche's Chair in the Moon" and "The Poker Night." From that apartment, he later wrote, he could hear the streetcar named Desire rumbling along its tracks on Royal Street and the one named Cemeteries running along Canal, six blocks away, and the metaphor of the two lines so appealed to him that he gave his drama a new title that would become one of the most memorable in world theater. Blanche's first line in the play, of course, is "They told me to take a street-car named Desire, and then transfer to one called Cemeteries and ride six blocks and get off at—Elysian Fields!" The St. Peter Street house now bears a plaque identifying it as the spot where *Streetcar* was created.

Through the years, Tennessee also stayed at a variety of hotels, the uptown Pontchartrain in 1946 and several in the Quarter. In 1951, he and his beloved grandfather, Rev. Walter Dakin, registered at the Monteleone Hotel for three weeks, and when they checked out discovered that the manager had taken care of all their expenses, presumably because the playwright had put New Orleans permanently on the literary map of the world four years before with *A Streetcar Named Desire.* On the other hand, the manager may have known that in *The Rose Tattoo* (1949), two Gulf Coast women on their way to New Orleans for an American Legion convention plan to stay at the Monteleone, which one of them describes as "old-fashioned." The other replies that what the Legionnaires are doing there is not old-fashioned.

During the 1950s and 1960s, Tennessee often registered at the Maison de Ville, across the street from 722 Toulouse Street. At this small, elegant hotel he always stayed in room number nine in the slave-quarter wing, which opens onto a patio with tropical foliage and a fountain. It was here that he was interviewed in the 1960s by Dick Cavett. On one occasion, he was scheduled to check out on the same day that a couple who had spent their honeymoon in number nine were arriving to celebrate their anniversary there. When checkout time came, the playwright, noted for his almost obsessive commitment to writing, usually five to eight hours a day, had not completed his work, and, despite repeated requests from the manager, continued to write for three hours while the couple waited impatiently in the lobby.

On at least one occasion, perhaps more, Williams stayed in the Royal Orleans, whose guests have included numerous other authors through the years, among them Lillian Hellman, Truman Capote, and William Styron. Tennessee's visit was in 1970, and at this time he gave Don Lee Keith the first interview that he had granted since his hospitalization in Barnes psychiatric unit in St. Louis. Part of the interview occurred in the hotel. Also during this visit he was interviewed by Rex Reed for *Esquire* magazine. In the 1990s, the Royal Orleans named two rooms on their second floor the "Tennessee Williams Suite."

Not surprisingly, since he loved shrimp, oysters, and fish, Williams relished the food in New Orleans. Among his favorite restaurants, none was dearer to him than Galatoire's, where his preferred table was in a corner from which he could watch the entire room. Mrs. Yvonne Galatoire Wynn, granddaughter of the founder, for many years presided over the dining room with elegance and grace. She recalled that when her father was alive, he would often go to sit with the playwright and they would carry on long conversations. In *A Streetcar Named Desire,* Williams paid a tribute to Galatoire's by having Stella tell Stanley that she is taking Blanche there for dinner. Other restaurants that he frequented included three old-line establishments, Antoine's, Arnaud's, and Maylie's and less fashionable but no less inviting dineries such as the Acme Oyster House and Victor's, where, after a long morning of work, he delighted in having a Brandy Alexander and a sandwich while listening to Ink Spots recordings on the jukebox. Then there was Solari's, a lunchroom and grocery store, which he memorialized in *Vieux Carré.*

Three times in the early years, Williams even worked in French Quarter restaurants, first in Mrs. Anderson's ill-fated "Eat Shop" on Toulouse in 1939. Two years later, after *Battle of Angels* closed in Boston without reaching Broadway, he was employed as a waiter at Gluck's, a German restaurant in the one hundred block of Royal Street. The restaurant and the building that contained it burned to the ground a decade later. On one occasion, he worked at the Court of Two Sisters during Carnival. None of these jobs was of long duration, one suspects because the aspiring writer, his mind occupied with creative projects, was not very efficient.

Also not surprisingly, Tennessee Williams was no stranger to many of the French Quarter bars during the nearly half century of his association with the area. In *Orpheus Descending,* Carol Cutrere refers to three bars, the Club Rendezvous, the Starlite Lounge, and the Music Bar, all of which were real night spots in the Vieux Carré. The Music Bar is unquestionably Dixie's Bar of Music, which flourished first on St. Charles Avenue in the 1940s and then on Bourbon Street under the direction of two sisters, Dixie and Irma Fasnacht. Miss Dixie, who still resides in the French Quarter, recalls the playwright's visits to the bar and his conversations with Miss Irma and her up until the 1960s, when the sisters sold the bar. In later years, he was fond of sitting at the piano bar in Lafitte's Blacksmith Shop and listening to Lilly Hood, the pianist, play old-time show tunes, many of which he requested himself. Through the years he also visited other bars along Bourbon and on other streets, some reputable, some sleazy, existing just on the edge between the legal and the lawless.

For one who knows the multiple, complicated, and symbiotic relationship between the life of Tennessee Williams and the Vieux Carré, I find it difficult to walk any block of the area without thinking of him and his deep attachment to his "spiritual home," which liberated him from the bonds that had constrained him and directed him down the path of a prodigious creativity. Who then can look at the old St. Louis Cathedral and not hear Blanche's description of the "only clean thing in the Quarter"? One month after his death in 1983, a memorial service was held in the cathedral to honor the writer most associated with the city. Next door to the cathedral is the Cabildo, whose arches are a prominent detail of Williams's poem "Mornings on Bourbon Street," and across the street, Jackson Square, where he was wont to sit in the afternoon after he had finished his long hours of work and had lunch. A few blocks away on Decatur Street is the site of the Morning Call coffee stand, where, until it was driven out of the Quarter by renovation of the French Market, he would sometimes start his day with black coffee or end the evening with café au lait and beignets.

Tennessee Williams put his indelible stamp on the community that provided him shelter and comfort all those years and made it his own so completely that anyone informed of his connections to all these sites will find the narrow old streets haunted by the ghost of the playwright who placed them permanently and unforgettably on the literary map of the world. He is a ghost not threatening or frightening but welcoming to those who appreciate the charming, mysterious qualities of the environment and the aura of magic he cast across it with the glow of the mythical paper lantern of his imagination.

Works Cited

Holditch, W. Kenneth. Interview with Charles Ayala. New Orleans, May 1994.

Tischler, Nancy M. *Tennessee Williams: The Rebellious Puritan*. New York: Citadel, 1961.

Williams, Edwina. *Remember Me to Tom*. As told to Lucy Freeman. New York: Putnam's, 1963.

Williams, Tennessee. Interview with Don Lee Keith. New Orleans, 24 January 1978.

——. Interview with Eric Paulsen, WWL-TV. New Orleans, April 1982.

——. *Memoirs*. New York: Doubleday, 1975.

——. "Mornings on Bourbon Street." *In the Winter of Cities*. New York: New Directions, 1956.

——. *Orpheus Descending*. In *The Theatre of Tennessee Williams, vol. 3*. New York: New Directions, 1971.

——. *The Rose Tattoo*. In *The Theatre of Tennessee Williams, vol. 2*. New York: New Directions, 1971.

——. *A Streetcar Named Desire*. In *The Theatre of Tennessee Williams, vol. 1*. New York: New Directions, 1971.

——. "Yellow Bird." In *"One Arm" and Other Stories*. New York: New Directions, 1954.

Windham, Donald, ed. *Tennessee Williams's Letters to Donald Windham, 1940–1965*. New York: Holt, Rinehart and Winston, 1977.

12

Tennessee Williams

The Angel and the Crocodile

Dan Sullivan

"The incontinent blaze of a live theater, a theater meant for seeing and feeling, has never been and will never be extinguished by a bucket brigade of critics."
—Tennessee Williams

As a former drama critic, I am saddened to think that Tennessee Williams saw us as people who went around raining on the theater's parade. But I do acknowledge the critic's temptation—and maybe the scholar's—to leave out the blaze when we discuss art: to explain away a writer's work according to some theory that we've devised. In my case no such theory about Williams has arrived. All I have to offer are some notions plus a couple of memories.

The first memory is a kind of ghost story. Time: the late 1980s. Place: New London, Connecticut, where I'm teaching at the Eugene O'Neill Theater Center. I'm staying at the Monte Cristo Cottage, the O'Neill family's summer home and the scene of *Long Day's Journey into Night*. It's an article of faith at the O'Neill home that the place is haunted. "Have you seen *her* yet?" my colleagues ask, meaning the ghost of Ella O'Neill, floating down the stairs in her wedding dress looking for her "medicine." "Not yet," I say.

In fact it's a perfectly friendly house; I love its quiet at the end of the day. Today being Sunday, I've got the place all to myself, and I've got plans. In a storeroom I've found a file cabinet filled with Audrey Wood's papers—Audrey Wood, Broadway's most powerful agent in the 1940s and 1950s. One of her top clients was William Inge, author of *Picnic* and *Bus Stop,* about whom I'm trying to write a book. I'm sure to find some Wood-Inge correspondence in the cabinet.

I don't. I find something more precious: a fat folder of letters from Wood's foremost client, Tennessee Williams, most of them typed on hotel stationery: Hotel Excelsior, Napoli; The Connaught, London; The St. Charles, New Orleans. Addressed to "Dearest Audrey," they're as personal as entries in a journal:

> Dearest Audrey, Are you mad at me? . . . I became very para-noiac as soon as I got here, fought with Frank, fell out with Natalia's sister and wrote Natalia a severe letter about her, prob-ably unjust and unkind. Why do I do these things? . . .
>
> Don't ask me why I've fallen into this state: because I couldn't tell you except to say that something "spooked" me somewhere, sometime, somehow, and I can't shake the spook. The lucky thing is that I'm writing about just exactly that thing. . . .
>
> There is a truth in this play [*Sweet Bird of Youth*] but I've got to cut to it, probe it out, with a very delicate blade, and no other hand on the blade but my own. I won't say this to Gadg [director Elia Kazan] when we talk, but I wish you would keep it in mind and help me to "hold the line" if he starts buying the meretricious values in the play instead of encouraging me to stick to finding its truth . . .
>
> When I get back, I will try to work out some kind of plan, some program, that might give me a chance to avoid, or at least temporize with, a total crack-up. It would certainly call for a very radical change in my way of life which has been so de-structive for such a long time now.
>
> I want to become a decent person, as I used to be.

The folder also contains long single-spaced letters from Wood to her client, assuring him of his talent, sharing her marketing strategy for the next play and rapping his knuckles about a naughty line in his latest script: "If 'Junior,' on page 69, is another name for that unmentionable object also referred to in another play by the tal-ented writer who wrote THE ROSE TATTOO, you know what you can do with it. If this character comes into another play by any writer—I'm going to scream aloud—in rage—not laughter." And al-ways ending on a note of tenderness: "Come home—dear Williams

—come home—we miss you and your friendly presence not to mention the best of your writing talent Come home before you become a memory to me—it's going on to 1954 sir."

Wood's earliest letter, dated Dec. 8, 1941, is addressed to an editor at Dodd Mead: "I want to thank you sincerely for your great kindness in sending the $20 check for permission to include Tennesee Williams' one act play THE LADY OF LARKSPUR LOTION in the Best One Act Plays of 1941. I have great faith in Williams and my biggest job is devoted to keeping him alive and eating. . . . Your special thoughtfulness in this instance is, therefore, doubly appreciated. Sincerely, AUDREY WOOD."

As I close the folder—which eventually went to the Harry Ransom Center at the University of Texas—I'm tingling. This house is haunted at that. Under the auspices of Eugene O'Neill, I've just had a séance with Tennessee Williams and Audrey Wood, two very classy human beings.

This memory takes some of the sting out of an earlier one from the early 1970s. Again it's a Sunday afternoon. *A Streetcar Named Desire* is being revived at the Ahmanson Theater in Los Angeles with Jon Voight and Faye Dunaway, and I'm in New York to interview Mr. Williams for the *Los Angeles Times.* Mr. Williams suggests over the phone that we meet at the Algonquin for brunch. "They know me there," he says—as if they don't know him everywhere.

We meet at the Algonquin, check our coats, and head for a table at the rear of the dining room. Seated at the banquette on our right is a tiny red-haired woman having lunch with a man I don't recognize. The woman I'm afraid I do. It's Audrey Wood, from whom Williams has been professionally divorced for two years, a devastating split for both parties and completely (so the gossip goes) his doing.

It's an awkward moment. Is Williams going to brush past the woman to whom he owes his entire career—his angel, shall we say? Of course he isn't. He stops at Wood's table and extends his hand. "My dear!" he says. Wood's hand slowly comes up . . . and, as slowly, is retracted. She stares at her plate, saying nothing. Williams stands there for the longest moment, then stalks to our table. "You can always tell a *lady* by her mannuhs!" he snarls, his voice loud enough to be heard several tables away. Wood and her friend immediately get up and leave the restaurant.

She wrote about this incident years later in her memoirs, *Repre-*

sented by Audrey Wood. Her intention, she said, wasn't to snub Tennessee. It was to protect herself. She simply couldn't bear to touch the man. The wounds were too deep: not just the brutal way Williams had fired her in public after the premiere of *Out Cry* in Chicago but also his litany of accusations through the 1960s: you hate my work, you think I'm finished, you wish I were dead, and so on. Fleeing Chicago, Wood told herself, "you'll get over this," but she never really did. Nor, perhaps, did her client.

This incident brings us to Williams the crocodile, every bit as toxic a creature as Andrea Del Lago in *Sweet Bird of Youth.* An exasperating person even when he wasn't "on" something—bourbon, pills, or paranoia—he could be a really nasty package when he was. Toward the end of his life, we have the impression of an emotional vagrant who has no choice but to trust in the kindness of strangers: he has exhausted the patience of his friends.

Often, though, Tennessee was the one who did the leaving. In the early 1960s, for example, he dismissed his longtime lover and major stabilizing force Frank Merlo for being unfaithful. This complaint probably translates as meaning "too controlling," which was Williams's real complaint against Audrey Wood. As members of his support system, his friends were supposed to know their place and stay there, whereas he reserved the right to come and go at will and especially to go.

Such an arrangement naturally led to "scenes"—which, as we know, is what stage plays are composed of. Some of Williams's latter-day cronies have even accused him of having provoked these confrontations on purpose, as if to scare up fresh emotional copy. "He required the constant exercising of his emotions, taking them to the breaking point and then coming back and writing what he had experienced," writes Dotson Rader in his tell-all memoir, *Tennessee: Cry of the Heart,* a book I urge you not to read.

My guess is that Williams's addiction to Sturm und Drang wasn't calculated. How can an unstable man be his own ringmaster? We do know, however, that in his twenties young Tom Williams had made a conscious decision to exorcise the prissy courtesies and repressions that his mother had drilled into him back in St. Louis—what he called his "Miss Nancy" side. "When I came out, I came out with a bang," he tells us in his memoirs, not just referring to his sex life. His crocodile side also began to emerge, and it would grow from year to year, causing much commotion. In the long run, however, Williams probably paid a higher price for his temperament than his friends did. He had to live with the crocodile. They didn't.

Toward his family his behavior was exemplary. Where Eugene O'Neill—a cannier sort of monster—virtually wrote his children out of his life, Williams not only supported his mother and sister but shared his time with them, often inviting them to New York and Key West for long visits, at considerable cost—from everything we know about Mrs. Williams—to his nerves.

His angels, then, proved persistent. One of the great virtues of Lyle Leverich's superb biography, *Tom*—which I insist you read—is to remind us how idealistic Tom Williams was before he became "Tennessee." This was a youth who really did believe that poetry could save the world or could at least save him. The spark never quite went out. Raking through the muck of Williams's memoirs, we occasionally uncover an absolutely gleaming line. "Mornings—how I love them: their victory over night." You don't give up on a writer like that.

And so Williams's career was exciting all the way to the end. Rather than writing him off, as he believed the critics had done, most of us kept hoping that he had one more piece of magic up his sleeve. If Verdi could father *Falstaff* at eighty, who could definitely rule out a return to form for Tennessee Williams at sixty, sixty-five, seventy? Despite the odds, we looked forward to the new Williams play, feeling that there would be plenty of time later to celebrate the old ones. Nearly twenty years after his death, we still don't know what to make of those last plays, but we were right about the earlier ones. They were built to stand.

I first came upon Williams's plays in my teens, not in the theater—we didn't have much live theater in my hometown—but in the corner drugstore, in ratty, thirty-five-cent Signet editions published to hype the movie version of the play. The cover usually featured a woman in her underwear and the back cover read like this: "In her need, she turned to the guitar player. And out of his tenderness, he gave her love. It was a wonderful love, wild with the sweetness of freedom. But in the minds of the townspeople it became corrupt, driving them to strike out at the lovers with a venomous, violent passion."

Into the schoolbag, quick! But when you got the book upstairs, it turned out to deal with human stuff, not hot stuff. The characters were exotic—at least to a fifteen-year-old growing up in New England—but they weren't from another planet. The language was high-flown, but there was mud on its shoes. The sex was suffused rather than in your face. There was a surprising amount of comedy. Best of all, you found yourself reading a play with as much enjoyment as a thriller, not at all like trudging through *Macbeth* and *Julius Caesar* for high school English class. I owe the cheesy paperbacks a good deal. Not only did they introduce me to Tennessee Williams, they introduced me to the pleasures of the theater. I'd be grateful even if they had turned out to be the pulp fiction they seemed to be.

Who would have guessed that they would turn out to be classics? After fifty years that's not too strong a term for *The Glass Menagerie* or *A Streetcar Named Desire*. Not only have Williams's plays endured, but they can also still surprise us. Faye Dunaway in that Los Angeles production of *Streetcar*, for example, suggested that Blanche's arrival at the asylum wasn't the end of her life, merely a temporary defeat. And nothing in Williams's script forbids that reading.

Another surprise for me, knowing *Night of the Iguana* only as a rather heavy-handed film, was the purity and youth that Richard Chamberlain and Dorothy McGuire gave Shannon and Hannah at the Ahmanson Theater later in the 1970s, suggesting a changeling brother and sister who could whisper absolutely anything to each other. Williams's angels really did sing that night.

Hannah Jelkes, the heroine of *Iguana*, is a hypersensitive quick-sketch artist who keeps her balance by fixing her attention on other people's faces and drawing what she sees. For the best part of his career, this was Williams's strategy as well. As long as he kept the observer in him as alive as the self-enchanted poet, he was on center. Unfortunately it was a balancing act that a temperament so divided couldn't sustain. The strain begins to show as early as *Camino Real* (1953) and pretty much takes control of the work after the mid-sixties, leading to near chaos in *This Is (An Entertainment)*, staged in San Francisco in 1975 and rarely produced since. Here was Williams trying to show that he could be as presentational and "with it" as the younger generation and falling flat on his face. Not for the first time, the new freedoms of the 1960s seemed to be exactly what he didn't need.

Which relates to the question of his sexuality. One of the dumber criticisms of his plays—also used against Edward Albee—is that they are gay fantasies in straight drag. There is no way to disprove this point. If Blanche and Amanda, Alma in *Summer and Smoke* and Serafina in *The Rose Tattoo*, Lady in *Orpheus Descending*, and Maggie in *Cat on a Hot Tin Roof* don't strike you as real women—so be it. Few actresses would agree with you.

As for Williams's male characters, are Stanley and Mitch and Big Daddy any less solidly drawn than the men in, say, Arthur Miller's plays? Like Hannah Jelkes, Williams wants to sketch all the people on the boardwalk and can identify with every face he sees. For all his fugitive leanings, he didn't consider himself an exile from the human race. He knew men. He knew women. He knew the heart. There's no indication that he yearned to write another kind of play if only he dared.

There is, however, an area of ambiguity in his plays that disturbs those who think he should have been more outfront as a gay artist. Even back in the 1950s, he was criticized for leaving up in the air the question of whether or not Brick and his friend Skipper in *Cat on a Hot Tin Roof* had gone to bed together.

For me, this ambiguity is one of his strengths. It reflects a fruitful détente between Williams the canny purveyor of whammo theatrical effects—sex! incest! cannibalism!—and Williams the poet, who knows the power of "something unspoken." Obviously his discretion is partly dictated by the conventions of public speech in the 1950s, a time when not everything could be called by its name; but it also reflects a good deal of theatrical wisdom. As Mae West replied when asked if she would ever perform in the nude: "Baby, once you're boned—where's the illusion?"

One could even argue that Williams's decline as an artist coincides with his loss of reserve. When the free speech dam broke in the 1960s, he let it all hang out, as in *This Is (An Entertainment)*—which I was unlucky enough to see in San Francisco—and the results are banal. One sees how much wiser the younger Williams was. "I give you truth in the pleasant guise of illusion," as Tom Wingfield says in *The Glass Menagerie*.

Illusion, indirection, the veil over the bulb—rather than being evasions, these point to a central truth in his best plays: that human behavior is rooted in mystery, that people aren't to be reduced to their case histories. Brick's feelings for his buddy are the point in

Cat, not their physical expression. Nor do we need to know whether Maggie the Cat really did make the lie come true—that is, succeed in getting herself pregnant by her reluctant husband (or, as some productions have suggested, by Big Daddy). Bad plays nail everything down. Good plays leave room for us to wonder.

Williams's angel was a recording angel, and it gave him little rest. Whatever the excesses of the night before, every morning found him at his typewriter, cranking something out—not always a play. There were novels, film scripts, short stories (*The Glass Managerie* began as one), poems, and some wonderful theater essays still available in a collection called *Where I Live.* One of the best of these pieces, "The Timeless World of a Play," explains Williams's aesthetic. It's a rather old-fashioned one. The theater was invented, he says, to arrest the rush for life for a couple of hours so that we can stop and look—really look—at our fellow creatures.

This is not the same process as appraising them over a desk. In real life we'd probably fire Willy Loman too. Or, Williams might have added, demand that Blanche come out of that damn bathroom this minute. Or throw a slipper at Amanda's eternal "Rise and shine."

But if we were to meet such irritating characters in some anteroom "outside of time," perhaps we could afford to treat them "with concern and kindness and even respect."

Fear and evasion are the two little beasts that chase each other's tails in the revolving wire-cage of our nervous world. Time rushes towards us with its hospital tray of infinitely varied narcotics, even while it is preparing us for its inevitably fatal operation. . . . About their lives, people ought to remember that when they are finished, everything in them will be contained in a marvelous state of repose which is the same as that which they unconsciously admired in drama. The rush is temporary. The great and only possible dignity of man lies in the power deliberately to choose certain moral values by which to live as steadfastly as if he, too, like a character in a play, were inured against the corrupting rush of time. Snatching the eternal out of the desperately fleeting is the great magic trick in human existence.

In his art, at least, Tennessee Williams managed it.

Postscript

Back at the Algonquin. With Wood gone, Williams relaxed and we had a pleasant lunch. "I feel like I've been giving interviews all my life," he observed, but it wasn't a complaint. He was ready to talk about his plays, his family, his "spaced-out" time in the 1960s (he liked hippie slang), anything I wanted to bring up.

Did he, as the grandson of an Episcopal priest, believe in the Ten Commandments? "Let's see, what are they? Well, I don't steal. I don't covet my neighbor's wife or my neighbor's ass. Hmmmm. Maybe I should correct that. I don't bear false witness. Ha! I bear *excessively* true witness for most people!"

How would he define his personality? "I'm a peculiar blend of the pragmatist and the romanticist. And the crocodile. And then I gotta be all those heroines. And all those heavies."

How was he coping with the seventies? "They think I'll be dead soon, so they're doing these elegiac things. I don't think they realize the longevity with which my family is gifted. Or afflicted. I don't know which!" Williams signed for the check, but the waiter couldn't read the signature.

"Could you print your name at the top so the girls in the office will be able to read it?"

"Tell 'em I'm Tennessee Ernie Ford and I'll come up and sing to 'em!" Big laugh.

Works Cited

Leverich, Lyle. *Tom: The Unknown Tennessee Williams.* New York: Crown, 1995.

Rader, Dotson. *Tennessee: Cry of the Heart.* New York: Doubleday, 1985.

Williams, Tennessee. "The Timeless World of the Play." In *Where I Live: Selected Essays,* edited by Christine R. Day and Bob Woods. New York: New Directions, 1978.

Wood, Audrey, with Max Wilk. *Represented by Audrey Wood: A Memoir.* New York: Doubleday, 1981.

Afterwords

A Panel Discussion

Colby Kullman, Moderator
Panelists: George Crandell, Albert Devlin, Allean Hale,
Barbara Harris, Kenneth Holditch, Philip Kolin, Michael
Paller, Robert Siegel, Dan Sullivan, Nancy Tischler

KULLMAN: This symposium on Tennessee Williams has offered an abundance of testimony to new approaches to Williams and his work. The symposium gave us realism and magic. New Williams and new plays. An apocalyptic reading to a renascence of Tennessee Williams study. The ten speakers who are happily on this panel ending the symposium have advanced Williams study; if they have brought him under a harsher glow of light, they have also made the footlights of his theater beam brighter.

I thought we might start out with some general questions about Williams. What kind of reappraisal is necessary in the light of his contributions to autobiography, letter writing, and nonfiction prose?

TISCHLER: I think that there's more interest in Williams because we're seeing more about his life in works that were previously obscure or not known at all. We're getting a revival of interest in those early works and also in his very late ones, some of which should be forgotten but some of which are really quite interesting. There must be some sorting out, but because we know more about his life and his contacts, I think we're also going to find revived interest in these other lesser known plays.

KULLMAN: How do you think these recent finds will work in terms of productions of them on the stage? One of the things we also want to be concerned about is not just the texts of the plays but the plays in performance. Do you think these new plays are going to work very well on the stage? Kenneth?

HOLDITCH: Well, *Not About Nightingales,* which Allean and I have seen, was excellent. It's a fascinating play, and one of the questions that came up on a panel at the Alley Theater [when the play was done in Houston] was, "Would Tennessee want these early plays produced?" And there were two people who very adamantly said, "No, he would be horrified." My response was that he would be delighted to see any good production of one of his works. That's because I think he believed that theater was a collaborative effort between the writer and the director and the actors and the set designer and everybody else. And so I think he'd be pleased. Certainly *Not About Nightingales* was well worth the effort.

PALLER: I think, given the way the theater works and the way the regional theater works especially, it takes someone of the stature of a Vanessa Redgrave—who was able to help get this play [*Not About Nightingales*] produced—to make a case for any of the very late plays, because they're so unknown. Regional theaters still love to do what's known. They weren't meant to do that, but regional theaters don't do *Vieux Carré* very much; they don't do *Small Craft Warnings* very much; they don't do *Something Cloudy, Something Clear* very much. And those are not great plays but are not nearly as awful as their reputation suggests. They're very interesting plays, but regional theaters are very timid, and it would take someone with a certain amount of stature to make the case for these plays—which is too bad, because they need to be seen. You don't need a thousand more productions of *The Glass Menagerie,* wonderful play though it is.

SULLIVAN: Well, that's true of the big resident theaters, but you know there are wonderful Off Broadway–style theaters all around the country—in my territory in Minneapolis the Jungle Theater, for instance—and I can well imagine some of them saying, "Let's take a chance on this. The critics will come. And the critics always *will* come, because we love novelty. If it's a play we haven't seen, and it's by Tennessee Williams, a playwright we know and are curious about, we will come and write about that. So I think it's a possibility *if* the theater really thinks it's a great play.

HALE: Well in sort of an antithesis to that question, "Should those early plays be produced?" I certainly think they should, because they have a strength of their own. But now a new sort of moral question, or ethical question, is arising with these very late plays, and I've known a couple of instances already: people are anxious to find out everything that isn't already found out about Tennessee Williams, and one person wants to publish his last play, for instance. Well, this last play is like three very strange fragments where you can tell he didn't know what he was doing yet, and these fragments are sort of . . . leftovers, and the people's names even change in the play, and to me, I hate personally to see this sort of thing published. But I see that in the future there will be more and more people wanting to do that. There's one of his last stories—you can tell that he hadn't worked his way through it, you know, and it had been discarded by his publisher. There was a little note on it, saying, "If Williams were himself, he would have thrown this in the trash, and I think that's where it belongs." Well, I sort of hate to see those things come to the surface. What do you think about the ethics involved? Do you just show everything the writer did and let people judge for themselves?

CRANDELL: My feeling is that these works should be made public. I think if a new manuscript by Shakespeare turned up, we'd want to publish it whether it was good or bad, and we'd make the same judgment for Tennessee Williams or Arthur Miller. I think one of the things the production of *Not About Nightingales* does is to correct one misconception, that the career of Tennessee Williams begins with *The Glass Menagerie*—that it was a sudden phenomenal success followed by a period of decline. I think there are grounds for a reappraisal, looking at the early works to see what was going on before *The Glass Menagerie*. And [*Not About Nightingales*] also calls for directors to follow the stage directions, to produce Williams not as a realistic dramatist but as one who uses various expressionistic devices, surrealistic devices, that sort of thing. Generally, I think bringing more to light is better than withholding certain pieces of evidence.

KOLIN: I agree entirely with what George says. I think there's another issue here; maybe we should call it "transbibliographic"—that is, what is the text of *Streetcar*? What is the text of *Menagerie*? We have a Dramatists' Play Service acting version; we have New Directions reading version. When we teach these things, people in the theater department use the acting text; people in the English department use the reading text. Should we have a conflated, collated variorum for Tennessee Williams? It's a difficult problem.

HOLDITCH: Well, I'm not sure I agree with George that these things should be produced, because I think if a writer is just working through notes and things, and what we find is clearly an early text, perhaps it shouldn't be published. I for one would not want to see the early versions of *Streetcar* published. I suspect the public should be kept in ignorance of those early things, because I have a thing about the mystery of creation. I don't think you want to show the writer's work before it's finished. I saw some parts, a staged reading, of some early scenes from *Streetcar* last year in New York, and they were absolutely fascinating to me. But I was worried about the wider perceptions of such scenes. I'm sort of like the old Hollywood Breen Office; I don't think that the public ought to get that stuff.

DEVLIN: I think George is right about the reasons for the positive reception of *Not About Nightingales,* and I suspect that New York will also find it to be a very intriguing and very novel production. It really is the first professional production of that part of Williams which is rooted in the sociopolitical theater of the 1930s. I wonder, though, how well *Spring Storm* will fare. It was originally entitled *April Is the Cruellest Month.* It apparently had a successful reading in 1995 in New York, and I suspect it too will probably be optioned and have tryouts and may indeed reach New York, but that play is going to run into competition with the well-known lyrical Williams. And I suspect that it's not going to fare very well and that it will bring the production of unknown plays into a more questionable financial realm.

HOLDITCH: And *Not About Nightingales* is more of a finished play, wouldn't you agree, Allean? That it's a play that was ready for production, more or less.

HALE: Yes, and you can definitely tell from his notes. He said he was interested in either the movies or the stage for that play. He was definitely trying to get that play produced. But I saw *Spring Storm* in New York, and it was surprisingly good. I think the reason it was never promoted is that it's probably too much like *The Glass Menagerie*. It gives a much harsher picture of Edwina, for instance; it's very satirical. But it's a good play on its own. Whether it would not succeed because it is too much like *The Glass Menagerie*, I don't know. I think it would have a lot more luck than maybe the one I'm working on now, which is *Stairs to the Roof*. It's hard to get really excited about *Stairs to the Roof*, because it's so much like Saroyan's 1930s things, and it does seem dated to me, but we'll see. I mean, if they get a powerful production like they did with *Nightingales*, that's what it takes.

KULLMAN: Okay, let's move on to another question about politics and Tennessee Williams. A lot of research has recently focused more on Williams as a political writer, someone who was very interested in the Vietnam War and had something to say about it, someone who was interested in ethnicity and race, someone who championed human rights. What would you like to say about Williams and politics? Kenneth?

HOLDITCH: Well, I think that he was very interested in politics, but I'm very happy that he was not one of those more doctrinaire playwrights. Even in *Not About Nightingales*, he doesn't really hit you over the head all the time with his message the way that some of those proletariat writers did in writing political plays. I do think he was concerned about improving the human condition without concentrating on a particular point —and that's what people often mean when they talk about "political writing"—but his concern with politics is very strong. I have a videotape that's never been published, in which Williams is interviewed in New Orleans by a rather inept television commentator, and Williams goes off into a violent diatribe against Ronald Reagan, who was president then, and says, "I didn't like him when he was Governor of California, and I don't like him now," and you realize he was very up to date about what was going on. And I was sort of surprised when I first heard that, because somehow, you know, we think about Williams—or at least I've always thought about him—as being up there writing for eight hours a day and not reading the newspaper and not particularly noticing what was going on.

DEVLIN: May I comment on that, just briefly? I think Williams is a political figure in this country. He has a deep, instinctive regard for American democracy, and he is deeply ingrained with the progressive ethos of the 1930s, however stymied it may have been. But I can't overcome the impression that Williams puts on and takes off political attitudes as though they were a light cape. I'm just not convinced that he was deeply aware of politics as a transforming dynamic. I think he was easily urged to become interested in political issues such as Vietnam in the late 1960s and early 1970s, but he always seemed to have a curious kind of detachment.

KOLIN: Yes, I'd like to address this issue. I think we're approaching it the wrong way. If you look at Williams plays in revival, you see a whole cluster of political issues emerging. C. W. E. Bigsby observed that *Cat on a Hot Tin Roof* is *the* play for the Watergate era, with its emphasis on mendacity. If you look at *Kingdom of Earth,* you have the whole issue of multiculturalism and anticolonialism. The issue is—maybe Williams's politics are so ingrained in the text that it's the revivals that bring them out.

SIEGEL: I'd like to say something about the texts, too, not knowing as much as other people do here about Williams the man. And that is, it seems to me that he does respond like any artist—he's a mirror of his times and does respond somewhat politically. Consider that the opening monologue in *The Glass Menagerie* has a very wry description of the depression, and even though there's a comment at the end that this is the social commentary of the play—somewhat ironic—it seems to me that other monologues in *The Glass Menagerie* clearly tell us what's going on around the world. For example, Tom counterposing the hot sex here in America with Guernica going on in Europe. And it also seems to me that *Cat* is very much a reflection of the 1950s, our materialism, in American culture at that time. And even in *Suddenly Last Summer,* the young woman, Catharine, tells us this is a tale for all of our times—she says this is a tale of our world, what happened to Sebastian. And clearly also in *The Night of the Iguana,* why does he have the Germans running around on that stage if not to comment on a kind of grotesque indifference in the world? So I think it's in his work, maybe not as directly as in Arthur Miller, but it's certainly there.

DEVLIN: Who else would be a provocative vacationer in 1940 if not a group of Germans?

PALLER: I think it also depends on what one decides is political, as opposed to what is ethical or moral. He certainly had a very strong moral sense and a very deep sense of empathy for the oppressed and the suffering. But we can't confuse him with someone like John Howard Lawson or some other very doctrinaire, programmatic political writer. He's more in a sense like Clifford Odets, whom Harold Clurman once described as someone who had the same kind of empathy but had no programmatic political plan. I think what interested Williams was more right and wrong, as opposed to politics, in the sense that one can separate those things.

SULLIVAN: I don't think he was a chameleon who would put on a mask and take it off. The attitude was always consistent: he was for the underdog and against the bully. Those are his politics. Maybe you can get one or two papers out of that, but I don't know if you could get a whole book. It's pretty simplistic. I think it's right; it's my politics too, but it's good, sort of a straight liberalism. He was even less political than Odets. He never got mixed up with any party; he was never called up before any committee; he stayed out of that pretty completely, and you don't see any overt interest in politics until the Vietnam days.

PALLER: In fact, he hired Elia Kazan to direct *Camino Real* even after Kazan testified.

HALE: Really, he was not an activist, but if you examine his plays carefully, you will find something in practically every play that you could call a political comment, an observation, and he goes out of his way for this. I saw the British production of *Orpheus Descending,* and it was done in a very political way.

That play has this character, Carol Cutrere, talking about going out and leading a protest, and it definitely alludes to the Scottsboro case. He didn't have to bring that material into the play, but he did it. And then he does something similar in every play. Even in *Iguana,* that little portion about the people eating off the dunghill—so he doesn't go out and say, "I'm going to fight this," but he puts it in his plays.

KULLMAN: Let's talk about another issue. One of our panelists, Michael Paller, is working on a book, *A True Story for His Time: Gay Characters in the Plays of Tennessee Williams.* My own university, last week, was looking at candidates in gay and lesbian studies, queer theorists, which is something at the University of Mississippi I never thought I'd see, and the times are changing. How is this new emphasis affecting Williams in terms of biography, interpretation of his works, or comments about criticism related to Williams's plays? Let's start with Michael Paller.

PALLER: It's a touchy issue, and I began my book—which actually began as my master's thesis—because I was so annoyed at some gay critics who were writing in the early 1990s. They were condemning Williams as nothing but a self-loathing, self-hating homophobe, because so much of his early work was inferential—because things were concealed rather than revealed —and because he would not come out until safely after Stonewall. Well, none of this is true. These charges made me want to look at the plays carefully and—not that Williams needed rescuing from anybody—try to defend him against this very myopic, politically correct 1990s point of view. This view is very ahistorical, because Williams was born in 1911 in the Deep South and grew up in a society that was deeply homophobic. Williams's own problems were about sex—as opposed to gay sex.

It's very easy, on the other hand, to turn him into a champion of gay plays and perform those plays as overtly gay, which is equally a mistake, I think. In *The Glass Menagerie,* for example, I think, there are a hundred clues that Tom is gay, and the actor has to know that, but can you *play* it? I don't think so. First of all, what does "playing gay" mean? It'd be playing a set of stereotypes. But it helps the actor to construct an inner life that is very specific. I think there was in Williams a very deep conflict between a need to reveal and a need to conceal. From that tension comes most of his very best work. And once the 1960s happened and a lot of the need to conceal fell away, he was deprived of a significant condition that earlier led to good work. I think it's then that some of that work becomes rather banal. Anytime the subtext becomes surface, it becomes banal. It's powerful because it *is* a subtext.

But even then, as I mentioned yesterday or the day before, he was not as concealing as a lot of these critics would like to think. I noted the character of Baron De Charlus in *Camino Real*, which was produced in 1953, the height of the McCarthy era, in which homosexuals were as persecuted as Communists. Williams presents this not only gay but sadomasochistic gay character on the stage. And I think if you read the play carefully, you'll see that Baron De Charlus is in the play for only about fifteen minutes, but he comes off, politically and morally and ethically, a lot better than Casanova, or Lord Byron, or Marguerite Gautier, who are famous romantics. He is someone who acts on his nature and befriends Kilroy when the other characters don't want to come near Kilroy because they're afraid to. I'm not a queer theorist; I'm not a theorist of any sort. I think that's my theatrical background. Theater is not a theoretical thing; it's a practical, real place where you solve problems. Sometimes Tennessee Williams is hijacked. As often as he's hijacked to make the case for homophobia, he's hijacked to make the case for gay rights. Again, he was not political in that sense. He was a human being who wrote plays from what he felt. And because he was gay, those feelings can't be denied, but they can't be separated from his historical context, either. So in my work I'm trying to recreate some of that context as well as look carefully at the plays, because then we might understand what could cause Allan Gray, Blanche's gay husband in *Streetcar*, to kill himself: was it out of shame, or out of genuine fear for being an outed gay man in the 1930s in the South? HOLDITCH: I think Michael made a very good point that Williams's not being able to write overtly of gay themes at that time, whether he wanted to or not, created a tension. I've always thought, with Cleanth Brooks and others as well, that tension is the origin of much great literature. The inner tension in Williams's work is wonderful.

One interesting thing about Williams's characters. You know the Williams estate forbids changing gender in the plays, and the Lady Maria St. Just found out that in Amsterdam they were doing an all-male production of *Streetcar,* so she dispatched Tom Erhardt to Amsterdam to end the production. He got there the last night it was running, so he said, "I just let them run for the last night." And the strange thing he said was that Rupert Everett decided he wanted to do Flora Goforth in *The Milk Train Doesn't Stop Here Anymore.* Rupert Everett has become a very popular movie star because of his appearance in *My Best Friend's Wedding,* and the Lady Maria said, "Oh, well, let him do it because I've known little Rupert since he was a child. If he wants to do this, it's all right." But the estate actually forbids that sort of thing.

KOLIN: Dakin Williams, in Key West several years ago, put on a one-person show of *Streetcar* and got rave reviews as Blanche.

HOLDITCH: But that's a spoof, Philip. I mean, he's doing that as a spoof. He laughs at himself doing that, you know.

HARRIS: I'd like to make a comment about that. Michael Paller and I have talked a lot about sexuality in Williams's work in the last couple of days, and it always fascinates me. Anyone who says that Williams was never overt, that this is all hidden, and so forth and so on, obviously has never read the fiction, which predates a lot of the plays, and in which he was definitely overt. That fiction, strangely enough, was rather well received, even among such traditionally conservative observers as William Peden at the University of Missouri. Where are these people coming from who obviously haven't read very much Williams?

TISCHLER: He was really obliged to hide much of the time. You can see it in the film materials. He couldn't get a film produced if he had overtly gay characters in it, so if he was going to sell material he had to make such things covert. But the other thing was family. I asked Dakin about that, whether anybody in the family was aware of Tennessee's homosexuality. He said, "Well, not really." Dakin knew fairly early on, but most of the family didn't. When those books of short stories like "Hard

Candy" were first brought out, he didn't want them sold in the St. Louis area, because he didn't want his mother to see them. [Laughter.] The other thing I wanted to mention is that Lillian Hellman talked about the homosexual character Allan Gray, who was cut out of the film of *Streetcar*. Allean was telling about that, about Vivien Leigh—Allean, could you tell us that story?

HALE: I think it was Vivien Leigh. When the filmmakers were doing all this censoring and they were going to cut out the passage in which Allan Gray's homosexuality is discovered— the account of Blanche going into a room and finding two men, another man with her husband, they said, "Well, we can't have that." The script called for Blanche to say "You disgust me" afterward. So Vivien Leigh asked, "So I have to say 'You disgust me' because he writes poetry?" [Laughter]

PALLER: I think Blanche's lines about "walking into a room I thought was empty" were the only lines in the play that the Lord Chamberlain's office in England demanded be cut when it was first produced there.

KOLIN: The Lord Chamberlain actually insisted on several cuts, including instructions about undressing onstage and verbal references to Stanley's kidneys. The Lord Chamberlain also had a revision about the Allan Gray episode and wanted Blanche to say that she found Allan in a room with a black woman. Responding to these changes, Irene Selznick, the producer, said, "Well, the play just won't open in England."

CRANDELL: I think these studies provide an opportunity for us to look again at Williams and his subversive strategies not just in terms of queer readings of plays but in terms of ethnicity and race as well. I am reminded by last night's production of *Twenty-seven Wagons Full of Cotton* that a character like Silva Vacarro can be made attractive. And he is of a different ethnic origin from the other characters in the play. Why does Williams do this? What is the subversive message of this particular play? He does this with characters in *Streetcar* too; he characterizes Stanley in terms that are stereotypically associated with black characters, which I think is another way of introducing racial issues into that play and specifically miscegenation. So while on the surface the plays seem wholesome enough for various committees and audiences, there is another way of reading the plays as well.

KOLIN: There is a history with *Menagerie* and *Streetcar* of a good number of traditional black theater companies doing these plays and doing them rather well. I'm very pleased to see that *Kingdom of Earth* is going to be done at the Tennessee Williams Literary Festival in March 1999. It's a play that hasn't been done very much—and the film version of it is dreadful—but that's one of the most important plays in looking at Williams and ethnicity and race, because that's the only play where you have a major character who is also a black man.

SULLIVAN: If we had such a thing as "male studies," Williams would be a wonderful playwright to look at there, because he's always asking himself, "What is a man?" "How many ways of being a man can there be?" He provides a stunning range of people, from Tom to Stanley, all kinds of different guys, and this is a deep artistic concern with him as well. I think this would be a fascinating topic for someone to look at. It means he is a playwright who wants to see the world and see all those faces and write about them and identify with them. The bad thing about studying anybody under one guise is that you tend to reduce him just to that. We must never do that. And remember that these plays live basically in the theater. They don't live under a microscope.

KULLMAN: Barbara Harris alluded to the fact that the short stories of Tennessee Williams have significant power. I've found that statement to be true in teaching a course called "The World of Tennessee Williams" to university seniors. They're amazed at the quality of the short stories. Williams also wrote poetry and nonfiction essays and was a painter. Would you like to say something about these other forms of Williams's creativity?

HARRIS: Rose was also a painter. And one of the most fascinating research experiences that I've had lately occurred when I was doing some research at Columbia in New York. Rose's paintings are there. They're absolutely fascinating. I took a painting of Tennessee's, which is a wonderful painting in and of itself, called "Amanda and Her Gentleman Callers," and I put it side by side with a painting of Rose's and asked all the staff if they thought these were done by the same person or by different people. All of them thought that the two paintings were done by the same person. I think that's very interesting. I had never seen any work at all on Rose's paintings. I hope whoever takes on the question of Williams's painting includes Rose's works, because they're very, very revealing.

HOLDITCH: Well, Allean has to speak on the paintings because she's written about them. I think that she'll verify the fact that as an earlier painter, Williams was more representational. Some people have even said he was a better painter then than he was later. I have one of his paintings, and I'm delighted to have it. I wouldn't part with it for anything, and I think it's wonderful, but it's not great art. Richard Freeman Leavitt says there was a woman in Key West who had an art gallery, and she represented Williams. She kept pushing him to paint more paintings because she was making money selling them. His friends would say, "Stop doing those paintings and get back to writing!" I don't know to what extent that painting interfered with his writing, but I think he was, as a later painter, a kind of Sunday painter.

HALE: I've been working on a project about his painting and more especially how he used painting as a metaphor in his plays. And there again, it's like the political aspect. If you really watch his plays—I mean if you read his plays carefully—there's almost always a painterly image. He creates one over and over again, so I've been tracing these, and it's been fun. You find a lot of examples. He often conceives a play, either from a phrase he's heard, like "cat on a hot tin roof," or often from a painterly image. As I said in my symposium presentation, for example, Jackson Pollock is a definite part of *In the Bar of a Tokyo Hotel*. As for his own painting, I guess you'd call it naive.

HOLDITCH: Yes, but isn't it true that his earlier paintings were more representational than the later ones? I've been told that many of the earlier paintings no longer exist. Somebody, I forget who it was, told me that it was unfortunate that he came under the influence of de Kooning.

HALE: I've just seen one or two of the earlier ones. There's a wonderful book put out by the curator of the painting part of the Harry Ransom Humanities Research Center at the University of Texas–Austin, which has about fifteen of his paintings. The

book's called *Doubly Gifted,* and it's a picture book of the paintings of maybe twenty or thirty writers. In it there's a picture
Williams supposedly did at age ten, palm trees and a lake, but
it's not all that representational—it's the only one I've seen.

DEVLIN: We're going to go down in March and look more closely
at the paintings in the Harry Ransom Humanities Research
Center, but we have seen, through the Internet, a description
of them, and they tend to fall into the category of portraits—
there are three or four portraits of Jim Parrott, for example.
And then fairly representational landscape paintings.

HOLDITCH: Those are the early paintings?

DEVLIN: Yes, those are the early ones. They tend to be the bulk
of the holdings of the Ransom Center, from what the Internet
descriptions reveal. We'll know more after we have a look. We
hope to represent at least a part of Williams's painting in the
book of Williams correspondence, using illustrations at appropriate points.

KOLIN: I think it's a truism to say that Williams was a renaissance man. One of the things that troubles me is that we all pay
lip service to the fact that he's the great lyrical dramatist, and
when *Streetcar* and *Menagerie* were reviewed, the poetry in the
plays was emphasized. And yet if you look at his poetic works,
such as *In the Winter of Cities,* very little attention has been
paid to his poetry. Even Williams aficionados sometimes recoil
and say, "Oh, this poetry is not very good" or "It's opaque,"
and I wonder why. I teach the poetry and I think it's important
to use it collaterally in looking at the plays, but I wonder why
more attention has not been paid to the poetry.

DEVLIN: I think one reason might be that the poetry was not
really integral—at least not apparently integral—to the composition of the plays, whereas the short fiction and the one-acts
were part of an organic process that tends to lead to the canonical works more than the poetry does. But I think you're
quite right, we have not paid adequate attention to the poetry.

HOLDITCH: One of the wonderful things about the poetry is its
wide range, because there are very, very funny poems, like
"Life Story," where one person falls asleep smoking a cigarette
in bed, and the narrator says that's the way people burn to
death in hotel rooms—it is funny, but that line doesn't sound

funny here, out of context. And then there are those rather folksy blues songs—the American blues songs that he did, that Paul Bowles set to music. There are also some very serious, tragic poems.

KOLIN: Some of the poetry is almost metaphysical. I hear echoes of Crashaw, Herbert, and Vaughn. In "Angels of Fructification," for example, there's a lot of metaphysical undertone.

TISCHLER: He read a lot of poetry. We've gone through the correspondence with Jay [James] Laughlin. Of course, Jay was one of the first to acknowledge Williams's poetic ability and publish him. All through his life Williams kept sending Jay poetry, and occasionally these poems would come out in little collections, but Williams never thought of himself as a very good poet. He just realized he was so much better a dramatist. He also never thought of himself very much as a painter, but one of the last letters—it may have been to Jay Laughlin too—said, "You know, I'm making so much money off these paintings, and they're so much easier to do." [General laughter]

HOLDITCH: I'm glad to hear that!

KULLMAN: Let's move on to another question. Every fall Nancy and Allean and Al and Ralph Voss and Kenneth and I attend the Clarksdale, Mississippi, Delta Tennessee Williams Festival, and perhaps the high point of that festival is the appearance of 100 to 150 high school students who perform scenes and monologues from Tennessee Williams plays. Most of us have been judges of that competition. The excitement among high school students from ninth grade up is very encouraging to us. What could we do to promote the presentation of Williams in high schools and colleges, in teaching in our country? I think Nancy asked this question, so we'll start with Nancy.

TISCHLER: I really think those young people at Clarksdale are delightful. I know Kenneth doesn't like me to say this, because he's opposed generally to young people. [Much laughter]

HOLDITCH: Not true! [More laughter]

TISCHLER: But they're really wonderful because they are so mixed: some are very sophisticated and come from art schools, where they've had lots of help in choosing an interesting play, and it's matched very neatly with the people working with it, and they've learned their lines, and they've got their gestures down, and so forth. But some are kids from country schools and couldn't have had a chance in this world to read anything. They've just gone to the library and found a play, you know, and they've worked it out, they've learned their lines, they do a few gestures, and some of those kids are really quite good. It really startles you. I think Williams's words speak to all of them. All of them seem to understand. They seem to know what they're doing. I really find it exciting. The whole theater is full. All the parents come, and schools from all over Mississippi bus these kids down there to play some Tennessee Williams. I think that's a wonderful event. I hope Clarksdale will do that forever.

KULLMAN: I encourage you all to teach a course in the world of Tennessee Williams at your school. At Ole Miss, the course closes four hours after registration opens with forty people in it. I have to take my phone off the hook for the next two weeks because students are trying to get in, and even the chancellor has asked to get his son-in-law in the class. So I think you'll find you don't need to be worried about the class not making. It will make, I promise you that, and it's very popular. It makes us feel good about what we do, because there are new generations who are going to do wonders for the world of Tennessee Williams. Any other comments?

SULLIVAN: Well, I get worried when scholars promote things, and teachers promote things, because the rebel in me says, "I don't want to read it." Don't make it *too* required a reading. If there's a way to make young people discover Tennessee Williams while thinking they're doing it on their own or on the sly, that can be very effective.

HOLDITCH: I think what you're saying is, if you suggest to students that this is really shocking material, you will pique their interest. I discovered this when I was teaching a sophomore-level survey of English literature, and we were required to teach everything from Beowulf up to the eighteenth century in the first half. I've always liked Edmund Spenser, and I've always liked *The Faerie Queene;* I think it's a wonderful poem, and of course needless to say, students don't like it [at first]. I discovered if I would read a little bit of it leading up to the "Bower of Bliss" scene, and I'd say, "Oh, I can't go into that in class because it's rather racy for a mixed audience" [laughter], then I would see *them* reading it, and the next time they'd be ready to discuss "The Bower of Bliss." I think you could do that with Williams.

KOLIN: Is "The Bower of Bliss" unteachable in New Orleans? [Laughter]

HOLDITCH: Well, yes, I'm just saying that to them, to attract their attention.

SULLIVAN: That's a good way to teach *Paradise Lost,* too!

KULLMAN: Well, Dan Sullivan gave a very fine presentation on "The Angel and the Crocodile" in Tennessee Williams, and with it came up terms that had been used to describe Williams. The subject made me think about myths about Williams that perhaps need to be debunked. Do you have your favorite myth out there that needs to be debunked?

PALLER: I think maybe the first place I read about [one myth in particular] was in an essay by Gore Vidal, who was certainly Williams's friend and a partisan, but Vidal seemed to make him sound illiterate and little-read—maybe he didn't read Gore Vidal, that might have been the problem—but there seems to be this notion that Williams didn't read, that he was not widely read, but when you read the plays, it's clear that he read an awful lot. I don't see how this idea got started that he was some bumpkin.

HOLDITCH: I think that was just a Gore Vidal pronouncement, don't you? He tends to make pompous pronouncements—he is a very good writer, but what he said was, "Well, I never saw him holding a book," which doesn't mean that he didn't read, because they may have been in situations where he didn't necessarily have a book in hand. Certainly it's clear that he was a reader.

HARRIS: I think if Vidal had said it in only one place, certainly we might be able to forgive him; however, he has said it a number of times in a number of places. This is what I call "The Gore Vidal Myth," and every time I run into it, it infuriates me even more, because Vidal *does* portray Williams not only as not much of a reader but also as not knowing much about anything else either. I don't know whether that characterization comes from a psychological envy, as Vidal's career has sort of peaked—I genuinely don't know—but it is an irritating thing, and it is a myth that needs to be corrected.

DEVLIN: Neither the letters nor the journals, which we've [Devlin and Tischler] read pretty thoroughly, will support a view of Williams as an omnivorous reader. There's simply no basis for this view in the body of the letters or the journals, I would say.

TISCHLER: But he read a lot.

DEVLIN: He read a lot, but he was not an indefatigable reader. He was not a devoted, intellectual reader. It's just a nuance that I would add.

HALE: No, I don't think he was an intellectual reader, but I think he read voraciously. I was amazed to find that even back in college at Iowa, when he was trying to write a play on Vincent Van Gogh, he read all the volumes of the Van Gogh letters. Now, that's a big chore. They're wonderful letters, but how many people read them? And he did the same thing with D. H. Lawrence when he was writing a play on Lawrence. He was not a researcher, but he certainly was a reader.

HOLDITCH: And as Jackson Bryer indicated, Williams read all those books about Zelda Fitzgerald for the play *Clothes for a Summer Hotel,* whether it was for the good or the bad, but he certainly read.

SULLIVAN: Can you tell, just from that evidence, that the man was a reader or not? You know you don't always jot down what you're reading in your diary or even in your letters. This is something you'd have to go to his friends for.

TISCHLER: And you do get evidence of that in the letters that he would send for books. He tended to read toward a purpose. You say that he read all of Fitzgerald at one point, or all of Van Gogh's letters. He was looking for an idea [for his own writing] in these books. At another point he said he wanted to write about Huey Long. He got everything he could find about Huey Long and read it. So he read the way a researcher reads, but Al Devlin's talking about wide reading for sheer intellectual interest. He didn't tend to do that. He rarely mentions abstract ideas except in connection with the intellectuals he met. He wanted to get together with Sartre, so he mentioned Sartre's work, but unless he was meeting somebody, he didn't seem to be reading for general intellectual enrichment. But his letters reveal, for instance, that even as a kid writing from Europe, he'd done his research on the "Grand Tour" and what all the countries were like. I thought for a sixteen-year-old those were really splendid letters.

KULLMAN: There's a wonderful book by Judith Thompson about myth and symbol in Williams, and it seems to indicate that there's a rich background of classical mythology and biblical analogies in his work, implying that he read incredibly. He had all this knowledge as general background, and it had to come from somewhere. Do you think she's wrong in presenting this material, or do you think he really did have all the knowledge Thompson indicates?

HOLDITCH: Don't you think a lot of that came from his grandfather Walter Dakin? His grandfather had that background from Sewanee and passed it along to him, I think.

CRANDELL: I think the important thing for us to consider is not how much he read but what he read and how he read it. We were talking earlier about whether we should publish his early or late materials. I think *The Notebook of Trigorin* is a good example of why we should publish those materials. Here he was obviously fascinated with Chekhov and so fascinated in his reading that he actually rewrites Chekhov in his own version. And I think it would be fascinating to study his process of reading, not so much listing everything he read, but asking how he reads Chekhov, how Williams reinterprets him, and what we can we learn from that process of thought.

KOLIN: Earlier, Colby Kullman mentioned teaching Williams. One of the myths that I think should be debunked is that Williams is a playwright of the grotesque. When people hear his name, they think of the sensational or the lurid, and that's not so, even though one of his first publications was in *Weird Tales*. There is a sense in which the classifications that are applied to Williams aren't applied to other great writers. You don't dismiss Ovid and *The Metamorphoses* as "lurid" and "grotesque" or *King Lear* as "grotesque."

HARRIS: Or *Titus Andronicus*.

KOLIN: Or *Titus Andronicus*. And so in what way do we counter that label with something that's more salient and more persuasive? The fact that Williams's events in the plays are graphic doesn't necessarily make them grotesque in a pejorative way.

SULLIVAN: I think the stories of his last years are very sad and tragic and at the same time rather colorful, because someone going down in flames is always interesting and dramatic. I think maybe we need to remember that this man, as far as I can see, was a gentleman almost all the time; this was not a roaring boy who breaks up bars and goes to hell that way. It's interesting that his decorum, at least the couple of times I met him, was just perfect. He was a southern gentleman, among other things, and all that other stuff was going on underneath. We don't want to overdo the decline and the flames and the damnation.

HOLDITCH: One myth that we've already brought up, that Michael Paller and others have brought up, is that his plays are thinly disguised stories of homosexuals. Blanche is not a man in drag. I think that's one of the major myths that need to be debunked. I think another myth is that the late plays are not worth anything, because they certainly are.

KULLMAN: As we begin the new millennium, the theme of the apocalypse is very prevalent in Williams's plays, and I thought maybe you'd like to say something about the apocalypse in the world of Tennessee Williams. Philip, you asked this question, so we'll start with you.

KOLIN: Apocalyptic imagery runs all through the canon. It seems to me that *Battle of Angels,* a very early play written in 1940, is filled with apocalyptic terror in a small southern town that really isn't a small southern town—it's a microcosm of hell. Apocalypse appears throughout the canon and in many forms. In *Kingdom of Earth,* it's a flood. In *Streetcar,* depending on how you read the ending, Blanche can go into heaven or she can just go into the snake pit.

HOLDITCH: I told Ralph Voss that one of the presentations I could make here deals with flame and fire in Williams. The title was going to be "Before I Start Screaming Fire!" There's fire all the way through the plays. In a minor play because it's a small play, *Auto-Da-Fé,* the protagonist, Eloi, talks about how there has to be burning like the ancient cities of myth that are destroyed, and he uses that figure over and over again.

TISCHLER: There's a book of literary criticism called *Landscape of Nightmare.* In it I remember the author talks about apocalyptic laughter. I thought that phrase fit Williams really neatly. He'll present a really hideous vision, and then the characters will seem to be laughing in the face of that vision, especially in the later plays. There's a grotesqueness in *The Gnädiges Fräulein* where the Fräulein is losing one eye after the other or one bit of her body after another. And she's really hilarious, even when she's facing mutilation. Good grief, how can you go through such an experience this way? I think that's part of the way he saw himself and his own tortured existence. Every time I hear descriptions of his own laugh, I think about apocalyptic laughter.

KOLIN: I don't know if anybody's ever made a case for Hawthorne and Williams, except maybe Blanche DuBois in teaching Hawthorne, but the sense of "My Kinsman, Major Molineaux" reminds me of some of the things in Williams. There's a Hawthorne strain in Williams that is clearly apocalyptic.

CRANDELL: I think we usually think of apocalypse as some big conflagration, but I think it can also take place on an individual level, where the destruction of a single character, like Chance Wayne at the end of *Sweet Bird of Youth,* represents the destruction of a certain way of life. Or the destruction of Blanche at the end of *Streetcar* can be seen as the destruction of a way of life that is being replaced by something less desirable. Through many of his plays, I think, we see a conflict between ways of seeing or ways of living, with the one that is supplanting the other not always desirable—and that is a kind of apocalyptic vision, if you will, the destruction of one world and its replacement by another.

SULLIVAN: I shy away from the term "apocalypse," because apocalypse is a final catastrophe, and it seems to me that what occurs in Williams is not that sweeping. As for Blanche, sure, one character may be sacrificed, but I think with Williams you always have the sense that some way life will go on, and the laughter is partly associated with this sense. Maybe there has to be some purging or some sacrifice, but there's redemption for somebody.

SIEGEL: I'd like to add something about that. If you look at apocalypse as destruction, in the same plays there's much creation too. In *Suddenly Last Summer,* you have this corruption, but you also have the doctor standing up to the bribe offered by Violet Venable, at least not willing to disbelieve Catharine's version of events surrounding Sebastian's death. The doctor puts truth before career. In *Cat* and in *Iguana* you have two terribly disillusioned men who are yet still willing to reach out to others, in Brick's case, Big Daddy; and in Shannon's case, Hannah Jelkes. Even though they are profoundly disillusioned, they're still willing to engage the world and struggle with their own disillusionment, so I think that creation is a very integral part of this destruction, too. It's not nihilistic at all.

HALE: That's one of the puzzling things you come up against in the very late plays, because in a couple of those, at least, there's really no hope at the end. Those really get apocalyptic. "The Chalky White Substance"—has anybody read that?—a short play, but it's the end, the doom at the end of everything. And the same thing is suggested in "The Lingering Hour," and even in "A House Not Meant to Stand." There really isn't any chance, any way out. It's sad, but I think Williams was probably very depressed at the end. Maybe that's what causes the difference. There *is* a difference.

KULLMAN: Well, we're nearing the end of our time for this session. Let's conclude with a discussion of the future of Williams studies. What needs to be done? Where do you think we're going? Allean, you asked this question, so we'll start with you.

HALE: One thing there doesn't seem to be at all, other than Brenda Murphy's book, is a book on directing Williams plays. Theater students ask me if there's any book on how you direct Williams's plays. I don't think there are any. I think they've done a study of Eugene O'Neill's stage directions, for instance, but they haven't ever done that with Williams, and his stage directions are wonderful. They are very thoughtful and tell you a lot about the play. Most of the studies have been from a critical or biographical standpoint, but there is little written from the standpoint of theater.

CRANDELL: Obviously the publication of his letters and journals will help. I'm in favor of continued publication of additional Williams plays. As the panel has suggested today, a study of the fiction and the poetry might be in order, especially one that doesn't see the fiction and poetry as some sort of prelude or preparation for the drama. I think that then we'll be able to see this material's merits apart from drama if there are any—and I think there are.

KOLIN: I'm editing a special issue of the *Southern Quarterly* for fall 2000 on the nondramatic Williams. Eight or nine essays deal with some issues that George Crandell has mentioned—poetry, of course—but Dean Shackelford is attacking a topic that no one today has mentioned, and that's Williams as a literary critic, with all of the prefaces, all of the letters to the *New York Times*, and all of the exchanges, including the interviews. What was Williams's view of literature? How did he approach literature? Was he a formalist? Was he a mythographer? I think there's ample material there to be dug up. Of course, production histories of the plays worldwide are needed. I've been working on *Streetcar* ever since I've been in long pants, but there's so much work to be done on the other plays, particularly on how a country overseas views American icons and how they're changed. I know there's an Eastern European production of *Streetcar* in which there are five people at the poker table, not just four, and the fifth one is a voodoo doll that the people in this culture believed was a vital part of the ambiance of New Orleans. Consequently, we need to explore Williams's role as an ambassador or interpreter of American icons.

SIEGEL: I'd like to agree with that statement in terms of the plays. It's fascinating for me to read in Arthur Miller's *Timebends* the process that went on with *Death of a Salesman* in Beijing, and I'd like to know a lot more about how Williams's works translate into other cultures—what is immediately grasped and what other productions have to work at, vis-à-vis their cultures.

KOLIN: Just obtaining props for the plays is interesting. Jean Cocteau, when he did *Streetcar* in Paris in 1949, went to all of the markets to try to find a New Orleans ambiance. At the end Cocteau simply said that New Orleans was just like a southern Marseilles.

TISCHLER: I'd like to see a variorum edition of Williams's major plays. We really need something on all of the variations on each play. I realize some of them don't deserve to be printed, but some of them are gorgeous; they're way too good to be just throwaways. If a director could choose among them, wouldn't that be wonderful? Brian Parker is working on this project now, of course, exploring different versions of the major plays. I'm really looking forward to more of those being brought out.

SIEGEL: Before the panel ends, there's something that's been on my mind the last few days. Maybe this idea's not appropriate because it's a Williams symposium, not one on Elia Kazan, but they were such close collaborators. You know, it's been easy for me sometimes to separate some people's personal life from their work or art if there are some things in their personal life that I find reprehensible but I can really admire their art. But I'm having a hard time forgiving Kazan. I wonder if that difficulty is on the mind of any other panelist here.

PALLER: Well, I think it's been deeply hypocritical of Hollywood for a long time to condemn Kazan for naming names. It was an ugly thing to do, although he did have the permission of at least a couple of people to name them. But the Hollywood blacklist worked because the studios enforced it. And so for Hollywood to be calling the kettle black I think is disgraceful, and I think it's about time that that blunder was acknowledged.

HOLDITCH: I agree. I think that Kazan was a wonderful director, although there are points at which he did damage to Williams's plays; there's no question about it. But I remember that wonderful line from W. H. Auden about Paul Claudel, the French poet who'd become a collaborator with the Nazis during World War II. In his poem "In Memory of W. B. Yeats," Auden writes, "And God will pardon Paul Claudel / For writing well." So maybe that's the way we should view Kazan now.

SULLIVAN: [to Seigel] Have you read the Kazan *Life*?

SIEGEL: No, I haven't.

SULLIVAN: First, you don't have to forgive him, but you have to understand what happened more from his point of view.

SIEGEL: I've read some excerpts from Miller's point of view in *Timebends*.

SULLIVAN: Okay, well, get *A Life*. [Laughter] No! I don't mean that! That came out very wrong. It's an autobiography called *A Life* by Kazan, and he makes his case there, and you can find him guilty or not guilty or somewhere in between, but it's a case to be considered. I figure if Miller could forgive him, if

Williams could forgive him, I can forgive him. He went on to do wonderful work, and you know, everybody errs, and he erred in a particularly public way. Anyway, read the book.

KULLMAN: I think it's clear that it's going to be very interesting what happens in the new millennium with regard to Williams's work. Thank you all very much.

Contributors

Jackson R. Bryer is professor of English at the University of Maryland and has written many books and articles about American fiction, particularly F. Scott Fitzgerald, and about American drama, particularly Eugene O'Neill. Bryer is the scholar's conference director for the annual William Inge Theater Festival.

George W. Crandell is professor of English at Auburn University. He has published articles on American humor and modern drama as well as *Tennessee Williams: A Descriptive Bibliography* and *The Critical Response to Tennessee Williams*. He is currently working on a descriptive bibliography of the works of Arthur Miller.

Albert J. Devlin is professor of English at the University of Missouri and has published *Conversations with Tennessee Williams* as well as extensive research (with Nancy Tischler) on Williams's correspondence. Volume 1 of Devlin's and Tischler's *Selected Letters of Tennessee Williams* appeared in 2000.

Allean Hale is adjunct professor of theater at the University of Illinois. A member of the editorial board of the *Tennessee Williams Annual Review,* she is a longtime Tennessee Williams scholar who has been particularly interested in the discovery and publication of Williams's previously unknown work. She has recently edited *The Notebook of Trigorin, Not About Nightingales, Stairs to the Roof,* and *The Fugitive Kind.*

Barbara M. Harris teaches at the University of Missouri, where she is completing her doctoral dissertation, "Shades, Shadows, Ghosts, and Doppelgängers in the Plays of Tennessee Williams."

W. Kenneth Holditch is research professor emeritus of the University of New Orleans and author of *The Last Frontier of Bohemia: Tennessee Williams in New Orleans*. He is also the founder and editor of the *Tennessee Williams Literary Journal;* cofounder of the Mississippi Delta Tennessee Williams Festival in Clarksdale, Mississippi; and one of the founders of the Tennessee Williams Festival in New Orleans. He recently coedited two volumes of Williams's *Plays,* 1927–1955 and 1957–1980, in the *Library of America* series, and coauthored the forthcoming *A More Congenial Climate: Tennessee Williams and the South.*

Philip C. Kolin is professor of English at the University of Southern Mississippi. He has done extensive research and has published a great deal on Williams's work, particularly the productions of his plays, and is the author of *Williams: "A Streetcar Named Desire"* in Cambridge's *Plays in Production* series. He cofounded, with Colby Kullman, the journal *American Drama, 1945–Present* and recently published *Deep Wonder,* a book of his own poetry.

Colby Kullman is professor of English at the University of Mississippi and cofounder, with Philip C. Kolin, of *American Drama, 1945–Present.* He and Kolin coedited *Speaking on Stage: Twenty-seven Interviews with Contemporary American Playwrights.* Kullman is also editor-in-chief of the two-volume reference series *Theatre Companies of the World.*

Jeffrey B. Loomis is professor of English at Northwest Missouri State University and the author of *Dayspring in Darkness: Sacrament in Hopkins.* He has also written articles on dramatists ranging from Shakespeare, Goethe, and Strindberg to Albee, Zindel, Sondheim, and Howe.

Michael Paller is a dramaturge, writer, and director in New York City. He has served as literary manager and dramaturge at the George Street Playhouse, the Berkshire Theatre Festival, and the Barrington Stage Company. He was Richard Corley's dramaturge for the Russian premiere of Williams's *Small Craft Warnings* and has taught at Columbia University and the Cooper Union. He is currently at work on a book on gay characters in Williams's plays.

Robert Siegel is a professor in the graduate creative writing program at East Carolina University. His plays have been produced in New York and regionally, and he has written screenplays for production companies in the United States and Europe. His contribution here was first read at our symposium and was then published by *American Drama*.

Dan Sullivan teaches journalism at the University of Minnesota and directs the O'Neill Critics' Institute at the Eugene O'Neill Theater Center in Waterford, Connecticut. He spent twenty-one years as the drama critic for the *Los Angeles Times*.

Nancy M. Tischler is professor emerita at Pennsylvania State University. The author of *Tennessee Williams: Rebellious Puritan* and *The Student Companion to Tennessee Williams*, she collaborated with Albert J. Devlin in collecting and publishing *Selected Letters of Tennessee Williams*, the first volume of which appeared in 2000.

Ralph F. Voss is professor of English at the University of Alabama. He is the author of *A Life of William Inge: The Strains of Triumph* and *Elements of Practical Writing* and is the coauthor of *The Heath Guide to College Writing*. He is a member of the national advisory board for the William Inge Festival and the Mississippi Delta Tennessee Williams Festival.

Index

New Orleans Athletic Club, 198
New York City, 14–15, 46, 66, 88,
    147, 164, 181, 188, 195, 198, 200,
    208, 210, 218–19, 226
New Yorker, 11
New York Public Library, 16, 100
New York Times, 11
Nietzsche, Friedrich, 91
Night of the Iguana, The, 2, 14–15, 21,
    24, 82, 111, 123, 147–48, 179–80,
    188, 211, 221–22, 236
nihilism, 124–25, 236
Noh drama, 5, 14, 149–51, 152–56,
    159, 161
Not about Nightingales, 2, 14–15, 131,
    181, 216–19
Notebook of Trigorin, The, 14, 181, 233

O'Casey, Sean, 148
"Occidental Noh Play, An," 150, 155
O'Connor, Flannery, 195
O'Connor, Jim, 132–35, 138, 140–42,
    143–45
Off Broadway, 83, 88, 147, 160, 182,
    188–89, 216
Off off Broadway, 88, 182
O'Hara, Scarlett, 52, 57, 186
Olivier, Sir Laurence, 54
"One Arm," 63
O'Neill, Eugene, 1, 206, 208, 210, 236
Orpheus Descending, 8, 21, 203, 212,
    221. See also *Battle of Angels*
Out Cry, 84, 159, 209. See also *Two-
    Character Play, The*

Page, Geraldine, 113
Paramount, 54, 56
paranoia, 102, 149, 158, 207, 209
Parker, Dorothy, 169
Parmenides, 111
Parrott, Jim, 37, 39–42, 45, 199, 228
Passion of a Moth, The, 62
Phelps, William Lyon, 36
Pinter, Harold, 14, 147, 149
Pirandello, Luigi, 4, 91, 93, 107
plastic theatre, 147

Plato, 111
Playboy, 178
"Poker Night, The," 61–62, 201
Pollitt, Big Daddy, 3, 23, 92, 94–108,
    112, 119–22, 179, 184, 212–13, 236
Pollitt, Big Mama, 92, 101–05, 122
Pollitt, Brick, 17, 92–103, 105–08,
    119–23, 125, 168, 212, 236
Pollitt, Gooper, 94, 97, 99–103, 106–
    07, 121–22
Pollitt, Maggie, "The Cat," 92–95,
    97–100, 102, 105–08, 119–23, 126–
    27, 168, 182, 187, 189, 212–13
Pollock, Jackson, 157–58, 227
popular culture, 3, 6, 44, 46
Portrait of a Madonna, 131
postmodernism, 1, 20, 183
Presley, Elvis, 190
Previn, André, 22, 182
"Primary Colors, The," 61
Production Code, 51–52, 54, 65
Provincetown, 1, 38, 88–89, 158
psychological, 20, 72, 107, 149, 231
Pulitzer Prize, 4, 8, 147
Purification, The, 75–78
puritanism, 71, 116, 179, 184,
    194, 198

Quintero, José, 163

race, 19, 212, 219, 225–26
race relations, 13
radical, 17, 65, 132, 142, 145,
    146, 207
Ravenstock, Chicken, 132, 142–45
realism, 20, 112, 158–59, 170, 172–74
reality, 111, 114, 116, 119, 133,
    170, 171
Red Devil Battery Sign, The, 8, 21,
    24, 188
religion, 12, 48, 67, 134, 143, 145,
    148, 149, 155, 159
Restaurant Jonathan, 194
revision, 15, 92–94, 97, 101, 103,
    107, 225
Rimbaud, Arthur, 14